Saltwater Aquariums For Dummies®

W9-AMA-361

Your Aquarium Maintenance Schedule

Every day, do the following:

- Turn the aquarium lights on and off. Most aquarists prefer to use an automatic timer. If you choose not to, try to turn the lights on and off in a consistent pattern.
- Check the fish and invertebrates for signs of stress, disease, or death. Be prepared to remove or treat fish that aren't well.
- Feed the fishes and invertebrates twice a day, removing any uneaten food.
- Conduct water tests until the water matures and the nitrogen cycle is established. Routine tests include ammonia, nitrite, nitrate, and pH. Record the test results.
- Check the water temperature and specific gravity or salinity. Adjust the heater, as needed.
- Empty the protein skimmer collection cup, as needed.
- Check the water level and top off, as needed.
- Check all aquarium systems: heater, filters, aerators, protein skimmer. Make sure they're running properly and smoothly and pay special attention to intakes and siphon tubes. Make sure that nothing is leaking.

Once a week, complete the following tasks:

- Remove excess algae, keeping beneficial algae at acceptable levels and getting rid of nuisance algae.
- Clean the glass, both inside and out, but don't use glass cleaner. Remove salt-creep deposits.
- Conduct water tests weekly after the water matures and the nitrogen cycle is established. Record all test results and add trace elements and buffers, as needed.

Every two weeks, do the following:

- Clean filters, as needed. Partially change or rinse the filter media on some filters if the bioload is high, the media is dirty, or the flow is restricted.
- Change 20 percent of the tank water while vacuuming the gravel.

Every month, be sure you complete these tasks:

- Conduct thorough filter checks. Replace the filter carbon and rinse the filter media and components, as needed and depending on bioload.
- Clean the protein skimmer.
- Replace airstones, as needed.
- Clean the outside of aquarium, removing salt and calcium deposits, dust, and dirt.
- Rinse any tank decorations that suffer from excess algae.

Every three months, conduct a thorough examination of all aquarium systems, including lighting, heating, filtration, aeration pumps, and tubing. Replace or clean parts, as needed.

For Dummies: Bestselling Book Series for Beginners

Saltwater Aquariums For Dummies®

How to Feed Your Fish

Use the following guidelines when feeding your fish and you will develop a working sense of how much and how often to feed them. It is definitely better to feed them too little at first than too much.

✔ **Offer as much food as your fish will eat in five minutes.** Flakes should sink no deeper than one-third the height of the tank. Provide tablets, pellets, or sinking food for bottom fish and invertebrates.

✔ **Feed your fish in very small portions over the five-minute period.** If any food is left over after this time, you're an over-feeder. Bear in mind, however, that some foods, like lettuce or spinach, are nibbled over time, so the five-minute rule does not apply.

✔ **If you're home during the day, feed your fish and invertebrates very small portions over the course of the day.** If you're not home, feed them twice a day at the same times every day: once in the morning, once at evening. Keep in mind that some critters are nocturnal, so you may have to feed them after the lights are out.

✔ **Always feed your fish at the same spot in the tank.** This lets you sneak food down to bottom dwellers while the surface fish are distracted.

✔ **Don't overfeed the fish, no matter how much you think they need more food.** Overeating stresses your fish and causes detritus to accumulate in the tank, degrading water quality.

Test Kits for a New Aquarium

Use the following table as a general guide for purchasing test kits. As your tank becomes more complicated, you can always add to your test kit collection.

Test Kit	Fish-Only Tank	Reef Tank
pH	yes	yes
Ammonia	yes	yes
Nitrite	yes	yes
Nitrate	yes	yes
Alkalinity	optional	yes
Dissolved oxygen	optional	optional
Copper	optional	no
Phosphate	optional	yes
Iodine	no	optional
Calcium	no	optional
Silica	no	optional

Test kits are made so you don't have to be a chemist to use them. While a couple of methods have been developed, the most common involves adding drops of a test chemical to an aquarium sample that changes the color of the water. You then match the water color with that on a color chart, which tells you the correct level of what you are testing.

Hungry Minds™

For Dummies: Bestselling Book Series for Beginners

Saltwater Aquariums

FOR DUMMIES®

Saltwater Aquariums FOR DUMMIES®

by Gregory Skomal

Hungry Minds™

Best-Selling Books • Digital Downloads • e-Books • Answer Networks • e-Newsletters • Branded Web Sites • e-Learning

New York, NY ◆ Cleveland, OH ◆ Indianapolis, IN

Saltwater Aquariums For Dummies®

Published by:
Hungry Minds, Inc.
909 Third Avenue
New York, NY 10022
www.hungryminds.com
www.dummies.com

Library of Congress Control Number: 2001099726

ISBN: 0-7645-5340-2

Printed in the United States of America

10 9 8 7 6 5

1O/RS/QS/QS/IN

Distributed in the United States by Hungry Minds, Inc.

Distributed by CDG Books Canada Inc. for Canada; by Transworld Publishers Limited in the United Kingdom; by IDG Norge Books for Norway; by IDG Sweden Books for Sweden; by IDG Books Australia Publishing Corporation Pty. Ltd. for Australia and New Zealand; by TransQuest Publishers Pte Ltd. for Singapore, Malaysia, Thailand, Indonesia, and Hong Kong; by Gotop Information Inc. for Taiwan; by ICG Muse, Inc. for Japan; by Intersoft for South Africa; by Eyrolles for France; by International Thomson Publishing for Germany, Austria and Switzerland; by Distribuidora Cuspide for Argentina; by LR International for Brazil; by Galileo Libros for Chile; by Ediciones ZETA S.C.R. Ltda. for Peru; by WS Computer Publishing Corporation, Inc., for the Philippines; by Contemporanea de Ediciones for Venezuela; by Express Computer Distributors for the Caribbean and West Indies; by Micronesia Media Distributor, Inc. for Micronesia; by Chips Computadoras S.A. de C.V. for Mexico; by Editorial Norma de Panama S.A. for Panama; by American Bookshops for Finland.

For general information on Hungry Minds' products and services please contact our Customer Care department; within the U.S. at 800-762-2974, outside the U.S. at 317-572-3993 or fax 317-572-4002.

For sales inquiries and resellers information, including discounts, premium and bulk quantity sales and foreign language translations please contact our Customer Care department at 800-434-3422, fax 317-572-4002 or write to Hungry Minds, Inc., Attn: Customer Care department, 10475 Crosspoint Boulevard, Indianapolis, IN 46256.

For information on licensing foreign or domestic rights, please contact our Sub-Rights Customer Care department at 212-884-5000.

For information on using Hungry Minds' products and services in the classroom or for ordering examination copies, please contact our Educational Sales department at 800-434-2086 or fax 317-572-4005.

Please contact our Public Relations department at 212-884-5163 for press review copies or 212-884-5000 for author interviews and other publicity information or fax 212-884-5400.

For authorization to photocopy items for corporate, personal, or educational use, please contact Copyright Clearance Center, 222 Rosewood Drive, Danvers, MA 01923, or fax 978-750-4470.

Hungry Minds™ is a trademark of Hungry Minds, Inc.

About the Author

Gregory Skomal is a marine biologist with the Massachusetts Division of Marine Fisheries. He has been an avid aquarist for over 25 years. Greg has a masters degree in marine biology from the University of Rhode Island and is currently working on his Ph.D. with the Boston University Marine Program in Woods Hole, MA. He is an accomplished photographer and writer, having authored several books on aquariums and numerous scientific articles.

About Howell Book House

Committed to the Human/Companion Animal Bond

Thank you for choosing a book brought to you by the pet experts at Howell Book House, a division of Hungry Minds, Inc. And welcome to the family of pet owners who've put their trust in Howell books for nearly 40 years!

Pet ownership is about relationships — the bonds people form with their dogs, cats, horses, birds, fish, small mammals, reptiles, and other animals. Howell Book House/Hungry Minds understands that these are some of the most important relationships in life, and that it's vital to nurture them through enjoyment and education. The happiest pet owners are those who know they're taking the best care of their pets — and with Howell books owners have this satisfaction. They're happy, educated owners, and as a result, they have happy pets, and that enriches the bond they share.

Howell Book House was established in 1961 by Mr. Elsworth S. Howell, an active and proactive dog fancier who showed English Setters and judged at the prestigious Westminster Kennel Club show in New York. Mr. Howell based his publishing program on strength of content, and his passion for books written by experienced and knowledgeable owners defined Howell Book House and has remained true over the years. Howell's reputation as the premier pet book publisher is supported by the distinction of having won more awards from the Dog Writers Association of America than any other publisher. Howell Book House/Hungry Minds has over 400 titles in publication, including such classics as The American Kennel Club's *Complete Dog Book,* the *Dog Owner's Home Veterinary Handbook, Blessed Are the Brood Mares,* and *Mother Knows Best: The Natural Way to Train Your Dog.*

When you need answers to questions you have about any aspect of raising or training your companion animals, trust that Howell Book House/Hungry Minds has the answers. We welcome your comments and suggestions, and we look forward to helping you maximize your relationships with your pets throughout the years.

The Howell Book House Staff

Dedication

This book is dedicated my family and friends who have supported my whimsical ideas to become a marine biologist since I was a young and naïve boy. I would like to thank my brothers: Bernie for pushing me into the water, Burt for exploring with me in the water, and Paul for fishing with me on the water. My sisters: Vickie for making me smile, Lenore for helping me think, and Maggie for inspiring me.

I would like to thank several childhood friends from the old gang who remain very close to me in adulthood. David Weis introduced me to aquariums, and Carlo DeVito and Bert "Condo" Condon spent countless hours with me setting up aquariums, running to the pet store, and getting drenched in aquarium water.

Special thanks to Carlo, with whom I have authored books, and his wife Dominique, for helping me initiate my book-writing career.

Most importantly, I would like to dedicate this book to my parents, Bernie and Irene. Affectionately known as Padre, my father provided me with the robust chest of tools that I needed to pursue a dream. His guidance, support, and wonderful sense of humor have taught me that life is truly an adventure. My mother persevered through countless hours of pet store visits, tolerated the slow destruction of her house, and eagerly tossed countless dollars into a glass rectangle to keep her son happy. I'll always remember her true love of the sea. She was truly a unique person and the consummate mother, and her early passing left a hole in my heart never to be filled.

Publisher's Acknowledgments

We're proud of this book; please send us your comments through our Hungry Minds Online Registration Form located at www.dummies.com.

Some of the people who helped bring this book to market include the following:

Acquisitions, Editorial, and Media Development

Senior Project Editor: Tim Gallan

Acquisitions Editors: Michael Singer, Kira Sexton

Copy Editor: Tere Drenth

Technical Editor: Ronald Shimek

Editorial Managers: Pamela Mourouzis, Christine Meloy Beck

Editorial Assistant: Carol Strickland

Illustrator: Ronald Shimeck

Interior Photos: Aaron Norman

Cover Photos: © VCG-FCG

Production

Project Coordinator: Dale White

Layout and Graphics: Jackie Nicholas, Shelley Norris, Jacque Schneider, Jeremey Unger, Mary J. Virgin

Proofreaders: Dave Faust, John Greenough, Angel Perez, Carl Pierce, TECHBOOKS Production Services

Indexer: TECHBOOKS Production Services

General and Administrative

Hungry Minds Consumer Reference Group

Business: Kathleen Nebenhaus, Vice President and Publisher; Kevin Thornton, Acquisitions Manager

Cooking/Gardening: Jennifer Feldman, Associate Vice President and Publisher; Anne Ficklen, Executive Editor; Kristi Hart, Managing Editor

Education/Reference: Diane Graves Steele, Vice President and Publisher

Lifestyles: Kathleen Nebenhaus, Vice President and Publisher; Tracy Boggier, Managing Editor

Pets: Kathleen Nebenhaus, Vice President and Publisher; Tracy Boggier, Managing Editor

Travel: Michael Spring, Vice President and Publisher; Brice Gosnell, Publishing Director; Suzanne Jannetta, Editorial Director

Hungry Minds Consumer Editorial Services: Kathleen Nebenhaus, Vice President and Publisher; Kristin A. Cocks, Editorial Director; Cindy Kitchel, Editorial Director

Hungry Minds Consumer Production: Debbie Stailey, Production Director

Contents at a Glance

Cartoons at a Glance

By Rich Tennant

page 7

page 271

page 187

page 229

page 111

page 281

Cartoon Information:
Fax: 978-546-7747
E-Mail: richtennant@the5thwave.com
World Wide Web: www.the5thwave.com

Table of Contents

Introduction

● ●

*G*reetings my friend! You have just taken the first step into the world of saltwater aquariums and I welcome you. Stop looking for complicated books with laborious equations on filtration and water chemistry. Don't grab a book just because it has a lot of pretty photos of elegant saltwater fish! The complete hassle-free guide to setting up a saltwater aquarium is *Saltwater Aquariums For Dummies* and, fortunately for you, it's in your hands right now.

Saltwater Aquariums For Dummies is a fun reference book that walks you through the entire aquarium process from selecting the proper equipment to choosing the right fish. I even help you choose the right pet store because, believe me, they are not all alike! I know, you've been told that saltwater aquariums are complicated, need constant attention, and cost a lot. But, my friend, times have changed since the introduction of the goldfish bowl, and new technologies are making the saltwater aquarium hobby a fast growing pastime very easily mastered by everyone with the average size pocketbook!

That being said, relax and read on. I'll keep it simple, but I won't skimp on the facts. If all goes as planned, your aquarium will be set up in no time and both you and your aquarium friends will be smiling for a long time to come.

About This Book

There's something about fish that I find fascinating, and the thought of keeping them in my home is very exciting! I am truly a fish fanatic. I find fish fun, so I guess that I'm really a fish "funatic" and hope that you are as well. We are not alone; people have been keeping fish in captivity for centuries. Among the first fishes to be kept in captivity were the common goldfish which date back to 265 A.D. in China. Care and husbandry of fishes have come a long way over the centuries.

The world of fish is both fascinating and complex. This reference will help you to understand this world and present what you need to know to set up and maintain a successful saltwater aquarium. Doing so requires a general knowledge of fish, their anatomy, and biology. You also need a thorough understanding of their proper care and husbandry.

In this book, I offer you a look at fish anatomy and show you what makes these animals so unique. I also examine the aquarium and the importance of meeting the biological needs of fish. In the process, I describe the critical differences between freshwater and saltwater aquaria. I walk you through the basics of aquarium set-up and proper maintenance. I cover proper nutrition and feeding as well as discuss fish health issues. And I even cover some advanced marine aquarium techniques. And, although I'm repeating myself, I present all of this info with a painless and simple approach!

Who I Am

I am a very avid fish enthusiast, but my passion does not only apply to fish. In general, all creatures of the ocean, including the ocean itself, are my playground and office. That's right, I not only study the ocean in my spare time, I do so when I go to work everyday.

I have been fascinated by the ocean and its inhabitants since the days when Jacques Cousteau was entertaining us with beautiful images of Earth's inner-space, the underwater world. I watched every episode as a kid and this inspired me to set up an aquarium when I was less than a decade old. Oh, like most, I started with a small freshwater system, which turned into a large freshwater system, which turned into a large saltwater system, which turned into multiple saltwater systems, and so on. And believe it or not, most of what I learned about aquariums was self-taught through a lot of trial and error with my buddies. As our aquariums became more elaborate, we learned slowly and often at the expense of my mother's pocketbook. Aquariums in those days were expensive and cumbersome to set up. Filtration was primitive and few people made the bold move to saltwater.

My passion for the ocean motivated me to become a marine biologist and I'm very fortunate to say that I am actually living my dream of traveling around the world studying fish both in the wild and in the aquarium.

What I Assume about You

First, I expect that you know little to nothing about aquariums, filtration, fish, and invertebrates. Second, I expect that you have no formal schooling in biology. Lastly, I expect that you have a genuine interest in these subjects to the point that you want keep saltwater creatures in captivity. That's it! If you've previously had a freshwater aquarium or you know a little more than I expect, then feel free to skip over sections of this book or merely breeze over them to make sure that you have a firm handle on the subject.

Why a Dummies Book?

As I developed my skills as a young aquarist back in the dark ages (the 70s), I made every attempt to read the saltwater aquarium books that were published in those days. A limited number of references were out there and I tried to read them as my aquarium buddies and I moved from fresh to saltwater systems. I recently unearthed one of those books from that box in the far corner of my storage unit and I looked it over. Whoa! Even after taking and teaching advanced college courses in biology, I found this antiquated relic a bit too hard to digest. In fact, it would have been easier to eat than to understand. Pages of equations on water chemistry, filtration, and aquarium maintenance are not my idea of a hobby. And that's why I am writing this book! Saltwater aquarium keeping does not need to be complicated. We all need a book to keep it simple, and that is exactly what this is!

However, I don't want you to think that you will not encounter problems on your journey through the aquarium hobby. The most advanced aquarists in the world stumble from time to time on this road. But this book is your map and companion and if you follow its advice, then you will not only minimize these problems, but you will know how to deal with them. And if this book does not answer your questions, then it will at the very least point you in the direction of the answer, because no matter what other books may tell you, no single book comprehensively covers it all. The world is full of literally hundreds of aquarium books, both technical and practical. To boil all of this information down into one book is impossible, but to condense the most basic and important information into one book is practical. Consider it done.

How This Book Is Organized

Like most *Dummies* books, this is a reference and not a step by step tutorial. Therefore, you can readily move to any part of the book to read about something that interests you. For example, you may be well versed in basic aquarium set-up, but you may want to know more about choosing fish. Simply skip to Chapter 10; no need to read the first nine chapters. And don't be afraid to take full advantage of the index.

You will find, however, that the book is written in a logical progressive fashion from the first step of choosing an aquarium to routinely maintaining it. I've divided this process into five parts, which proceed as follows:

Part 1: The Basic Aquarium

The eight chapters in this section will help you move from having no aquarium at all through the process of selecting one and setting one up. If you read all these chapters, that empty space in your home that you have been eyeing as a perfect spot for an aquarium will be filled with a well-chosen, well-equipped aquatic ecosystem.

Part 11: Fish and Invertebrates

Of course, what good is an aquarium if you don't have something living in it? Hence, this part will introduce you to and help you select your new roommates. I start with the basics of fish biology and move you through the process of selecting the right tank inhabitants for your aquarium. These chapters are, in my opinion, the most enjoyable part of the book because fish and invertebrates are truly unique creatures and enjoyable pets. Just as selecting a new dog or cat can be fun, so can finding the right fish for your aquarium.

Part 111: Caring for Your Aquarium

If I had to choose a part of the book that is the most important, then this is it. Unfortunately, it is also the part that most people find to be the most complicated! If you were reading a book written 20 years ago, then perhaps it would be. But not any more. In these chapters, I introduce you to what you need to know about water chemistry; the ugly "n" word, nitrogen; the common aquarium nuisance known as algae; and the simple steps of aquarium upkeep. Trust me, these are not difficult topics, and you will agree with me after all is said and done. Think of this section as having to go to the gas station to fuel your car. Everybody loves having the luxury and joy of a car, yet nobody really enjoys having to stop for gasoline every couple of hundred miles, but you can't have one without the other! So to enjoy the benefits of your aquarium, you need to keep it moving smoothly with some basic maintenance.

Part 1V: Caring for Your Pets

Much like the last part on basic aquarium upkeep, this part shows you how to keep your fish running smoothly. In these chapters, I discuss how to feed your fish and how to keep them healthy. There are not a lot of effective treatments for fish and invertebrate diseases, so the best care is preventative care. In the final chapter of this section, I discuss some of the basics of fish and invertebrate observation. This is very important for assessing the health of your pets.

Part V: Part of Tens

Here, I've compiled some fun lists of do's and don'ts of saltwater aquariums. These provide helpful hints like what kinds of creatures not to keep in your home as well as fun facts about fish and invertebrates that will dazzle your friends.

Part VI: Appendixes

Here's where you find a list of additional resources as well as a glossary of fish and aquarium terms.

Icons Used in This Book

As is typical of *Dummies* books, there are a number of small pictures called *icons* in the margins of this book that highlight various aspects of the text. Here's what they mean:

When you see this icon, it means that the paragraph next to it is simply good advice that will help you accomplish the task at hand or information that will keep your aquarium and its inhabitants healthy.

As you would expect, this icon is indicative of a potential problem or dangerous situation associated with the topic being discussed. Pay particular attention to these because they may involve your fish, but are more likely to affect you and those around you.

In most cases, this icon highlights information that is technical by nature and not critical to the task at hand. If you are simply not interested in the topic, pass over it.

If I use this icon it means that I want you to make a special effort to remember the point that I am making. I try not to do this too often, but some information needs to be emphasized and re-emphasized so that it sinks in. Most of this is common sense. For example, while the correct temperature for a tropical aquarium is important to remember, I won't ask you to commit the chemical composition of seawater to memory!

Where to Go from Here

Well, now that we have had an opportunity to meet, it's time to move on to the real important stuff: saltwater aquariums. Where you go from here largely depends on your personal level of expertise. If you have never owned an aquarium, then simply turn the page and let's start at square one. If, however, you already have a saltwater aquarium and want to add some inhabitants, go to Part II. Perhaps you want to review the index and see what topics tickle your fancy. Go for it. Enjoy!

Part I
The Basic Aquarium

The 5th Wave — By Rich Tennant

Kyle spent many happy hours admiring his handcrafted fish/reef/flooded basement aquarium

In this part . . .

The first eight chapters of this book provide the nuts and bolts of the saltwater aquarium. They present everything you need to know about setting up a basic saltwater aquarium.

Chapter 1

Your First Steps to Keeping Fish

*W*hen I decided to set up an aquarium all those many years ago, my immediate impulse was to go out and buy, buy, buy. Well, I did that and learned a few costly lessons right from the start.

Think of setting up a saltwater aquarium as building a small house. Actually, you are building a small house — for your marine pets! To build a house, you first have to decide why you are building one. Then you have to decide what kind you want and where to purchase your materials. Setting up your aquarium is no different (just a lot cheaper) and this chapter will help you take those important first steps.

Understanding What's So Great about Aquariums

You can find a variety of reasons to purchase, set up, and maintain a healthy aquarium in your home. Perhaps your child wants a saltwater aquarium, and you're wrestling with the decision. In this section, I give you a bunch of great reasons to have an aquarium in your favorite room.

Perhaps the best way to describe to the experience of having an aquarium is to tell you why I started keeping an aquarium when I was young. Prompted by the early television shows of underwater explorer Jacques Cousteau, I was in awe of the ocean and its inhabitants, particularly tropical coral reefs and all of the beautiful creatures that inhabit them. During those same years, I was fortunate to travel to the coral reefs of the Caribbean and swim among those very creatures. Swimming about the reef with a mask and a snorkel, I explored all the nooks, watched the fish, and admired the beauty for hours and hours. Soon I learned to scuba dive and take underwater photos, but that wasn't enough, especially when I had to return to the cold Connecticut waters. I had to have these animals in my home all the time. So I set up an aquarium and was able to experience much of what I enjoyed while swimming with the fish in my own home. Later, I also became a marine biologist.

Not everybody has had the opportunity to explore the coral reefs of the Caribbean, but most have seen the beauty of these areas and all their inhabitants on television. But why watch a TV when you can see the creatures live and at a fraction of the cost of traveling to the tropics?

If you can't think of a reason to have an aquarium and none of mine in this section suit you, perhaps you should reconsider.

Fish watching

I can watch fish for hours, but, admittedly, I'm a bit strange. Still, the more you watch your aquarium, the better off your aquarium will be. You'll get to know all the subtleties of your fish; you'll name them; you'll know about their individual personalities (oh, they have them); you'll watch as they interact; and, most importantly, you'll know immediately if something isn't quite right. Each animal in your aquarium is your pet, and, like any pet, by watching it daily, you'll know when it acts normally and when something is wrong. You can diagnose problems as they arise and not after it's too late.

Relaxation

Fish and invertebrates are entertaining creatures, and just sitting and watching them can be very relaxing. As far as I'm concerned, relaxation is one of the very best reasons to have an aquarium. Studies show that spending time in front of the aquarium reduces stress. Also, if you have insomnia, try fish watching — it sure beats counting sheep!

A fishy family affair

I know that this is going to sound a bit corny, but fish keeping is fun for the whole family. By bringing the kids into the process, you help them learn the responsibility involved in taking care of pets. Every child will want to feed the fish, and you can show them how to do it properly. Daily, weekly, and monthly maintenance duties become easier if they're shared by all. Also, if everybody has a vested interest in the aquarium, the aquarium will be better off. In fact, family pets often get more attention than those owned by a single person.

Your child may want an aquarium and promise to take care of it. Please realize, however, that with any pet, he or she has to commit to maintaining the aquarium. The responsibilities are similar to those associated with keeping a dog or cat. The child may not always have the high level of interest he or she expresses early on. You have to be prepared to not only emphasize the importance of aquarium maintenance to your child but also be willing to pick up the slack for him or her.

Fishy friends

You aren't the only one who will enjoy your aquarium. How many times have you been to a friend's house who has an aquarium, and you couldn't help but check it out? So, too, will your friends when they visit. Think of your aquarium as a pet and piece of furniture combined! People appreciate a house that's nicely decorated, and people generally like pets. Your aquarium will offer both amenities at once, and you'll be the talk of the town!

It's a natural thing

Perhaps you too are an aspiring marine biologist. I can think of no better way of getting started than by owning an aquarium. Many studies on fish biology have been conducted on those kept in aquaria. In fact, much of what scientists know about marine life comes from studies on captive fish. Fish and invertebrates are living animals that eat, grow, exhibit unique behaviors, and act and react to their environment and to other animals. As an amateur biologist, you can discover a lot about fish in your own home. The whole family will understand the importance of and gain a respect for nature by having a piece of it in your own home.

The study of fish is known as *ichthyology*. Scientists who study the biology of fish are known as *ichthyologists*. That means that by owning an aquarium with fish in it, you become an amateur ichthyologist.

The ideal pet

Have you ever had to quiet a dog, clean up an unsightly pet mess, go find the cat, or hope that the mailman doesn't get bitten? If you answer "yes" to any of these, you know what owning a typical pet is like. Fish, on the other hand, never give you these problems. They don't bark or bite or scratch. If you're tired of dealing with the typical pet, try the tropical pet, instead!

Keeping an aquarium requires a commitment. If you can't commit to your tropical fish, either drop the idea or wait until you can make that commitment. You wouldn't get a dog if you didn't have time to feed it, so don't get an aquarium if you can't take care of it.

Knowing Your Responsibilities for Your Wet Pets

Most of the ornamental fishes sold in pet stores are freshwater fish, many of which are spawned and raised in captivity. Although they represent only a fraction of the number of fishes sold, almost all of the saltwater species are harvested from the wild. This means that almost any fish that you buy for your saltwater aquarium has been captured and taken from its native habitat.

The most popular of these saltwater fish come primarily from coral reefs. Of course, natural reef systems can be hurt if great care isn't taken to protect them and harvest fish wisely. If managed properly, the coral reefs around the world can be harvested without harm because they are extremely productive. Take care, however, not to purchase fish that may have been harvested in areas that don't adhere to the sound conservation of natural reefs. If you can, try to purchase *captive bred* fish.

Aquarium pets include fish and invertebrates. You probably know what a fish is with its scales, fins, and gills. Invertebrates, however, are different from fish. In general, they belong to many kinds of groups like insects, clams, corals, and worms. The basic feature that unites invertebrates is the fact that they lack a backbone. Invertebrates for the aquarium include shrimp, coral, and anemones, to name a few. I discuss invertebrates in great detail in Chapter 11. For the purpose of this chapter's discussions about fish needs, I'm referring to invertebrates as well.

Fish in their natural environment, whether on the reef or the New Jersey shore, are subjected to many challenges in order to survive. Most of these involve natural processes of predation (big fish trying to each little fish), feeding, reproduction, and disease. In addition, natural catastrophic events that change the quality of the water in which fish live are rare, but they can generally avoid this lowered quality by moving to other areas. In many ways, fish living in their natural environments are very much responsible for themselves. (A possible exception to this would be fish that are living in areas assaulted by man-made pollution.)

Fish kept in an aquarium live in an artificial environment but are also faced with several challenges in order to survive. However, most of these challenges can't be met by the fish and must be provided by you, the *aquarist*. When you take it upon yourself to set up an aquarium, you're accepting the responsibility of meeting all of the needs of its inhabitants. Without you, your aquarium and all its inhabitants are doomed. Your responsibilities include insuring high water quality, proper feeding, correct water temperature, a balanced fish community of the proper density, appropriate habitat and shelter, and sufficient lighting — to name a few. Your fish are no longer in the wild, they are your pets, and they need you! The fish are totally dependent on you to meet their everyday needs. If they get sick or diseased, you must treat them.

As you gain experience as a fishkeeper, you may want to go beyond the basic needs and try to establish specialty tanks. But first, start slowly with your aquarium and take time to develop your talents as an aquarist; you will gather a tremendous amount of knowledge through your own experiences and with the help of this book. If you're an experienced freshwater aquarist, you'll discover that marine fish are less tolerant of poor water quality and that you must be meticulous in the quality of your care. You may want to keep a log of all your experiences so that you can learn from them.

In Table 1-1, I've put together a short list of the biological needs of your fish and invertebrates in order to survive. I've also included the kinds of equipment that will provide for these needs in order to introduce you to some common aquarium components.

Table 1-1	What Exactly Do My Fish Need?	
Biological Needs	*Equipment*	*Chapter Numbers*
Water	Aquarium tank	2
Clean water	Filters, protein skimmer	3
Oxygen	Aerators, power heads	3
Correct water temperature	Aquarium heater	4
Adequate lighting	Aquarium light	5
Housing and protection	Aquarium ornamentation	6
Food	Aquarium foods	17
Disease treatment	Aquarium treatments	19

Getting Started with Your First Saltwater Aquarium

The steps you take now, as you begin to plan your aquarium, are important to the success of your setup. By taking the time to properly plan your aquarium now, you can save a lot of time and money down the road. Your complete system will require little time and a small investment if you plan it properly. You want to set it up once and set it up right, though.

Your first saltwater aquarium should be simple — not necessarily small, but simple. That means trying to avoid planning a complicated specialty aquarium. You can always add to your system as you gain experience in aquarium keeping, but for now, keep it simple.

At this point you have a number of decisions to make about your aquarium. I can't overemphasize the need for you to plan your aquarium completely — from what kind you want and where you want to put it to what kind of fish you keep. In this section, I walk you through the process of making these decisions.

Some basics

When you bought this book, you made a choice to set up a saltwater aquarium. As you're probably aware, freshwater systems are extremely common — you may even own one yourself. While both kinds of aquaria are similar and much of the same equipment is used by both, the most significant difference is the chemical composition of the water they hold. This book doesn't discuss freshwater systems, but here, I briefly address the differences between fresh and saltwater aquaria and their upkeep.

Saltwater aquariums can also be referred to as *marine aquariums* or *seawater aquariums.* In this book, I use these three terms interchangeably.

Just add salt, right?

While some people think that fresh and saltwater aquariums differ by just one ingredient (salt), they're only partially right. If the differences were that simple, more people would have marine systems.

Consider first the most basic differences: Fresh water is found in most inland lakes and ponds, it contains low concentrations of salts and minerals, humans need to drink it to live, and most fish that live in it can't tolerate salt water. On the other hand, salt water is the ocean's water, it contains high concentrations of salts and minerals, humans can't drink it, and most fish that live in it can't live in fresh water. In Chapter 9, I discuss the biological differences between fish that live in salt water and fish that live in fresh water.

In the wild, fish and other aquatic life have adapted quite well to these two different kinds of water, and the problems they've encountered have little to do with the amount of salt in the water. However, in the aquarium, these differences in water chemistry affect your success in the following ways:

- A saltwater aquarium has less room for error when compared to a freshwater setup. Marine fish and invertebrates are more sensitive to slight changes in water quality because they have adapted to a stable environment: the ocean.

- Saltwater fish are more difficult to find and tend to be more expensive because almost all are caught in the wild.

- Saltwater fish don't breed in captivity the way freshwater fish do, so you don't have an opportunity to produce your own fish.

- Marine aquariums are more expensive because they require more equipment in order to maintain excellent water quality.

- You can generally place more freshwater fish in an aquarium than saltwater fish because of their differences in sensitivity to the toxicity of ammonia in seawater (see Chapter 13).

- Freshwater fish survive quite well on flake food while saltwater fish require a mixture of food that includes not only flakes but also frozen and live foods.

As a matter of common sense, most authors of aquarium books recommend that a first-time aquarist start with a freshwater aquarium. That is the road I traveled when I started with aquarium keeping, and it's sound advice, but that doesn't mean that you have to take it. Sure, the marine aquarium is a bit more sensitive. But with the right planning, this book to guide you, and a commitment to high water quality, you can jump right into a marine aquarium (but not literally, of course!).

After all, freshwater fish don't have the brilliant and riveting colors that draw people to saltwater fish in the first place. Freshwater aquariums also don't offer the beauty and splendor of the invertebrates available to saltwater aquarists.

Brackish water

If you've never heard of brackish water, don't panic because I'm not going to spend any time on this kind of aquarium. Brackish water is actually a kind of aquarium that is neither pure fresh water nor pure salt water, but something in between. Basically, brackish water areas occur where salt water meets fresh water, providing a mix. Brackish water occurs naturally along the coastline in many bays and coastal ponds. These areas are called *estuaries,* and many species of fish use these areas to spawn and their young spend much of their early lives there. Brackish water aquariums are specialized and complicated, accommodate special species that are difficult to obtain, and are definitely not for the beginner. Therefore, in this book, I don't address this type of semi-marine aquarium.

Types of saltwater aquariums

Saltwater aquariums aren't all the same, and you can style your system to whatever you like. The best way to think about the different kinds of marine aquaria is to look to nature and see the unique environments in the ocean. If you live in the north, you know that the ocean tends to be darker with very different kinds of fish than the crystal clear coral reefs of the tropics. While most people prefer a tropical reef aquarium, you may want to recreate the habitats of the northern coldwater fishes in your home. The choice is yours, and your options are limited only by the level of your commitment and the size of your pocketbook.

You can classify the kinds of marine tanks in many ways. Some experts go by the types of organisms that you put in it, while others group them based on the type of environment that you're trying to recreate. Both methods are valid, and I present all the options available, starting with what occurs in nature.

Tropical

By far, the most common saltwater aquarium contains the brilliantly colored fish and invertebrates that come from warm tropical waters of the world. These creatures are clearly the most beautiful, most social, and most entertaining. These systems are typically referred to as *tropical marine tanks* or *reef tanks,* and these tanks are further classified by the types of animals that they hold. A tropical marine aquarium typically has a heater to maintain its high temperature requirement (see Chapter 4).

Coldwater

As the name implies, coldwater tanks hold fish that come from the more northern, or temperate, parts of the world. In the eastern United States for example, these would include animals that live in the ocean from Maine to Virginia. Fish and invertebrates from these areas prefer cooler water, come in fewer varieties, and are less colorful than their southern friends. These aquaria don't need heaters but do require chillers to keep the water temperature between 60° and 66°. Because you may heat your home in the winter, chillers aren't needed only in the summer. Unfortunately, chillers are expensive, and you can plan on adding a couple of hundred dollars to your equipment tab to set a coldwater marine aquarium. Because coldwater systems aren't very common, I don't plan on spending a lot of time discussing this option in this book.

Most coldwater species are collected by aquarists and aren't readily available in pet stores. If you plan on collecting your own fish, be sure to check with local fish regulations to be sure that you don't inadvertently break the law. You may save money on fish, but the fine will certainly defeat that purpose.

The type of saltwater aquarium you set up can be further characterized by the way you populate it. In other words, you have the option of putting only fish in your tank, only invertebrates, or a mix of both, which is typically referred to as a *reef tank*. Of course, these are rough classifications. You won't find any set rules as to how you stock your aquarium, as long as everybody who lives in it gets along.

The marine fish aquarium

This is by far the simplest and most popular type of saltwater aquarium. As the name implies, it's stocked with only fish (and no invertebrates) — usually tropical fish, but coldwater systems may be fish-only as well. Before the days of live rock, this type of aquarium was the only type of saltwater aquarium available to the average home aquarist. Because there are no live invertebrates in the tank, the decorations include dead corals and other unnatural settings. These aquaria are the simplest, employing the same basic equipment as a typical freshwater setup. Marine fish aquariums are typically less expensive and require less maintenance than the more complicated reef tanks. As long as the fish that you chose get along, you won't have much to worry about except maintaining high water quality.

Marine fish tanks are not only less trouble but also allow you to collect more aggressive species of fish that would normally feed on the invertebrates of a reef tank. Lighting in these tanks isn't critical, and the proper number of fish to stock is easily estimated. You have only to worry about feeding the fish, and disease treatment is less complicated.

After all is said and done, the marine fish aquarium is a good place for the first-time saltwater aquarist to start. Remember, you can always add to your setup as your skills develop.

The invertebrate aquarium

At one time, only advanced aquarists and fish dealers kept invertebrates. But new advances in technology, new collecting and transporting techniques, and the availability of live rock allows the average home saltwater aquarium to house healthy invertebrates. An invertebrate aquarium is a more natural setting than a marine fish aquarium, but invertebrates are extremely sensitive to water quality, so advanced filtration systems are required. Other equipment, including protein skimmers and specialized lighting, is essential, as well. I talk more about protein skimmers in Chapter 3, but suffice it to say that this important piece of equipment removes waste from the water. But why more light with invertebrates? A lot of people don't realize that invertebrates, like corals and anemones, have tiny organisms in their bodies that capture light the way plants do, providing energy for their hosts. Without intense light, these organisms and their hosts will die.

Live rock (not a concert)

Live rock isn't actually rock that's alive, it's rock that is inhabited by large numbers of tiny animals and plants. The rock is either harvested from the sea or cultivated in tropical areas for the aquarium trade. By adding live rock to your aquarium, you're adding a well-established, healthy invertebrate, plant, and algal community. This will basically jump-start your aquarium and provide a foundation for your mini-community. The reason that live rock isn't typically added to fish-only tanks is because the fish will eat the inhabitants of the live rock.

Live rock provides the foundation of the invertebrate tank to which corals, sponges, anemones, and other invertebrates are added. Without fish in the aquarium, you don't have to worry about fish predation on the more delicate invertebrates, and you can expand the diversity of your tank inhabitants. The invertebrate aquarium is extremely attractive, but if you like fish with your invertebrates, you may want to consider a mixed species aquarium.

As with any aquarium, take care to choose animals that are compatible, even if they're all invertebrates. For example, lobsters are known to eat many kinds of invertebrates, so don't place one of these bad guys in the tank.

The living-reef aquarium

Also known as a *mixed-species aquarium, mini-reef aquarium,* or *micro-reef aquarium,* the reef aquarium is by far the most natural setup. If you've ever snorkeled in the ocean, seen underwater television shows, or visited an aquarium, you know that a balanced natural underwater setting includes both fish and invertebrates. As a matter of fact, even the most diverse fish habitat in the world — the coral reef — contains far more invertebrates than fish! In the wild, fish eat invertebrates and invertebrates eat invertebrates, but the whole community lives in harmony because of the size of their community (the ocean is huge!). With a home aquarium, you're limited by space, so this harmony is simply not possible. Therefore, when you set up a mixed species aquarium, take great care to buy only species that get along; that is, don't eat each other. Therefore, the reef aquarium is really an invertebrate aquarium with a few docile species of fish.

As you may expect, the setup is similar to an invertebrate aquarium, relative to water-quality equipment and lighting, but the extent to which you outfit your aquarium depends on the number and types of invertebrates that you add.

You won't find any set rules when putting together your mixed species aquarium, as long as you provide the right amount of filtration and light and keep a community that gets along. Your reef aquarium isn't limited to those found in the tropics. You're more than welcome to establish a coldwater reef community if that's what you desire, but most enthusiasts prefer a tropical reef aquarium. The most advanced mixed-species aquariums contain only species that occur naturally together in the same geographic region, for example, a Caribbean reef aquarium or a Hawaiian reef aquarium. Some even prefer a more specialized setup that contains more aquatic plants and algae, invertebrates, and just a single delicate species of fish, like the seahorse.

No matter what kind of mixed-species tank that you set up, when you mix fish and invertebrates, you'll need to grapple with important issues.

✔ Some species of fish eat invertebrates, and the reverse is true as well. So take care when selecting fish.

✔ You may have difficulty treating your fish if they contract a disease because many of the common disease treatments, like copper, kill invertebrates.

✔ Because invertebrates require very clean water that's low in wastes, you're going to have to keep the number of fish to a very low number in a mixed-species tank. The more fish, the more toxic fish waste, and the higher the probability of causing harm to the invertebrate community.

✔ Reef tanks require more sophisticated filtration equipment, tend to be more costly, and clearly require a bit more attention.

Don't let these aspects of the reef aquarium deter you from setting one up, because the pros far outweigh the cons. These tanks are the most beautiful aquarium setup that you will encounter, representing a balanced mini-version of the natural environment. This, in itself, makes the effort worthwhile. In Chapter 3, I discuss the filtration needs of the reef aquarium, and in Chapters 5 through 7, I point out the other special kinds of equipment you need.

Planning Your Aquarium

To determine which type of saltwater aquarium you can set up, ask yourself what kind of tank you want. Your answer hinges on whether you want a fish-only tank, whether you want invertebrates, whether you want both, and how much time you're willing to commit to the aquarium. This section may help you sort out your answers.

Search and research

Just the mention of the word "research" conjures up thoughts of a laboratory or a dusty old library. Fret not, I'm not talking about that kind of research, but the fun kind of research. Perhaps a visit to an aquarium dealer or a public aquarium will help you refine you preferences. When I was young and had the time, I spent many hours in the pet store watching the fish and choosing the kinds that I wanted in my aquarium. (Because not all dealers are alike, feel free to check out a few dealers.) Strike up a conversation with some of the shopkeepers and employees so that you can start laying the groundwork for choosing the right dealer right from the start. I discuss choosing the right dealer in the "Find a really fishy dealer" section later in this chapter.

Almost every major city has some kind of public aquarium. These are the places where you really see a wide variety of fish and invertebrates from all over the world. The folks who run aquariums are professionals who can't afford a bad display, so most displays are well kept and truly beautiful. At public aquariums, marine animals are often kept in aquaria that mimic their natural habitats, so you can get a full appreciation of the diversity of marine life. Granted, you won't be able to set up such elaborate surroundings in your home, but nothing says that you can't get ideas about the kind of system that's right for you. Don't walk up to the shark tank and say to yourself "that's for me:" It's simply not feasible. Besides, sharks can be a pain to feed, literally! However, perhaps that aquarium of Indo-Pacific butterflyfish tickled you fancy? Now that's a setting you can copy! After visiting a public aquarium, go to an aquarium dealer and put your ideas in motion, price out your options, and check for availability. It's decision time.

Organize it!

Make sure you put all your ideas on paper as you plan your aquarium. Write down what kinds of fish and invertebrates you're looking to put in your aquarium. Keep a running tally on costs. Even sketch out your tank setup with all its components, both inside and out. Make many of the decisions in the planning stage instead of trying not to make it up as you go along. Set up a game plan, so to speak. Oh, you'll have to make some changes as you encounter small problems, but a course to follow makes it easier.

Find a really fishy dealer

Finding and establishing a rapport with the right dealer is important to the entire aquarium process, from the initial purchase to treating diseases to troubleshooting. This book gets you started and helps you keep a healthy aquarium, but this book can't anticipate all the new developments in the aquarium trade that your dealer will have immediate access to.

The first step in finding a qualified dealer is, of course, to find out how many near you carry and outfit saltwater aquariums. Depending on where you live, you may have access to a single pet store or many. Keep in mind that a lot of aquarium stores carry freshwater setups because they're more popular and less expensive, yet they don't have any saltwater aquaria. The store that has primarily freshwater tanks and just one saltwater aquarium is not the ideal place to purchase your supplies. Remember that you're looking for expertise as well as equipment, and the part-timer generally lacks an extensive supply of both.

I hope you have access to a number of dealers that you can evaluate. You want to establish a good working relationship with your aquatic dealer because you need someone to advise you during the setup and maintenance of your system. You want somebody who maintains a good, clean business, has healthy fish in his or her aquariums, and is always willing to answer your questions and spend time with you. A good dealer gives you invaluable information on new products and reliable products. He or she is motivated by the desire to help you maintain your system correctly — not solely by money. Choose someone with the right attitude: someone who will be consistently available to help. Try to avoid dealers who don't take the time to explain details to you or find the specific fish that you desire. I prefer the pet shops that cater to the needs of all levels of enthusiasts, are willing to special order supplies, and would rather send you elsewhere than sell you an improper choice.

If you've worked successfully with a freshwater aquarium dealer in the past, this would be the logical place to start with your marine interests.

Sometimes it's worth spending a few more minutes in your car or spending a little more money to get to a qualified dealer if your options are limited. One thing I stress to all aquarium enthusiasts is that if you find the right dealer, establish an excellent rapport, and get great service and advice, be sure to stick with that dealer for all your needs. Why? Just like a good family doctor, you want to establish trust and a good business relationship. To shop around for a little savings simply isn't worth compromising a good source. If, however, the quality of help starts to diminish, all bets are off and you can move on to a different dealer.

To evaluate a dealer, go to the shop and spend some time. See how many saltwater aquaria the dealer has; look for well-stocked shelves of aquarium supplies, equipment, and food options; and seek advice to see what kind of response you get. Don't be afraid to ask the proverbially stupid question (even if you already know the answer)!

It's all about the fish

Sharpen your fish-watching skills by taking the time to take a good, hard look at every saltwater aquarium the dealer carries. Make sure the water looks clear and clean. If not, the water may be medicated. If it is, why? Some dealers keep some tanks under continuous copper medication for new fish arrivals, and although this isn't a bad thing, you definitely don't want to buy new arrivals until they have settled in and survived the rigors of capture and transport. Feel free to ask the dealer when a fish arrived and how long he or she has had it.

Inspect the fish for signs of fatigue, disease, and stress. A healthy fish has clear eyes and skin, good balance in the water column, and clean healthy fins that respond rapidly as the fish moves. (See Chapter 9 for more on fish anatomy.) These fish usually have their wits about them and respond readily to your moves, as well. You can also evaluate the health of the animal by watching it feed. If a fish or invertebrate feeds in captivity, it's a pretty good sign that it's well adapted to its surroundings and its aquarium is clean and healthy.

The water column refers to the body of water from the surface to the bottom. Some fish live at the top of the column, some live on the bottom, and others prefer the middle. A healthy fish can maintain its balance and position in its preferred part of the water column.

Obviously, dead fish in the tank are a very bad sign, and if the dealer has a propensity to kill fish, drop him from your preferred dealer list.

And don't forget about service

Some dealers go above and beyond simply providing fish, equipment, and advice. Some stores offer water quality testing, aquarium seminars, maintenance and repairs to your equipment, and disease diagnosis and treatment. As far as I'm concerned, these services put these stores into the preferred status.

Where to go

You may have a lot of options when finding a dealer that sells saltwater aquariums, fish, and supplies. Options may range from your small pet shop to a mega-mart to the Internet. Each of these has its advantages and disadvantages, but you want to select the one that offers you the best advice and the right choices. Don't typecast any kind of store: Your local neighborhood pet store may prefer to sell cats and dogs and dabble in fish, or they may prefer to sell fish and dabble in cats and dogs. The pet supper store that's part of a chain may have a lot of supplies, but the fish person may be a part-time high school kid who's more interested in his or her clothes. Alternatively, that same store may have hired a fish specialist who treats each tank and the trade as a true vocation. This may also apply to a small pet section in the back of a department store.

So what's the bottom line? The person behind the counter! If that person loves the hobby of aquarium-keeping, he or she will take the time to be well versed in the trade, stock the store with the right supplies, and take excellent care of fish and invertebrates. If you find a dealer like that, give the shop your business. The dealers wants to stay in business to keep getting paid for doing what makes him or her really happy. And you don't stay in business if your employees are disrespectful, your shelves are poorly stocked, and your customers' fish die.

Chapter 2

Choosing an Aquarium

- -

In This Chapter

▶ Figuring out where to put your aquarium

▶ Choosing the right aquarium for you

▶ Covering your aquarium

▶ Supporting your aquarium

- -

*I*n this chapter, I discuss one of the most important parts of the aquarium system: the aquarium itself. You can probably get away with leaving one or two aquarium components out of the system and having your fish survive. They may live only one day, but they will live nonetheless. However, without the aquarium tank itself, you and your marine friends don't have a chance. Fish and invertebrates simply don't deal well without water, in a box or permanently in a bag: They need a tank to live in. Not just any container sold at a pet store will do.

For marine creatures, the old-fashioned goldfish bowl isn't a comfortable option. I liken it to forcing someone to live in a closet without ventilation! Keep away from goldfish bowls, Siamese fighting fish bowls, small rectangular plastic ornamental tanks, or homemade wooden contraptions. I can guess what you're thinking: Who would use such things? I'll keep the names to myself, but it has happened before. Simply put, the aquarium tank isn't the piece of equipment that you decide to save a few bucks on.

As you may expect, you have quite a few options. Aquariums come in many shapes, sizes, and styles. They can be glass or acrylic, tall or short, rectangular or multi-sided. What you choose depends on several factors, which include the amount of space you have available, the amount of money you want to spend, the number of fish you want to hold, and, last but not least, what tickles your fancy. This chapter helps you sort through those options.

Deciding Where Your New Aquarium Should Live

After you set up your aquarium system, you're not going to move it unless you take it completely apart. So choosing a permanent site for the aquarium is something you don't want to take lightly. (In fact, you want to decide this during your planning process.) This section shares a few tips and reminders.

Fish watching

I think I can assume that you're not setting up an aquarium for exercise. Instead, you, like me, find marine fish and invertebrates fun, beautiful, peaceful, and exciting. So, you need to place your aquarium in an area of the house where you will enjoy it most and where you're likely to spend a lot of time. (That doesn't mean the garage if your other hobby is working on cars!) Generally, the living room or den is a great place to put it. Well-used living areas provide an excellent setting for your aquarium because the fish acclimate to people entering and leaving the room. Poorly used areas will render fish skittish and timid when people enter or approach the tank. Don't, however, choose the busiest room in the house. Too much activity can spook your tank inhabitants or cause damage to your tank. For example, the kids' playroom may be a fun place for the aquarium, but jumping children and flying objects don't blend with a peaceful aquarium.

Aquariums can be fun, but they also require some attention. Routine system checks are easy if the aquarium is in a place where you can spend a lot of time watching fish. You don't want to be forced to make a special trip out to the aquarium room in the very back of your house, past the dog that really doesn't like you.

Windows and doors and floors

You may have the perfect room for your aquarium picked out because you spend a lot of time there. But a few other factors may change your mind. Suppose the spot you chose is right next to a huge picture window, behind a swinging door, on the third floor of a house built in 1850. Good location? Not! Here's why: First, while windows illuminate the room and the aquarium, they cause problems for your little ecosystem. Light and temperature are two very important parameters that you will keep an eye on in your aquarium (see Chapters 4 and 5). You don't want either of these to change greatly from day to day. An aquarium too close to windows will be illuminated by direct sunlight, causing changes in water temperature and promoting extensive growth of algae. Algae can be good, but too much is not!

Similarly, doors let in drafts and sunlight, causing light levels and tempera-ture to fluctuate. In addition, a swinging door may hit your aquarium, and a cracked aquarium is a disaster!

The strength of your floor is also very important. Make sure the part of the house you have chosen can hold your aquarium when it's chock full of water, gravel, rocks, coral, and equipment. Keep in mind that salt water weighs 8.4 pounds per gallon, so a fifty gallon tank weighs at least 420 pounds and that's without the other system components. The floors in older homes may not be able to support this kind of weight.

Hot and cold

Bearing in mind that you have to maintain a relatively constant aquarium temperature, you can see why room heaters and air conditioners can cause problems. If you live in an area with hot and cold seasons, all your rooms have some kind of heat source. I don't expect you to remove it for the aquar-ium, and you shouldn't. The room heater will actually assist the aquarium heater in keeping the water in your tank at the right temperature. (If you didn't have a heat source in the room, the aquarium heater would be running almost constantly.) On the other hand, if the room's heat source is too close to the aquarium, it may overwhelm the heater in the tank, causing water-temperature problems.

Much of this information is also true for room air conditioners, which can cool a tank.

Water and electricity

Now when I think about water and electricity, I see a dangerous mix. But the fact of the matter is that when you set up an aquarium, you positively need both to make it work. Normally, placing electric motors and gadgets in and around a tank full of water is a no-no. (So parents, don't let your children set up the aquarium alone!) More than once, I've felt the odd sensation of 110 volts being conducted through my body because I wasn't paying attention. This wasn't pleasant and was potentially lethal! Keep in mind (and teach your children) the dangers of electricity and the importance of following the proper steps of aquarium setup.

All electrical equipment for your aquarium should plugged into connectors with ground fault interruption capability. These types of outlets are inexpen-sive, easy to install, and go a long way in preventing electrocutions.

When you choose the final resting place for your aquarium, you must have access to water and power. Moving buckets of water through a living room loaded with 17th century furniture may not be the greatest idea. Running extension cords across the room to power as many as ten electrical components doesn't sound good, either. Instead, find a spot with easy access to a water source and a power source.

Keep in mind that no planning in the world will keep an area from getting wet from the aquarium and its maintenance. You may not want to set the tank on your favorite Oriental rug. Choose an area that can tolerate a little moisture from time to time. Set your tank so that you have easy access on all sides for cleaning and maintenance.

Marine tanks suffer from *salt creep,* which is caused by the bubbling of salt water. When water is bubbled or is splashed, the water evaporates, leaving the salt deposit on the tank glass, filter unit, and just about everything that the water contacts. You can reduce salt creep with an aquarium hood (and I talk about that in the "Putting a Lid on It" section of this chapter), but you must have access to all sides of your tank so you can clean it.

Determining What Size Tank Is Best

The general rule is to buy the largest aquarium you can afford and accommodate in your home. The reason for this is straightforward: Would you rather live in a one-room apartment of a five-room suite? Fish and invertebrates require space to swim and sufficient oxygen to live, and both are dictated by the size of the tank.

The oxygen content of water is related to the surface area of the tank. *Surface area* is the amount of area on the surface of the tank that's exposed to air. The more surface area a tank has, the more room for gas exchange at the surface and the more oxygen enters the water and toxic gases, like carbon dioxide, leave the water. Oxygen content is also related to the temperature of the water. Warmer water has less oxygen than colder water. Because most marine tropical fishes prefer water in excess of 75°, the amount of oxygen may be limited in the tank, so you have to increase your surface area. How do you do that? By choosing a tank that has a large area on top that's exposed to air.

Tanks come in all sizes and shapes. Although two tanks may have the same volume, their shape dictates the amount of surface area, which may be different. Tall slender tanks don't have a lot of surface area relative to the volume of water, so you don't get a high rate of gas exchange with one of these. On the other hand, a short, wide tank has more surface area and is better for gas exchange. For example, consider two 55-gallon tanks; one measures 48 inches long × 12 inches wide × 21 inches high, and the other measures 36 inches long × 12 inches wide × 28 inches high. The volume of these tanks can be calculated by multiplying length by width by height; the surface area is equal to just length times width. Both tanks have a capacity of 12,096 cubic inches, but the first tank has a surface area of 576 square inches and the second tank has a surface are of 432 square inches. Clearly, the first tank is preferred. These are simple calculations, so don't be afraid to go to your dealer with a measuring tape and a calculator before you pick out your aquarium. You should already have a general idea of the size you want, given the space available in the spot you chose for the tank.

Room at the inn

When choosing your tank, the number of aquarium inhabitants your aquarium can accommodate may factor into your decision. If you put too many fish into your tank, you will overcrowd it, the filtration system will be overwhelmed, and you will have serious water quality problems. In addition, fish become stressed when they're crowded, and stress leads to disease and death. (Have you ever been in an overcrowded elevator?)

Several different methods have been used to determine fish capacity and there are several general rules. Most aquarium enthusiasts use fish length and tank volume to estimate the number of fish that a marine aquarium can hold. Larger fish consume more oxygen and, therefore, require more aquarium space.

You can probably accommodate one inch of fish per four gallons of water for the first six months. Gradually increase fish density to one inch per two gallons after this initial period.

For example, a 40-gallon aquarium should contain no more than 10 inches of fish for the first six months. These may be comprised of one three-inch queen angel, two one-inch clownfish, one two-inch regal tang, one one-inch bicolor blenny, and two one-inch Beau Gregory's. After six months, additional fish may be added gradually to increase the total number of inches to 20. Keep in mind, however, that fish grow, so your two-inch regal tang may grow to three inches in those six months. Also, realize that this general rule doesn't compensate for the shape of the fish. The width of a fish is called its *girth*. For example, the girth of an eel is much smaller then that of a grouper. The six-inch eel is likely to require less space than the six-inch grouper, so the general capacity rule doesn't apply. If you plan to keep heavier fish, be more conservative in your tank capacity calculations.

In my opinion, it's better to err on the side of too few fish than too many.

Bottom line

You may be saying to yourself, "if you leave it up to me, I'll buy the smallest and least expensive tank because I want to minimize my investment." This is one approach, but generally not the best.

A saltwater aquarium is a big investment in money and time, so don't go halfway. All the time in the world won't keep a very small tank from becoming a problem. Buying the wrong tank will lead you to either go buy the right one down the road or discourage you from becoming a long term aquarium enthusiast, resulting in a waste of money either way. The bottom line is this: If you can't afford or accommodate an aquarium that's at least 30 gallons, don't make the investment.

Looking at the Types of Tanks

After you've decided on the appropriate size and shape of your aquarium, choosing the tank itself is largely a matter of personal taste. In my early years of aquarium-keeping a few decades ago, plate glass tanks and goldfish bowls were the standard. In those days, many of these tanks were framed in metal and came in standard 10-, 20-, and 55-gallon rectangular sizes. Wow, how times have changed with the development of plastics! Modern aquariums now not only come in a variety of sizes, but also come in a number of interesting shapes. Have you ever seen an aquarium table? It's out there. Both glass and acrylic tanks are available to you, and each has its distinct advantages and disadvantages. Both styles can be purchased *reef-ready,* as well. That means that the tanks have predrilled holes for equipment and plumbing, but this feature can be a bit more expensive.

Good old glass

Glass tanks, like the one shown in Figure 2-1, are sealed with a silicone rubber cement. Although the most common design is rectangular, glass tanks are also available in a variety of multi-sided shapes like octagon and hexagon. They are built for the sole purpose of housing living animals and are, therefore, nontoxic. Glass also doesn't scratch as easily as acrylic does.

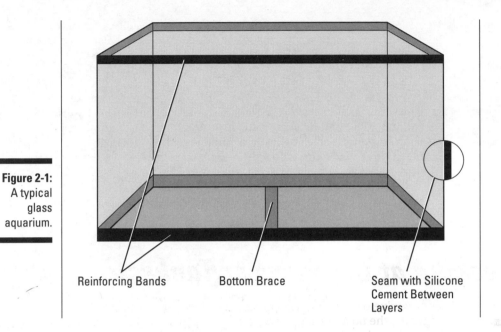

Figure 2-1:
A typical
glass
aquarium.

Reinforcing Bands   Bottom Brace   Seam with Silicone
Cement Between
Layers

Glass is heavy, however, and the larger the tank, the thicker the glass. Keep this in mind when you're finding a good location for the aquarium. Most glass aquariums are equipped with plastic frames that provide some stability as well as attractiveness. The frames come in a variety of colors and styles, so you can pick one that matches the drapes, if you so choose.

In today's aquarium market, the glass used in these tanks may be either plated or tempered. I don't have the space to get into the specifics of how each glass type is made, but suffice it to say that plate glass won't shatter like tempered glass will, and plate glass is more common than tempered, but not as strong. If you plan to drill holes in your glass aquarium for filter plumbing, make sure it is plate glass.

In general, glass aquariums are still by far the most common and practical to buy. Glass happens to be my preferred choice because I'm a bit old-fashioned.

Crazy-looking acrylic

Acrylic aquariums are molded as a single piece with few seams. This makes them more transparent, but you will get some viewing distortion of the tank inhabitants at the corners. Acrylic is also lighter than glass and is offered in more shapes and sizes than standard glass aquariums. Acrylic tends to be stronger than glass, so it doesn't break or shatter as easily.

However, acrylic tanks do scratch easily and can be quite a bit more expensive than glass. Algae scrapers and tank decorations can also cause damage to the tank when not properly handled. Although not easy to repair, scratches in the acrylic can be buffed out with special scratch-remover kits.

When choosing your tank, either glass or acrylic, be sure you select one with no scratches. Also check that no areas are devoid of silicone by closely inspecting the aquarium seams. Also, although I don't recommend this if you're a beginner, some enthusiasts build their own tanks. If you have some technical expertise in handling glass or plastics, go for it, but be sure to use non-toxic silicone cement to seal the seams.

Putting a Lid on It

An essential item for any aquarium is a *hood* (also called a *canopy* or cover). This important piece of equipment performs a variety of functions that will make your life and those of your friends in the tank easier.

- ✔ It prevents unwanted items from entering the tank and injuring the fish. If little Johnny decides to throw the sand-covered Nerf ball in the house, it's nice to know that the ball, the sand, and little Johnny will not end up in the tank.

- ✔ It prevents overzealous fish from jumping out of the tank. No doubt about it: Fish will jump. Sometimes, they're motivated by another member of the aquarium community; sometimes they're spooked by sudden vibrations or movement in the room. Other times, they simply run out of water while swimming toward the surface. The guy next door who knocks or raps on the aquarium can also cause skittish fish to jump. Remember, fish can't breathe air, and nothing is worse than finding your pet on the floor next to the aquarium in the morning.

- ✔ The cover prevents water from splashing to the walls and floor, causing damage to the aquarium surroundings and salt creep. You don't want to ruin your upholstery!

- ✔ The hood slows the rate of water evaporation from the tank. A properly working aquarium will have a lot of water movement and bubbling from aeration and filtration. In most aquariums, the water temperature is over 75°. Water evaporates when it bubbles and when it is kept at a high temperature. Now when water evaporates from a seawater aquarium, the salts don't leave the tank but become more concentrated, thereby increasing the salinity. (Salinity is discussed in Chapters 7 and 14.) This disturbs the fish and water quality if not carefully monitored. No matter what you do, you need to routinely add water to the tank. To reduce the amount of water that's required, you use an aquarium hood. Water will condense on the cover and re-enter the tank instead of evaporating to the room.

✔ The hood helps the aquarium retain heat, thereby reducing the use of the heating unit.

✔ The hood keeps water from damaging the aquarium light and prevents a potentially dangerous electrical problem. Remember, water and electricity are both important for the aquarium, but you still want to keep them apart.

The hood is generally fitted to the dimensions of the tank and can be adjusted to allow for aquarium accessories. Make sure that it's composed of thick (⅛-inch) glass or plastic so that it can support the weight of other aquarium components if needed. In addition, it should be segmented so that the entire assembly need not be removed to feed the fish or work in the tank.

I strongly recommend the type of hood that also houses the aquarium light. These units are self contained and properly designed to keep water away from the lighting unit, to minimize danger, and to cover the entire tank thoroughly. I've always felt that the tank, stand, and hood should be purchased as a package built by the same manufacturer. This ensures that aquarium components won't be mismatched, and the package may be less expensive than separate components.

Standing under Your Fishy Friends

The best support for the heavy weight of the aquarium and all its components is a commercially manufactured *aquarium stand.* This type of support is built to hold a full aquarium (hundreds of pounds). Homemade stands and common household furniture may look sturdy, but they can fail under such a heavy load. Stand failure can be costly to both the aquarist and the homeowner. Thirty-plus gallons of water can wreck havoc on a room, so don't try to save money on your support for the aquarium.

Of course, if your aquarium is very large, you can place it directly on the floor. But even if your tank is tall enough, you'll still have to look down to enjoy the action, and that can be a pain in the neck.

The most common commercially built aquarium stands are made out of iron or wood. Which one you buy depends on your personal preference.

Iron

Wrought-iron and angle-iron stands are the simplest and least expensive to buy. The design of these stands is open, which doesn't provide much room to hide aquarium components, but they are very sturdy.

Wood

If you're willing to spend more for something more decorative, buy a wooden cabinet stand. The aquarium sits on a cabinet that can house aquarium supplies and equipment behind doors on the front. These cabinets come in a variety of styles and finishes that will likely match your room décor, if that's important to you.

The most expensive aquarium stand is the aquarium enclosure. This is really a cabinet stand that includes a canopy that covers the top of the tank. The canopy may or may not be attached to the cabinet as one piece. These stands can be quite elegant, making the aquarium a handsome addition to your room.

 Be careful to stay away from cabinet stands made of particleboard because they will come apart after long-term exposure to water.

 If you decide to use a piece of furniture for an aquarium stand, place under the tank a ⅝-inch sheet of plywood and a ½-inch sheet of polystyrene cut to the dimensions of the tank. These layers will even out any imperfections in the supporting surface and distribute the load of the tank. Homemade stands aren't uncommon, but if you go this route, make sure that you use materials that can hold hundreds of pounds level.

The specialty tank

The standard community aquarium represents a peaceful compilation of fish originating from multiple areas around the world. Aquarists who desire a more natural aquarium will set up what is referred to as a specialty tank. Don't confuse this aquarium with a species tank. A *species tank* generally houses just one species of fish that may be temperamental, may require special water conditions, or is being kept for breeding purposes.

The *specialty tank* generally contains multiple species of fish and/or invertebrates that originate from one area. In essence, the specialty tank makes every effort to fully mimic one particular habitat. It contains only the animals, substrate, and decorations that come from that habitat.

Marine fish originate from and occupy an incredibly diverse range of habitats. The coral reefs and temperate waters of various oceans contain fish that you can purchase. These geographic areas can be recreated in your home when you set up a specialty tank. To maintain a specialty aquarium, therefore, you need a thorough understanding of the habitat and the ability to recreate that habitat in the aquarium.

Specialty tanks are beyond the scope of this book, but putting one together doesn't require making major changes in your water chemistry. Unlike freshwater habitats, the characteristics of seawater are not radically different among the coral reefs around the world. Therefore, if you intend to stick with a tropical aquarium, you need only consider changing the species composition and some of the decorations to construct a specialty tank. In other words, you won't need to alter your water chemistry if you want to mimic an Atlantic coral reef, an Indo-Pacific coral reef, or a Hawaiian coral reef. When the specialty tank is finished, you'll have recreated another part of the world within your home. Enjoy!

Chapter 3

Figuring Out Filters

*T*he most important requirement of healthy fish is clean water. Just as air is to humans, water is to fish and marine invertebrates. Imagine how you would feel if you were literally forced to inhale bad air, like car exhaust, all the time. Fish in the natural marine environment are generally exposed to an open system where water quality isn't a problem. Products of respiration (breathing) and digestion are readily swept away and naturally filtered. The sheer volume of water keeps problem substances at levels that are virtually nonexistent.

On the other hand, fish housed in the aquarium live in a closed system where products of respiration and digestion remain until they are removed. The primary piece of equipment that removes toxic substances from the aquarium is the filter. An aquarium without a filter is like living in a house without plumbing. Ugh!

In Chapters 13 and 14, I discuss the chemistry of water and how it affects your fish. You don't need to read those chapters before making some important decisions on filtration, however. Basically, all you need to know is that fish and invertebrates are living creatures that, like all living things, take substances from the environment and give substances back to the environment.

Understanding Respiration and Digestion

Fish and invertebrates need to breathe oxygen to stay alive. When they remove oxygen from the water, they put back carbon dioxide. We call this *respiration*. Humans respire as well, only we can't do it underwater. So, not only do fish need oxygen in the water, but they also change the chemistry of the water by putting back carbon dioxide. When fish excrete urine, they also get rid of waste substances that are high in nitrogen, namely ammonia.

Fish and invertebrates in your aquarium also need energy to live, and this comes from the food that you feed them. Just like other living creatures that eat food, these animals process it internally, taking away important nutrients and disposing of wastes. These wastes, which break down into ammonia, need to be removed from the water, as well.

The inhabitants of your aquarium aren't the only ones that put substances into your aquarium water. So do you! Not all the food that you feed your pets is consumed, and those morsels that aren't consumed become aquarium waste that breaks down into its chemical components like carbon, nitrogen, and hydrogen.

As you can read more about in Chapter 13, ammonia and other compounds with nitrogen are harmful to fish and invertebrates, so they need to be removed from the aquarium. This is the job of the filter.

Flirting with Filters

Just as the name implies, the filter is a piece of equipment that filters the water in your aquarium. When the aquarium water is filtered, certain substances are either removed from the water and retained in the filter or converted to less harmful compounds and returned to the aquarium. This process is called *filtration*. Substances that are retained in the filter need to be disposed of when the filter is cleaned.

Not all filters are the same, and no filter removes all the harmful substances from the water. So, while filters help you clean the water, they don't do all the work for you. You still need to make partial water changes to remove some substances, and you also need to clean your filter (see Chapter 16).

Not all filters do the same kind of filtration. The part of the filter that actually does all the work is the *filter medium* (more than one medium is "media," and some filters have several kinds of filter media). For example, the typical power filter has synthetic filter floss in it. This floss filters the water by removing large debris but also provides an area for bacteria to grow. These bacteria act to filter the water, as well. Therefore, filter floss really provides two kinds of filtration.

We categorize filtration into three different kinds: mechanical, biological, and chemical. Some filters provide only one kind, while others provide all three. It's like having ice cream that's just vanilla or ice cream that's vanilla, chocolate, and strawberry. For your saltwater aquarium, you want all three flavors (of filtration that is, not ice cream).

Mechanical filtration

Filters that provide mechanical filtration physically remove suspended particles from the water by passing it through a fine filter medium, which sifts out particles. The filter floss does this. Many filters that you find at the dealer provide at least some degree of mechanical filtration. You can think of mechanical filtration as being very similar to skimming debris from the surface of a pool, only the debris isn't only from the surface of the water but from the entire aquarium.

If not removed, these larger particles that are suspended in your aquarium eventually break down into smaller molecules that mess up your water chemistry. Getting them out when they're larger saves your aquarium from a lot of potential trouble. Obviously, smaller molecules aren't removed by mechanical filtration, so they need to be removed by other means. External power filters and canister filters provide rapid mechanical filtration using filter floss. (How many ways can _you_ use the word filter in a sentence?)

Biological filtration

Biological filtration uses the most abundant form of life in the world — bacteria — to remove harmful molecules, like ammonia, from the water in your aquarium. Although when you think of bacteria, you probably think of nasty little buggers that cause problems, in all honesty, we would be in serious trouble if we didn't have bacteria in our lives. In an aquarium, bacteria drive the nitrogen cycle, which is the conversion of a harmful nitrogenous substance, like ammonia, into a less harmful substance, like nitrate. In Chapter 13, I discuss the nitrogen cycle in detail because it is essential to the successful maintenance of your aquarium. For this chapter, suffice it say that the bacteria that live in a filter or filter media provide biological filtration of your aquarium water, thereby removing molecules that mechanical filtration can't.

An excellent example of a biological filter is an undergravel filter, which draws water through the aquarium substrate. The _substrate_ is the stuff that you put on the bottom of the aquarium — the gravel. The gravel is actually filter media because it contains the necessary bacteria to convert nitrogenous wastes to nitrate. Some filters provide both biological and mechanical filtration. A good example is filter floss. It not only acts as a mechanical filter, it also provides a substrate for bacteria to colonize for biological filtration. Although this type of filtration requires a bit more time to establish a healthy bacterial colony, it provides the best kind of filtration — and every saltwater aquarium requires biological filtration.

After your biological filter is well established, don't throw it out to clean it — you would have to start from scratch to re-establish a new bacterial colony. Biological filters that allow you to simply rinse the media and reuse it are the best ones to purchase so that your bacterial friends are saved and can help you another day.

Chemical filtration

When you add activated charcoal to your filter, you're providing chemical filtration to your water; that is, the filter is using a chemical treatment to remove toxic substances from the aquarium. Some aquarists consider chemical filtration to be another form of mechanical filtration, but at the molecular level. Think of mechanical filtration as the removal of debris that's suspended in the water and chemical filtration as the chemical removal of substances that are dissolved in the water.

For example, activated carbon in your power filter absorbs dissolved molecules from the water by trapping them. Other filter media, like zeolite and ion-exchange resins, similarly remove toxins from the water by taking advantage of their molecular shape. You can turn a filter that provides mechanical filtration, biological filtration, or both into a one that also provides chemical filtration by adding one of these media to the filter. Many of the commercially available filters on today's market allow you to do this, primarily with activated carbon.

Chemical filters get used up over time and need to be replaced. Whereas some mechanical and biological filter media can be rinsed, chemical filter media, like activated carbon, should be thrown out every month or so (see Chapter 16).

Your Filter Choices

Most commercially manufactured aquarium filters provide all three kinds of filtration (mechanical, biological, and chemical), but they do so to different degrees of effectiveness. For example, an external power filter mechanically removes particles, chemically removes toxins (if it contains activated carbon), and biologically converts nitrogenous wastes via the nitrogen cycle in its filter media.

However, you must match the filter with the aquarium. For example, imagine that you're shopping for a vacuum cleaner. A lot depends on what kind of floor you're cleaning and on how big the room is. You're not going to need a really powerful vacuum for wood floors, but a mini-vac may be too small for a living room. The same is true for aquarium filters. The extent to which you need to clean your water is dependent on the type of aquarium you're planning.

Invertebrate and reef aquariums need to have the highest possible water quality for their inhabitants. Invertebrates like corals, sponges, and anemones are sensitive to even the smallest amounts of harmful substances, like ammonia. On the other hand, if you're the owner of a marine fish aquarium (see Chapter 1), you don't need to keep sensitive invertebrates alive, so the filtration system can be less efficient and, perhaps, a little less expensive.

The size of the aquarium is important, as well. Just as a mini-vac won't clean a large room efficiently, a small filter won't keep up with a large aquarium. Size your filtration system to your aquarium — a good dealer can assist you in doing so.

Some of the filters available to the aquarist include internal box filters, external power filters, canister filters, undergravel filters, trickle filters, fluidized bed filters, protein skimmers, and complete external water management systems. In addition, water sterilization techniques are also available in the form of ultraviolet (UV) sterilizers and ozonizers. Choosing the right system for your new aquarium can be a bit confusing given all the different kinds and manufacturers. For the marine aquarium, I thoroughly recommend multiple filter systems, which include all three types of filtration discussed in the preceding section.

In this section, I describe each filter type, give you an idea of what kind of filtration it provides and for what kind of saltwater aquarium it applies, and offer some specific recommendations so that you don't leave this chapter overwhelmed by the options. Keep in mind that because this book is a reference, I'm obliged to at least introduce you to the current technology. By doing so, I don't want to confuse you, I only want you to be familiar with all types of filters so that you're ready when an aquarium dealer tells you that you "must" buy a particular system.

Inside box filter

Also known as a *corner filter,* an *internal box filter* is one of the most basic forms of aquarium filters. Usually relegated to the corner of the aquarium, this small, clear plastic box is filled with filter floss and activated carbon, working its little heart out to keep the aquarium clean. Air is driven from an external air source down into the center of the box, creating a vacuum as it exits and drawing water into the filter. The water pulled in is filtered through the floss mechanically and through the carbon chemically (see Figure 3-1). If the filter is allowed to mature over time, the floss provides a substrate or medium for bacterial colonies to establish, providing biological filtration. Sounds great, right?

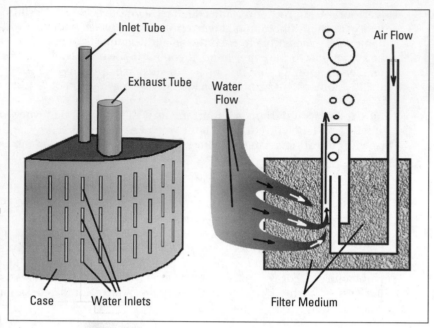

Figure 3-1:
The internal
box filter,
also known
as a corner
filter.

Wrong! Although very inexpensive (less than $5), the box filter is by far the most primitive filter — I haven't had one since my famous freshwater guppy tank of 1971. It's simply too small and inefficient to handle the wastes and debris that accumulate in the aquarium. That doesn't mean that there's no place for the box filter in the saltwater aquarium system. Some aquarists use the simple box filter to keep their smaller quarantine tanks clean (see Chapter 12). Box filters are maintained by replacing the activated carbon and the filter floss, although some of the latter should be retained for the bacteria that they harbor.

Sponge filter

Sponge filters, like the one shown in Figure 3-2, have rapidly replaced box filters in most small saltwater aquarium tanks, like a quarantine aquarium (see Chapter 12). As the name implies, the filter is composed of a sponge material that's highly porous. Like the corner filter, the sponge filter sits in the aquarium and sticks out like a sore thumb. Air is driven into the sponge from an external air pump, and water is pulled into the filter as the air escapes. These filters provide some mechanical filtration, but more importantly, they have enough surface area to support a lot of beneficial bacteria for biological filtration. The sponge itself provides the filter medium, so you don't need additional media. These filters provide no chemical filtration. Sponge filters are easy to maintain (simply rinse), are very inexpensive (less than $10), and come in sizes that can filter tanks up to 125 gallons. However, they are simply too inefficient for a typical saltwater aquarium, except for smaller quarantine tanks.

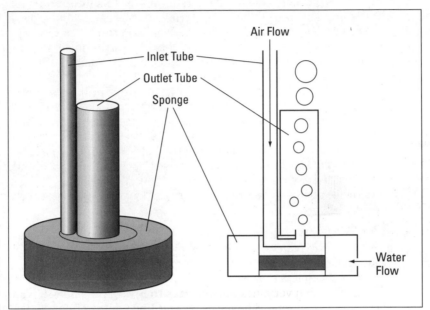

Figure 3-2:
The sponge filter.

Undergravel filter

Undergravel filters are the old workhorses of the saltwater aquarium hobby. For many years, they have been considered the most efficient filters for saltwater aquaria, and no successful tank was found without one. While times have changed and more advanced filtration systems are now available, the undergravel filter is considered by many to still be an effective filtration choice. This filter has also evolved and improvements in this technology make the undergravel filter an excellent choice, particularly for a fish-only aquarium.

The original variety

A basic undergravel filter consists of a perforated plastic plate that rests on the bottom of your aquarium tank under your gravel. At each rear corner of the plate is a lift tube that extends up into the aquarium. Air is pumped to the bottom of each lift tube, and bubbles that come right back up the tube create a water vacuum. This pulls aquarium water down through the gravel and the filter plate and out the lift tube. Therefore, you get water circulating from the aquarium down through the gravel.

In an undergravel filter, your gravel acts as the filter media. Particles and debris get trapped in the gravel providing mechanical filtration. More importantly, excellent biological filtration is provided when the gravel becomes the home of millions of bacteria that break down harmful ammonia. For this reason, certain kinds of gravel are required for this filter, and a longer setup time is necessary to establish bacterial colonies. Most undergravel filters are covered by two grades of gravel: fine gravel on top of coarse, separated by what is known as a *gravel tidy.* After a healthy filtration system is established, this filter can be used for months without intense maintenance and cleaning.

A basic undergravel filter, however, has its share of problems. Debris accumulates in the gravel and needs to be routinely vacuumed out so that the filter doesn't get clogged. Cleaning can be difficult if too many corals and rocks are sitting in the tank, and that's why they aren't well suited for the reef aquarium. Most undergravel filters don't provide chemical filtration, but carbon cartridges that fit on the lift tubes are now available. Also, while air-driven undergravel filters provide aeration, they tend to be noisy and may not be strong enough to provide for adequate water circulation, particularly as the gravel clogs.

Reverse flow

How do you avoid clogging the gravel in an undergravel filter? Reverse the flow of water through it and instead of pulling water through, push it. This way, the filter media doesn't get clogged, and the efficiency of the filter is maintained. There are a couple of ways to reverse the flow of water through the filter: The most common involves adding another filter to the process. By pumping water from the output of a canister filter down the lift tube of the undergravel filter, you can easily reverse the flow of the entire system. You won't have the mechanical filtration of the gravel, but the canister filter will do that for you. (I discuss canister filters in more detail in the "Canister filters" section, later in this chapter). The reverse flow gravel filter provides excellent *biofiltration* (biological filtration) without some of the problems associated with the basic system.

Powerheads

As a major improvement to the undergravel filter, *powerheads* were invented to replace the less efficient air-driven system. The powerhead is a small pump that sits on top of the lift tube and literally pulls water through the gravel from the aquarium (see Figure 3-3). This not only improves filter efficiency but also increases water circulation. These are two big bonuses.

What about aeration? Powerheads now come with a *venturi aerator,* which introduces air into the outflow. But wait, there's more! Reverse flow powerheads are now available that allow you to have a reverse flow undergravel filter without a canister filter.

However, as good as powerheads sound, they don't provide filtration, they just move water efficiently.

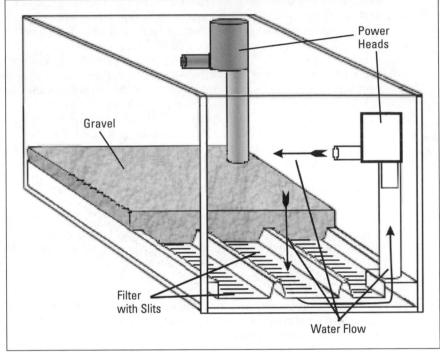

Power
Heads

Gravel

Filter
with Slits

Water Flow

Figure 3-3:
The
undergravel
filter with
power-
heads.

Undergravel filters are relatively inexpensive filters that provide excellent
biological filtration for a fish-only aquarium. If you're going to use an undergravel system, reverse flow is the most efficient, either with powerheads or,
preferably, with a canister filter for added filtration.

Power filters

A power filter is the one of the easiest and least complicated filter systems
for you to employ as a beginner aquarist. The design is simple: Water is
pulled into the filter media and pumped back to the tank. But, as is the case
with most filter systems nowadays, power filters have improved over the
years, and now a few kinds are available.

External power filter

An *external power filter* looks like a big square cup that hangs on the outside of
the tank and is powered by its own motor. The filter generally contains filter
floss or filter sponges and activated carbon as filter media. Water is drawn
into the filter by a U-shaped intake tube, flows through the filter media, and is
pumped back to the tank either through a tube or a spillway. The filter media
provide mechanical and chemical filtration; biological filtration is established

as the filter matures and bacteria colonize it. Therefore, these filters provide all three kinds of filtration and are specifically designed to turn over large amounts of water. The power filter also circulates the water, providing valuable aeration.

These filters are easy to maintain — most have simple cartridges that can be routinely replaced. However, retain some of the used filter floss or use a sponge-type media so that you can hang onto helpful bacteria.

External power filters are ideal for fish-only tanks (see Chapter 1) that also have an undergravel filter system.

Biowheels

Some external power filters come with a nifty option called a *biowheel* (see Figure 3-4). The biowheel comes into contact with both the air and the water in the filter. As water moves through the filter, the wheel spins, exposing millions of bacteria that live on the wheel to the air and the water. Because these bacteria need air to efficiently convert ammonia, this system provides enhanced biological filtration in your power filter. Also, the biowheel allows you to retain these bacteria even though you have to replace the internal filter media. Biowheels aren't available only on external power filters but are also offered as separate units that hang on the back of your aquarium and are powered by a powerhead or canister filter.

Internal power filters

I mention *internal power filters* not because they are an improvement to the external power filter but because they are currently available on the market. These filters are similar to the external power filter, but sit inside the tank, taking up valuable space and obstructing the view. Although most models provide mechanical, chemical, and biological filtration, I don't recommend them as a permanent filter system.

Canister filters

A canister filter (see Figure 3-5) is really just an external power filter that doesn't hang on the tank but sits on the floor or under the aquarium. I'm treating it separately because the canister filter is a different category of power filter that's much more efficient. The canister filter is a self-contained high-pressure pump that draws water from the aquarium with an intake tube and returns it with a output tube that can directed anywhere the aquarist desires (preferably back to the tank). As discussed in the "Undergravel filters" section earlier in this chapter, output from a canister filter can be directed at another filtration system, like a reverse flow undergravel filter or a biowheel.

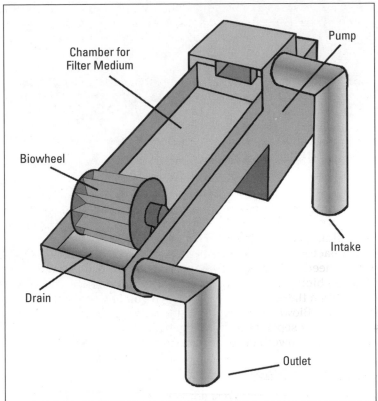

Chamber for
Filter Medium

Pump

Biowheel

Intake

Drain

Outlet

Jee
ible
n th
Glow
ith a

Figure 3-4:
An external
power filter
with a
biowheel.

The filter itself contains compartments with various kinds of filter media, like activated carbon, filter sponges, filter floss, and ceramic bodies. Water is pumped over all the media layers, providing mechanical, chemical, and biological filtration. These filters are more expensive yet provide excellent efficient filtration at a high rate. These filters don't need to be cleaned frequently, and the use of multiple filter media allows valuable bacteria to be retained when the filter is cleaned every three or four months.

If you intend to have more than a fish-only saltwater aquarium, the high efficiency of a canister filter makes it one of my recommended filter options.

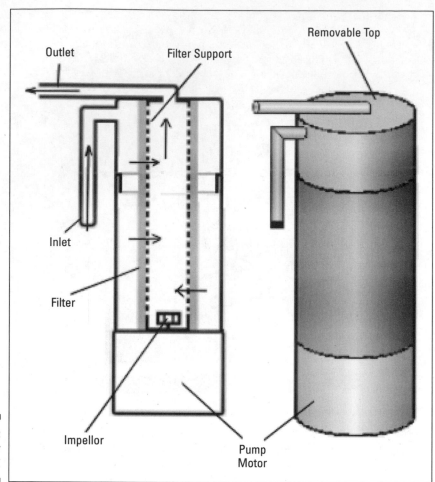

Figure 3-5:
The canister
filter.

Trickle filters

Trickle filters, also known as *wet-dry filters,* were once reserved for aquarists who built their own filter systems. Now, many companies commercially manufacture a number of styles and sizes for home aquariums. In essence, the theory behind the trickle filter is to maximize the exposure of the aquarium water to bacteria and air at the same time (like a biowheel does) so that bacterial conversion of ammonia is most efficient.

An overflow box on the back of your tank delivers water from the aquarium to the large acrylic trickle filter box. The filter box is generally divided into two compartments. The main compartment contains multiple layers of filter media for mechanical, biological, and chemical filtration. This compartment is mostly dry except for the lower few inches. The other compartment contains a pump and other optional equipment. Water from the aquarium is sprayed or trickles evenly over the first compartment through the filter media where it collects at the bottom (or *sump*), moves into the other compartment, and returns to the aquarium (see Figure 3-6).

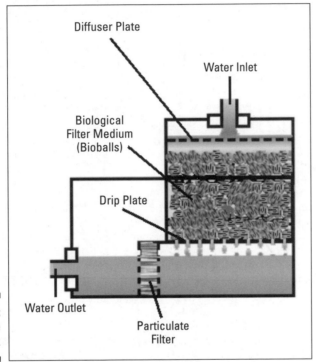

Diffuser Plate

Water Inlet

Biological
Filter Medium
(Bioballs)

Drip Plate

Water Outlet

Particulate
Filter

Figure 3-6:
The trickle
filter.

The filter is called a *wet-dry filter* because of a basic division of bacterial labor in the system. The dry part involves the multiple layers of filter media above the wet part. These media include coarse and fine matting for mechanical filtration and plastic spheres known as *bioballs* for bacterial colonization. Bags of activated carbon are typically placed in the sump for chemical filtration. In the dry part of the filter, water dripping through the system has maximum exposure to air and bacteria for efficient conversion of ammonia to nitrate. The wet portion of the filtration in the sump involves the further conversion of nitrogen compounds (nitrate) to less harmful nitrogen gas. The bacteria that do this don't need oxygen, and the wet portion of the filter allows this to happen. Unfortunately, in most trickle filters, the dry part works very well (up to 20 times better than an undergravel filter) but the wet part is not as efficient, so nitrates must be removed by other means. I discuss this in greater detail in Chapter 13.

Trickle filters offer great advantages over other filter systems relative to filtration efficiency and effectiveness. In addition, many trickle filters on the market today allow you to add other aquarium components to the second compartment of the filter. These include heaters and protein skimmers (see the following section).

Partial Filters

This section contains information about those filters that don't provide all three kinds of filtration but are lacking in one or two types. I've separated these filters from the previous section to emphasize the fact that these filters need to be matched with others for a complete system. Think of these filters as components of a stereo system. The receiver may work beautifully, but you need speakers to make it a complete set.

Fluidized bed filters

Although a relative newcomer to the aquarium world, the *fluidized bed filter* is considered one of the most efficient biological filters. The operation of this filter is quite simple. The unit consists of a sand-filled chamber that either hangs on or sits under your aquarium. An inlet port directs water into the filter and outlets return water to the aquarium. In the filter, your aquarium water comes into contact with millions of sand grains populated by beneficial bacteria for extremely efficient biological filtration.

Some manufacturers claim that these units have 20 times the biological filtering capacity of the same volume trickle filter. The problem is, that's all they do. Therefore, if you intend to have a fluidized bed filter, you need some other filter, like a canister filter or external power filter, for mechanical and chemical filtration and aeration. Fluidized bed filters also need some kind of pump to move water through them. Therefore, you must purchase a powerhead or a similar pump in addition to the filter.

The efficiency of a fluidized bed filter makes it a perfect candidate for a reef aquarium, but other filters are required to provide mechanical and chemical filtration.

In-line filters

I briefly mention in-line filters here because they can be used in conjunction with fluidized-bed filters to provide mechanical and chemical filtration. *In-line filters* are just chambers that contain cartridges with filter media. Water must be supplied to the filters via a powerhead or similar pump.

Protein skimmers

At one time used only in the advanced marine aquarium, the protein skimmer is now commercially available for all saltwater enthusiasts. This piece of equipment utilizes *foam fractionation* to remove dissolved organic wastes from the water. What does that mean? Basically, the protein skimmer is a tube that hangs in the back of your tank. Air is delivered to the bottom of the tube by an external source, generating a cloud of fine bubbles that flow to the surface. Proteins and other wastes adhere to the bubbles, travel to the surface, and collect in a removable cup that's emptied. This is really just a form of chemical filtration, but unlike other filters, wastes are actually removed from the water and not converted to something else. So the protein skimmer takes a lot of burden off the other filters.

 With so many protein skimmers on the market, keep in mind that their effectiveness depends on how long the air bubbles are in contact with the water of the aquarium. In general, the different types of protein skimmers carry out this process in a couple of different ways, which are discussed in the two following subsections.

Counter-current

Counter-current is just a fancy way of saying that the water in the protein skimmer moves in the opposite direction of the air flowing through it. Therefore, in these units, water is pushed down the skimmer cylinder by a powerhead or water pump and air supplied by an air pump to a wooden airstone rises from the bottom of the cylinder. These units typically hang in the tank, thereby obstructing your view and taking up valuable aquarium space. One is shown in Figure 3-7.

 The effectiveness of this kind of protein skimmer depends on the height of the cylinder, which is limited by the height of the tank. The longer the skimmer column, the more air-water contact and the better the cleaning efficiency. Keep this in mind when you select your protein skimmer.

Venturi

These units allow water and air to be injected into the skimmer at the same time by the same water pump. They are situated outside the tank and can be kept out of sight. Although they tend to cost more, you don't have to worry about a separate air supply and wooden airstones.

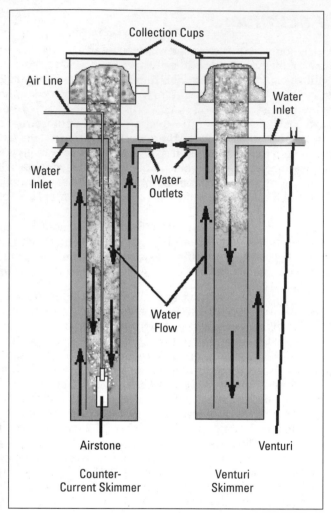

Figure 3-7: A counter-current skimmer.

You can add protein skimmers to your trickle filter sump — several models are designed for that application. So if you plan on having a trickle filter system, you probably want to consider a protein skimmer that will fit into it and be kept out of sight.

No matter what kind of saltwater aquarium that you have, I strongly recommend that you outfit it with a protein skimmer. This minimal investment will save you and your filtration system a lot of time and trouble. Your fish and invertebrates will like it, too!

Diatom filters

This unique aquarium filter system takes advantage of technology that has been deployed by swimming pool filters for decades. *Diatoms* are tiny single-celled algae that are encased in tiny shells composed of silica. Diatom filters use powder-like filter media comprised of these tiny skeletons, which have tiny pores capable of filtering the smallest particles.

Diatom filters are mechanical filters that are actually too efficient, because they remove even the beneficial free-floating tiny animals that your aquarium invertebrates feed on. They are so efficient that they clog rapidly if used for more than an hour. Therefore, diatom filters aren't good for permanent filtration and are best suited to short-term water "polishing" after the bottom is stirred up.

Denitrators

These relatively new pieces of aquarium equipment are designed to reduce the nitrate load in your tank. Nitrate is the end product of the nitrogen cycle (see Chapter 13) and is usually removed with frequent partial water changes. The *denitrator* (which sounds like a killer robot) uses bacteria to break down nitrate, providing biological filtration and reducing the need for partial water changes. Most denitrators consist of a simple airtight chamber filled with substrate for bacterial growth. While most fit nicely into the sump of a trickle filter, some models can be placed in the aquarium.

Denitrators are a relatively new innovation for the aquarium trade and as far as I'm concerned, the jury is still out relative to their effectiveness. If your budget allows for the purchase of one or if one comes with your trickle filter, fine. Otherwise, consider this piece of equipment optional.

Complete water-management systems

For your new aquarium, you can buy a complete water management system that incorporates the biological filtration of trickle filters with chemical and mechanical filtration, heaters, aerators, denitrators, and protein skimmers. These units can be very expensive, but represent the future of water-quality management in home aquariums. Before you purchase your aquarium components, at least look into one of these new systems.

All natural

This discussion of filtration would not be complete if I didn't mention natural filtration. Live rock and sand contain millions of bacteria that assist in the breakdown of ammonia and other harmful compounds. If you plan on having live rock in your aquarium, you will be providing a natural form of biological filtration. Some enthusiasts rely exclusively on this type of aquarium filtration, but I think that this method is a bit too extreme for a new aquarist.

Water Disinfection

There are two common methods for disinfecting water that are commercially available to the home aquarist: ultraviolet sterilizers (UV) and ozonizers. Although some authors recommend one or both of them for the marine aquarium — and, therefore, I discuss them in this section — I don't think they're necessary because they can cause more problems than they are worth.

UV sterilizers

Ultraviolet sterilizers are self-contained units that kill some microorganisms that may be harmful to your fishes. Water is passed from your power filter or canister filter to the UV unit, where it is exposed to ultraviolet light before being returned to the tank. However, the effectiveness of this method depends on many factors, and its usefulness for the home aquarist has been questioned. I recommend UV disinfection only if you intend to maintain delicate species of fishes and only to treat severe outbreaks of disease.

Ozonizers

Ozonizers produce ozone, a compound consisting of three atoms of oxygen, that kills microorganisms in the aquarium. However, the chemistry of ozone in seawater is poorly understood, and ozone can be harmful to humans. Therefore, I don't encourage the beginner to use ozonizers for water disinfection.

Which Filter System Is Best for You

Table 3-1 gives you an idea of the kinds of filter combinations to consider, depending on the kind of aquarium you want. For example, there are four basic filter combinations for the fish-only aquarium, but notice that the reef tank (discussed in Chapter 1, along with the fish-only tank) has fewer options. That's because this type of aquarium requires the most efficient filtration. In addition, I assume that all of these setups include a protein skimmer.

Table 3-1	Filter Combinations for Your Aquarium				
Type	*Undergravel*	*Power*	*Canister*	*Trickle*	*Fluidized*
Fish-only	x	x			
	x		x		
				x	
			x		x
Reef tank			x		x

Aeration and Circulation

In Chapter 2, I discuss the needs of fish and invertebrates — one of these needs is oxygen. The process in which you add oxygen to the water is called *aeration,* pronounced air-AY-tion. Of course, you're really just adding air to the water, but when you do so, oxygen diffuses into the water, and your pets love you for it. Aeration and circulation go hand in hand. Adding oxygen is one thing, but it must be distributed throughout the tank. Circulation is particularly critical for reef tanks because it not only delivers oxygen but also sweeps away wastes, delivers food, and helps the animals' own internal circulation.

By keeping the water moving in the aquarium, you're also evenly distributing the temperature of the water. What good is a heater if it heats only one corner of the tank? (See Chapter 4 for the lowdown on heaters.)

Most of the filter systems discussed in this chapter aerate the water in some way, shape, or form. The undergravel filter with venturi powerheads, for example, provides circulation and aeration. However, input piping from a canister filter or trickle filter provides circulation and some aeration, but you will need to add more aeration in one of the three following ways.

Air pumps

Although most filters provide water circulation and aeration to the aquarium, it is a very good idea to have an external air pump moving air through one or more airstones in the tank. An air pump increases circulation in the tank, promotes oxygen exchange at the surface, and increases the escape of carbon dioxide, carbon monoxide, and free ammonia from the tank. In addition, this increase in circulation acts to mix all the aquarium levels so that a uniform temperature is maintained throughout the tank.

There are two general air pump designs: the diaphragm type and the piston type, both of which are shown in Figure 3-8. The diaphragm pump, also known as the vibrator pump, is the more common of the two and generally provides enough maintenance-free usage for most aquariums. It can, however, be a bit noisy. The piston pump, however, is more powerful and should be used in larger aquariums, particularly if an undergravel filter and multiple airstones need to be powered. In this air pump, air is generated with a piston mechanism.

The size and power output of air pumps vary. Although many are meant to correspond to the size of the aquarium, buy one based on what you're going to do with it. If you plan on powering a protein skimmer and an undergravel filter in your thirty-gallon tank, you need a high-capacity air pump. However, this would not be the case if you simply want to run air to a mermaid ornament in your ninety-gallon tank; you can buy a smaller one.

Airstones and airline tubing

An *airstone,* also known as an *air diffuser,* is generally made of porous stone or perforated wood that allows air to pass through it, splitting the airstream into tiny bubbles. Too fine a mist will cause bubbles to adhere to various tank decorations and to fish. You want the bubbles to travel slowly to the surface and agitate the water. Airstones come in a variety of sizes and shapes, and the ones you choose depend on how much you need to aerate and on your personal preference. Some airstones on the market today can create dramatic effects.

Be sure to keep a watchful eye on your airstones because they will degrade and clog over time, making your air pump work harder and increasing wear and tear. Airstones are relatively inexpensive, so replace them when the bubbles they generate become inconsistent.

Your air pump and airstones will require *airline tubing* to form the link between the two. This is plastic or rubber tubing that delivers air from your pump to the airstone. This should fit snugly at all joints so that air doesn't escape from the system. Air leaks reduce the efficiency of the system (filter, airstone) and may ultimately burn out the pump.

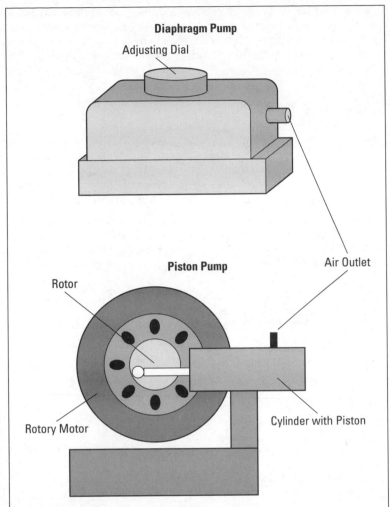

Figure 3-8:
A
diaphragm
and piston
pump.

Make sure the tubing is manufactured for use in the aquarium; other grades may be toxic to fish. Also, airline tubing will degrade over time, so if it starts kinking or cracking, replace it to save your air pump and maintain the efficiency of the air delivery.

If you intend to run multiple airstones or additional devices, like filters, from a single pump, you need one or more air valves. These will enable air flow to be directed to multiple devices from a single pump. The use of several air valves will allow you to turn on and shut off devices as you see fit.

Wavemakers

The most conscientious reef aquarists use a *wavemaker* to increase circulation in their aquariums. The rhythmic movement of water in the tank actually simulates the motion of the ocean, creating a natural setting for the invertebrates in your aquarium. This is not an essential piece of equipment if you have other kinds of equipment, like powerheads and airstones, that circulate the water.

Chapter 4

Heating Your Aquarium

*T*he oceans of the world are different in many ways. One of the most fundamental differences is water temperature. Because many kinds of fish and invertebrates are distributed all over the world, they have adapted over time to these differences in water temperature.

Most fish and invertebrates are cold-blooded animals. That means their body temperatures are the same as the temperature of the waters they live in. In general, their bodies function best at specific water temperatures and, therefore, all fishes have temperature preferences that depend on where they originate.

Based on their temperature preferences, fishes are sometimes grouped in general categories. *Temperate* fishes include many species that inhabit cooler waters. If you set up a coldwater aquarium, it will likely contain temperate fishes.

However, the most common fishes in the marine aquarium are tropical coral reef species. The term *tropical* refers to natural habitats where the waters are warm throughout the year. It should come as no surprise, therefore, that you must heat your aquarium water to a specific temperature range. This is the job of an aquarium heater. This essential piece of equipment maintains your aquarium water at a constant temperature, regardless of the room temperature. This chapter delves deeply into the subject of aquarium heaters.

Feelin' Hot, Hot, Hot

Suppose you live in a warm place, like Florida, year 'round. You may be thinking that you don't need an aquarium heater. Not true. Remember, fish that live in the tropical seas of the world experience few changes in the temperature of the water that they live in. In your aquarium, therefore, you want to mimic the natural environment and maintain as constant a temperature as possible.

Even though your fish and invertebrates can tolerate a range of water temperatures, water that fluctuates even a few degrees can stress your animals and possibly kill them. In Florida, the outside temperature isn't always constant: It too fluctuates. This ultimately creates problems for your pets if you don't have an aquarium heater.

Getting the Right Temperature

Unless you're planning to set up a coldwater aquarium of temperate fishes or invertebrates, tropical marine fish and invertebrate species require that the aquarium temperature be maintained at 75 to 79°. However, this range is entirely dependent on the species you choose, so consult your local pet dealer or one of the many fish encyclopedias (see Appendix A) for the temperature requirements of your specific pet. Make sure that you don't mix species that have very different temperature preferences.

Temperature can be reported in either Fahrenheit (°F) or in the metric Celsius (°C). Don't let this confuse you — it's simply a difference in scale. Throughout this book, I use Fahrenheit. If you want to convert from Fahrenheit to Celsius, simply apply the formula in Chapter 24.

Understanding Hot Parts

As you can expect, a lot of heaters are available on the market for today's home aquarium. Some designs are clearly better than others, but the most popular aquarium heaters work off the same principles and have many parts in common.

With the exception of some specialized heater designs that are relatively uncommon, a basic aquarium heater looks like a big test tube with a bunch of wiring in it and an electrical cord coming out of it. This wad of wiring is actually a heating coil contained in a glass tube that gets submerged in your aquarium. (The extent to which it is submerged depends on the type of heater.). Of course, the heating coil has to be turned on and off, and this is the job of the thermostat, the mechanism that usually determines the quality of the heater. You can set the thermostat with the control knob, and you know that the heater is operating because an indicator light fires up.

Taking a Peek at the Types of Heaters

By knowing the basic parts of a heater (discussed in the preceding section), I can more easily explain the differences between the various types to help you choose the right one.

Hanging heaters

A *hanging heater* is also referred to as the *clamp-on, clip-on,* or *semi-submersible* heater. This is the oldest style of aquarium heater and has been around since my early aquarium days, way back in the '70s. As you may expect, the hanging heater is so named because it hangs on the upper part of the aquarium clamped to the rim of the tank. The glass body of the heater is submerged in the aquarium, but the controls remain out of the water.

Although these heaters are the least expensive, they also tend to be the most primitive, and I don't consider them to be the best choice for the saltwater aquarium. First, their placement at the top of the water column is not the most efficient location for heat exchange. This location also makes them extremely vulnerable to being disturbed by both you and the tank's inhabitants. The more either of you bang into the heater, the higher the chance that it will be damaged (the glass body can crack). These heaters also tend to have less efficient thermostats for controlling their operation.

A damaged heater is a dangerous electrical appliance for all living things near it. Remember, electricity and water don't mix!

After you've made such a significant investment in your aquarium, don't jeopardize the success of the entire system by saving $20 with a cheap heater. Many of your tank's inhabitants are worth more than the amount you'll save!

Submersible heaters

A *submersible heater* (shown in Figure 4-1) is the preferred heater choice for the saltwater aquarium. Also known as an *immersion heater,* the submersible heater is placed fully in the aquarium in any location that you desire. This means that you can put it near the bottom, out of the way of the aquarium's inhabitants, out of your view, and in a more efficient location for heat dispersion. You can even put the submersible heater in the sump of your trickle filter (see Chapter 3), keeping it completely out of the way of the aquarium. In addition, most submersible heaters have advanced thermostat controls that make temperature selection and control easier.

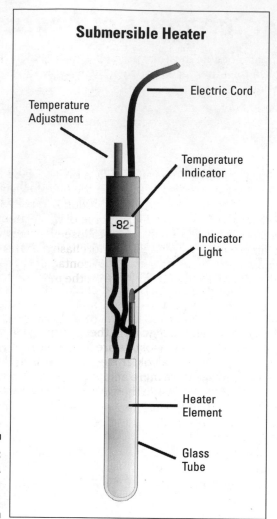

Submersible Heater

Temperature Adjustment

Electric Cord

Temperature Indicator

-82-

Indicator Light

Heater Element

Glass Tube

Figure 4-1:
A
submersible
heater.

Looking for Hot Options

Whether you choose a hanging heater or a submersible heater, look for the following features.

Thermostat

The switch that controls the operation of your heater is the *thermostat,* and it comes in a variety of styles. Most heaters have a built-in thermostat, but others have a separate one. The external thermostat is either placed on the side of the tank or has a separate probe that's placed in the water. Although this style is not common, it offers excellent temperature control because it is electronic, and digital temperature displays are more accurate.

Bimetallic strip

The most common aquarium heater is regulated by a built-in thermostat. Older models have a mechanical thermostat called the *bimetallic strip.* As your aquarium cools, the strip contracts until the circuit is closed and the heater is turned on. This system is the old workhorse of the heater thermostat world, but it has flaws. Bimetallic strips tend to lose efficiency with time and ultimately fail to function properly. If you do purchase a heater with a bimetallic strip thermostat, be sure it has magnetic contacts. These close the circuit more effectively, decreasing wear and tear on the unit.

Electronic

Although heaters equipped with bimetallic strip thermostats tend to be less expensive, heaters with electronic thermostats are better. An electronic thermostat operates more efficiently than an older mechanical thermostat. These units usually detect water temperature more accurately from the glass body of the heater, instead of from the air inside the glass body. In addition, more advanced electronic heaters are designed to fail in the "off" position, so that your fish aren't cooked if the heater has a problem. This gives you time to detect the problem, which is why you want to keep a watchful eye on your aquarium water temperature every day.

Hot spots

Place your heater close to an area of high circulation so that heated water can be rapidly and evenly distributed throughout the tank. This is usually near the filter system, the filter input from an external filter, or the airstones (see Chapter 3). The fully submersible heater should be placed at the bottom of the tank so that heating convection can be optimized. The sump is also a great place, because water is always moving through it.

Temperature control

All heaters have some kind of temperature control that you use to set the proper temperature. The knob that controls the operation of the heater is closely related to the thermostat. I treat it separately because you use this part of the heater to set up its operation. Now some heaters are user-friendly and others aren't.

Older style heaters with bimetallic strip thermostats have control knobs that you use to set the temperature, but you need to calibrate it using a thermometer. Although a fancy sounding word, "calibrate" really just means that you set the heater to operate at a desired temperature, usually about 75°. How do you do that? After your tank is filled and long before you add animals, you place the heater in the tank and then plug it in. Your thermometer will tell you the temperature, and you hope that it's close to 75°. If it's cooler, adjust the control knob just until the point that the heater turns on and the indicator light is on. If the temperature is too high, adjust the knob until the heater is off. Over the next several hours, repeat these steps until the temperature stabilizes at 75°. Perhaps you can see why these heaters aren't very convenient.

On the other hand, you can avoid having to calibrate the heater by buying one of the more advanced electronic heaters. These units usually have a control knob that lets you select the desired temperature. Therefore, all you have to do is set the control dial to 75° without doing any adjustment.

I recommend that you double check the temperature even with electronic heaters after initially setting it up, just to be sure that it's operating correctly.

Thermal protection

Consider this: You're putting a glass tube with electrical elements inside of it into a tank full of water and a bunch of live animals. To most people, that spells an accident waiting to happen. And believe me, any time you put water and electricity together, you're going to have an element of danger. That's why some protective options are available in heaters.

Fish are inquisitive creatures and are bound to investigate your heater. If the heater is hanging an the side of the tank or just lying on the bottom, it's only a matter of time before it gets pushed into the wall of the tank or a piece of coral — and cracks. Make it a point to buy a heater with suction cups, which will keep the heater in one location and buffer it from occasional strikes from both you and your fish. If your heater doesn't come with suction cups, you can purchase them separately to protect your heater.

You can also protect the glass body of the heater itself. I know of at least one manufacturer that markets a protective guard for the heater to protect both the heater and the fish. Some heaters also have protective finishes on the glass body of the heater. These protective coatings include ceramic, Teflon, silicone, and even stainless steel. They may cost more, but the health of you and your fish are worth it.

One Size Doesn't Fit All

You may have selected a type of heater, but now you need to know what size to buy. Size depends on a few factors.

Power

Aquarium heaters come in a variety of sizes based on their power output. This is measured in wattage (just like light bulbs) and ranges from 25 to over 200 watts. It is extremely important to buy the right size heater for your aquarium set up. The general rule is five watts per gallon of water up to 50 gallons. Then, because larger aquaria tend to hold heat better, three watts per gallon is enough power for tanks greater than 50 gallons. So, for example, a 30-gallon tank would require a 150-watt heater while a 60-gallon tank would require a 180-watt heater.

It's not only the size of the aquarium that dictates the size of the heater. You should also take into account how hard the heater has to work. In other words, how cold is the room that the aquarium is in and more importantly, what's the difference between the room temperature and the aquarium temperature? For example, some folks prefer to keep their room temperature at 55°, yet a tropical aquarium should be at 75°. That means that the heater must work to maintain the aquarium temperature 20° above the room temperature. On the other hand, a warmer room would allow the heater to work less.

With this in mind, some heater manufacturers and aquarists size the heater not only to the aquarium, but also to this room-aquarium temperature difference. Basically, if your room temperature is just a little cooler than the aquarium, you can buy a smaller heater than the general rule dictates. If your room is much colder, you need to go bigger. Table 4-1 guides you through the selection. For very large tanks in very cold rooms, I recommend two heaters and this is indicated by a (2) next to the wattage.

Table 4-1	Heater Size Selection		
	Heater Size at Room-Temperature Difference of		
Aquarium Size	*10°*	*20°*	*30°*
15	50W	75W	150W
20	75W	100W	200W
30	100W	150W	250W
40	150W	200W	300W
55	200W	250W	200W (2)
65	200W	250W	250W (2)
75	250W	300W	300W (2)

Hot number

In Table 4-1, you see that larger tanks require more than one heater if the room temperature difference is large. But you don't need to have a large room temperature difference to have two heaters: Here's why. If your single aquarium heater fails or malfunctions, your fish and invertebrates can potentially die. If, however, you have two heaters, the other heater can pick up the slack if one fails. I only recommend this for larger tanks because hiding *one* heater can be difficult, let alone two.

If you opt for more than one heater, simply divide the recommended power by two. For example, instead of a single 200W heater for a 55-gallon tank, you can use two 100W heaters. You may want to put one in your aquarium and one in your sump. A little back-up heater power is a sound investment.

Length

Aquarium heaters come in a variety of lengths ranging from six to fifteen inches. In general, heaters that are more powerful are longer. This is not a problem for the fully submersible heater, but hanging types should be at least three inches shorter than the tank height to account for gravel and other ornamentation.

A word of caution

As with all electrical components, please handle your heater with extreme care. Don't plug your heater in until it is submersed in water regardless of what kind of heater it is. A hot heater will readily burn you, can potentially start a fire, and will crack if you submerse it in water. As a matter of course, keep all of your electrical components unplugged until the tank is completely set up and full.

Conversely, never remove your heater from the aquarium unless it's unplugged. Also allow it to cool even after unplugging it before you take it out of the water.

Choosing a Thermo Meter

Of course, I mean a thermometer, but you should think of it as something that measures the amount of heat in your aquarium, hence a *thermo meter*. This is an essential piece of equipment that I recommend even if your electronic heater has a temperature probe or sensor. A standard thermometer is a minor investment that assures you that your heater is operating properly. A number of kinds are on the market today, and some are more accurate than others.

Floating thermometer

This style has literally been around for decades. It floats in the aquarium, but tends to wander about in the currents if it's not restrained in one area. Finding and reading a floating thermometer can be a hassle, particularly if you have to lift the hood (see Chapter 2) to retrieve it.

Sticking thermometer

Just like a floating thermometer, but it has a suction cup that adheres it to the inside glass of the aquarium. A bit more easily read, but it's something for your fish to play with.

Hanging thermometer

This glass thermometer attached to a stainless steel bracket that hangs on the inside of your aquarium. It stays in place, but may interfere with your aquarium hood and, again, is something for your fish to bump into.

Sinking thermometer

This is really just a floating thermometer that's weighted and sinks to the bottom. It drifts about the aquarium if not secured and provides a toy for your fish, which is not good.

Thermometer-hydrometer

This is a thermometer that's inside your hydrometer and floats in the aquarium. The hydrometer is used to measure the amount of salt in your water. This is called *salinity*. I discuss salinity and hydrometers in Chapter 7.

Liquid crystal thermometer

This thermometer sticks to glass wall of your aquarium on the outside. There's nothing for your tank inhabitants to interfere with, and they are very easy to read but not as accurate as other thermometers. After one is in place, it is difficult to move.

Digital thermometer

A bit more expensive, but a digital thermometer provides electronic accuracy. These are external units that have a temperature probe that goes into the tank. Most also tell you room temperature, and some have a built-in alarm that alerts you when the temperature is too hot or too cold.

Temperature controller

This is a very expensive unit that integrates with a heater and actually controls your aquarium water temperature electronically. These are best for extremely large systems and not essential for you as a basic home aquarist.

Hot tip

This chapter covers a lot of heater options for your aquarium. When in doubt, don't be afraid to buy a little larger unit than you need. A heater more powerful than you need won't hurt, but one that's too small won't be able to keep up. Thermometers are inexpensive (less than $2), so buy a couple, perhaps a liquid crystal stick-on and a floating type. The latter can be kept out of the aquarium and used to double-check the temperature or to check the temperature of water that you're adding to the tank. Ideally a digital thermometer is the best, but the added expense (more than $15) may not be in your budget.

Chapter 5

The Light Choice

*W*hen you think of the tropics, what comes to mind? Bright sunshine and crystal-clear turquoise waters teeming with colorful living creatures, right? Well, sunshine, clear waters, and colorful creatures go hand in hand. In the tropical waters of the world, the water is clear, and sunlight is able to penetrate deeper than in more northern temperate (cooler) waters. This allowed for coral reefs to develop in the areas specially adapted to the right combination of light and water depth. With the coral reefs came a huge diversity of other invertebrates and fishes.

Did you ever notice that where there is no intense light, there is no coral? Coral isn't a plant; it's an invertebrate animal that actually houses tiny plant-like organisms in its body that feed it. Therefore, coral needs light and a lot of it.

Fish need light, as well, but not as much of it. They need to see what they eat, and their lives are adapted to changes in light intensity over the course of a day and over the course of a year. Daily changes in light dictate rest periods for fish. A *diurnal* fish is active during the day and rests at night, and a *nocturnal* fish does the opposite. In addition, monthly changes in light intensity stimulate spawning in many tropical reef fishes and invertebrates. So light is extremely important in the natural environment.

Now, here's the challenge: Bring enough light into your aquarium so that your reef creatures live and act naturally. Is it possible? Yes. Even though it's highly unlikely that you'll get them to spawn, you will be able to mimic natural lighting so that they resume their diurnal or nocturnal habits.

Oh, by the way, a light in your aquarium is good for you as well your fish. What good is an aquarium if you can't see what's in it?

Understanding Light

By definition, light is electromagnetic energy from the sun that's measured in wavelengths. Visible light is what humans actually see, it's composed of light of many wavelengths, and it's called the visible light spectrum. Visible light with the longest wavelength is red. Light with wavelengths longer than this visible light is called *infrared,* but you can't see it without special equipment. As visible light wavelengths decrease, the colors change from red to orange, yellow, green, blue, and violet. Light with wavelengths shorter than this is called *ultraviolet* (UV), and you can't see it, either. UV light can also be damaging to your skin and your eyes.

Before I'm through boring you to tears, I want to add one more bit of knowledge to this physics lesson. The shorter the wavelength of light, the deeper it penetrates in the ocean. Therefore, blue and violet light goes the deepest while red and yellow light are filtered out quickly by the properties of water. This is called *light attenuation,* and fish and invertebrates have adapted quite well to it.

What does all this have to do with aquarium lighting? Well, it turns out that reef invertebrates, like coral, are very dependent on short wavelength light like blue, violet, and even ultraviolet. This light is very important because these animals have photosynthetic algae living in them. These are called *zooxanthellae,* and they are able to take wastes from the coral, harness the energy of the sun, and convert it to energy for the host. What does that tell you? If you plan on having a reef aquarium, you need to increase the intensity of your lighting and include light from the blue side of the spectrum.

Fish, on the other hand, don't have such special needs for high-intensity lighting. Thus, a fish-only marine aquarium shouldn't have high intensity lighting because it promotes excessive growth of algae in the tank, and most fish don't prefer it.

Furnishing Fishtures — er, Fixtures!

Aquarium lighting comes in two general types of fixtures: strip lights and hanging spotlights. Strip lights are simply long lighting fixtures that are either built into your aquarium hood, sit on top of your glass canopy, or hang suspended over your tank. A good example of a strip light is standard fluorescent hood fixture. Most hanging fixtures are high intensity lights that generate a lot of heat and can't be kept on top of the aquarium. Dome-shaped hanging fixtures are referred to as *pendants,* and they deliver a concentrated spot of light.

Watt is power

If you've ever replaced a light bulb at home, you know that the intensity or power of the bulb is measured in watts. This is the case for most standard aquarium lighting, as well. Depending on the type of light, aquarium lighting can be as powerful as 400 watts.

While power is rated in watts, the color of light is rated in degrees Kelvin. I'm not going to get into the specifics as to why, because I think you've had enough physics already. Suffice it to say that aquarium bulbs can range from 5,400°K to 20,000°K, and the greater the number, the more blue light is produced. Typical reef aquar-

ium lighting is about 10,000°K because it produces a lot of blue light. I tell you this because when you're shopping for light bulbs, you'll encounter these numbers.

Another specialized term that you will undoubtedly encounter is *actinic lighting*. Actinic light bulbs produce light at the blue end of the spectrum near UV light. They are ideal for corals and other photosynthetic invertebrates but they aren't full-spectrum bulbs, so additional lighting may be needed. These bulbs are produced for most lighting choices.

Because aquarium fixtures come in a variety of styles, make your choice while you plan your aquarium. The type of lighting you choose depends on your tank's inhabitants and the visual effects you want to achieve. For example, high-intensity lamps that hang above your aquarium will create a much different lighting effect than a standard hood fixture that distributes even lighting. It will look like sunlight rippling through clear tropical waters, creating a truly dramatic natural look. However, if you're going to go with this type of lighting, you really don't want to buy a full plastic aquarium hood (see Chapter 2). Instead, use a glass canopy.

Lighting the Way

You can find a number of choices for lighting your aquarium. In this section, I run through your options and give you an idea of the benefits of each type, including the qualities of the lighting, the initial expense, the amount of electricity a unit consumes, and the life of the bulb.

Natural light

While natural sunlight is an ideal source of light for your aquarium, it is also the most difficult to harness in the right quantities. It certainly is inexpensive, and it does provide the entire spectrum of wavelengths, called *full-spectrum light*. Nonetheless, direct sunlight is difficult to control, it's not predictable, and therefore, it's not a logical source of aquarium light.

Tungsten

If you started with a ten-gallon setup a few years back, you may have had an incandescent light on top of it. This is also called *tungsten lighting*. Your typical light bulb provides tungsten light.

- ✔ **Quality of light:** Incandescent lights burn hot, they don't provide full spectrum lighting, and they promote the growth of nuisance algae.

- ✔ **Bulb longevity:** Tungsten light bulbs don't last long and require frequent changing.

- ✔ **Expense:** The initial cost of these units is low, but they consume a lot of electricity.

- ✔ **Recommendation:** Not for the saltwater aquarium.

Fluorescent

Considered by many to provide the optimum lighting for the aquarium, fluorescent lighting is popular for saltwater aquariums. If you think that you're unfamiliar with fluorescent lighting, think again. It's very common in commercial office buildings, and we've all seen it and used it in our everyday lives. There was a time when the same type of lighting was used in the aquarium, but times and technologies have changed. Now, fluorescent lights are made specifically for saltwater aquariums. If you choose this type of lighting, make sure that you buy it from your fish dealer. These fixtures usually come as full hood aquarium lights or may be purchased separately as a strip lights for glass canopies. (See Chapter 2 for more on hoods and canopies.)

- ✔ **Quality of light:** Fluorescent fixtures produce cool, bright light that spreads evenly from the light into the aquarium. This doesn't allow for natural surface ripple effects, but it does distribute light evenly in the tank. Fluorescent bulbs or tubes come in a wide variety of choices and power outputs. Full-spectrum lighting is available and ideal for reef tanks (discussed in Chapter 1). Multi-bulb fixtures are available so that light of different spectral qualities can be mixed. Fluorescent lighting is also pleasing to the eye.

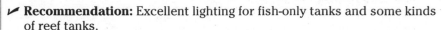

- **Bulb longevity:** Fluorescent tubes generally retain their spectral qualities until they fail. They are known to last from several months to two years, depending on the bulb.

- **Expense:** Initial cost is less expensive than other aquarium lighting, they operate very efficiently, and they consume relatively low amounts of electricity.

- **Recommendation:** Excellent lighting for fish-only tanks and some kinds of reef tanks.

Power compact fluorescent

This type of lighting is really just a U-shaped fluorescent tube instead of a straight tube. However, they have a much higher light output than a standard fluorescent fixture. Power compact fluorescent lights are sold as strip lights, or you may purchase a retrofit kit for a standard hood.

- **Quality of light:** These fixtures have the same benefits of standard fluorescent lights, but they produce higher intensity lighting. Full-spectrum and specialty lighting is available and works well for deeper reef tanks. Multi-bulb fixtures are available so that light of different spectral qualities can be mixed. Like fluorescent lighting, power compact is also pleasing to the eye.

- **Bulb longevity:** Power compact fluorescent tubes also retain their spectral qualities until they fail. They are known to last from several months to two years, depending on the bulb.

- **Expense:** Initial cost is more expensive than standard fluorescent lighting, but they operate more efficiently and consume less electricity.

- **Recommendation:** Excellent lighting for reef tanks.

Mercury vapor

This lighting uses mercury vapor to produce light from spotlights suspended above the aquarium.

- **Quality of light:** These fixtures provide spotlighting, which can create dramatic natural visual effects with water rippling. Although intense, the spectral quality of the light is lacking on the blue side of the spectrum, so they're not good for reef tanks without additional lighting. These lights produce heat, so they need to be ventilated.

- **Bulb longevity:** Can be quite short with a significant loss of efficiency in less than six months. Bulbs need to be replaced frequently.

▸ **Expense:** Expensive to purchase and operate.

▸ **Recommendation:** Good for deeper saltwater tank but not for reef tanks without additional blue lighting.

Metal halide

Like mercury vapor lighting, metal halide lights produce powerful spotlighting that penetrates deep and produces dramatic visual effects. Metal halide light bulbs look like standard light bulbs on steroids. Metal halide lighting is available in hanging lamps, hanging pendants, or ventilated canopy fixtures.

▸ **Quality of light:** Provides intense deep-penetrating full-spectrum light that's ideal for invertebrate tanks. Bulbs that favor the blue side of the spectrum are available for special reef lighting.

The lights need to be suspended above the aquarium and ventilated because they run hot. Because they may produce ultraviolet light, they can be damaging to the human eye, so take care around them.

▸ **Bulb longevity:** Need to be replaced every eight to twelve months to maintain maximum efficiency.

▸ **Expense:** Expensive to purchase and operate.

▸ **Recommendation:** Ideal for reef and invertebrate tanks.

Combination

It is now possible to purchase lighting systems that offer a combination of lighting types. Most of these are offered as light strip fixtures that sit above your aquarium. The most common are metal halide fluorescent fixtures that include multiple light sources.

Although expensive, these systems offer the best of both worlds: high intensity light for photosynthetic invertebrates and soft fluorescent lighting for pleasant viewing.

Switching from Day to Night

An often overlooked component to a lighting system is also one of the most critical: the on/off time switch. Tropical marine fish and invertebrates come from regions where day length ranges 10 to 15 hours, so you can't expect your pets to be exposed to 24 hours of light. Remember, some animals are diurnal and some are nocturnal, so you really need to simulate day and night in your aquarium.

An inexpensive automatic timer will turn your lighting system on and off at the same time so that a consistent day length can be maintained. A 12-hour day is generally recommended for most aquariums.

Consider making an effort not to startle your fish with the sudden switching of lights. In nature, the sun doesn't drop like a rock, so neither should the one in your aquarium. You can mimic a more natural sunset and sunrise in a couple of different ways. First, if you have more than one lighting fixture, you can have another automatic timer. Stagger the timing of the lights so that one shuts off and turns on about an hour before the other. If you don't have more than one light fixture, control the lighting in the room, instead. Simply put room lights on automatic timers or control them yourself so that lighting changes gradually. This little detail helps keep your fish happy and, therefore, healthy.

Chapter 6

Fishy Furnishings

*I*n the wilds of the ocean, the name of the game is eat or be eaten. Most of the small fish and invertebrates that you keep in your aquarium are the ones that end up on the short end of the stick. In nature, these little critters are always wary of potential predators. The coral reef ecosystem, however, provides hiding places, caves, and nooks for protection. Many species of fish even set up small territories that they defend. Thus rocks, sand, plants, macro-algae, and coral reefs are important structures that fish and invertebrates need to survive.

When you introduce your new aquatic guests to their new home, they will undoubtedly be looking for the same nooks and caves they left behind. To make them feel comfortable and keep them healthy, you need to decorate and aquascape.

Accessorizing: A Matter of Taste

Just how you *aquascape* (that is, underwater landscape) your saltwater aquarium is entirely up to you as long as you take into account the following basic rules:

✔ Don't put anything into the tank unless you're positively sure it won't harm your fish. The best way to ensure this is to avoid collecting your own decorations. Buy them instead from a reputable dealer.

✔ Make an effort to give your aquarium creatures some creature comforts, like caves and crannies.

- ✔ Don't overstuff your aquarium with decorations. The most important element in the tank is water. Every piece of rock or coral you put in the tank will displace water and space, and your pets need both. In general, cover only about 50 to 60 percent of the bottom of your tank.

- ✔ Stick with calcareous ornamentation whenever possible. This just means that the decorations are calcium-based, like coral and dolomite. This will help stabilize the chemistry of the water, which needs to be alkaline. I talk more about this issue in Chapter 14.

- ✔ When you stack rocks and other ornamentation, make sure the structure is stable. Rocks, by definition, are heavy and you don't want one changing the décor in your living room, if you know what I mean. A good rule is to make the base of structure as wide as it is high.

- ✔ Take the time before you buy to design the décor of your aquarium. Sit down with a pencil and paper and draw it. Get creative, pulling ideas from books and public displays, and try to make it a reality.

Getting the Natural Look

There is no such thing as a typical freshwater-aquarium look because so many kinds of ornaments, gravel, plants, and weird toys are available to suit the many tastes out there. Remember the kid next door who had the purple gravel, bubbling skeleton, and plastic plants? Must have been the '70s!

On the other hand, the norm for the saltwater aquarium is the natural look. As you may expect, I'm a true believer in the use of natural-looking ornamentation. The use of corals, rocks, and dolomite not only looks good, it also helps water chemistry and gives your fish a more natural setting.

Most freshwater decorations are simply not for the marine aquarium. Of course, if your child wants to put a ceramic skin-diver in the tank, go ahead and have some fun.

Conducting a Background Check

I don't know about you, but if I didn't have a background on the back of my tank, my guests would see not only all my aquarium wiring and tubing but also the wall behind it (which needs painting very badly). The aquarium background masks these poor views and also provides a pleasing backdrop to the beauty of your aquarium inhabitants. I've always felt that the ideal aquarium background is one that blends with the aquarium and becomes barely noticeable. The wrong background will pull attention away from your pets. I tend to lean toward a darker background because it highlights the colors in the tank.

A word on conservation

Marine fish, invertebrates, live rock, and corals are harvested from the wild for the marine aquarium trade. Much of it comes from Pacific islands with small, rural, low-income areas that have few options for employment. Without proper management, these areas become quickly overharvested, and a great deal of natural habitat is destroyed. This doesn't happen everywhere, but the extent of the damage is really not known.

The marine aquarium trade is a billion-dollar industry that has a vested interest in staying alive. That's why industry leaders, conservationists, and dealers from around the world got together in 1998 to form the Marine Aquarium Council. The primary goal of this important international body is to transform the marine industry into one that's based on quality and sustainability. If all goes according to plan, you'll be able to walk into your dealer and buy a piece of live rock or a fish and know that it was harvested properly and in a way that didn't impact the natural ecosystem.

But the Marine Aquarium Council is a little ways off from getting to this level of control. In the meantime, the best thing that you can do to insure that your aquarium isn't set up at the expense of a piece of nature is to buy from a reputable dealer. In the United States, you can find several member associations of the Marine Aquarium Council. One of them is the American Marinelife Dealers Association. If your dealer is a member, there's a good chance that he or she is reputable. Don't be afraid to reach out and contact any of these organizations (see Appendix A) to find out what you can do to keep your aquarium thriving without upsetting Mother Nature.

Simply paint

The least complicated background that I've seen is a paint job. That's right, many aquarists paint the rear wall of their aquariums to give them a uniform "underwhelming" appearance. This is not a bad idea if the right color is chosen, but these backgrounds are somewhat permanent and don't lend themselves to spontaneous change. I've seen black and dark blue painted backgrounds, and both can be pleasing to the eye.

Stick-ons

The most common backgrounds used today are taped or self-stuck to the back of the tank. Underwater scenes, solid colors, or mirrored foil backdrops are available at every aquarium dealer. These can be purchased pre-cut or cut from a big wrapping-paper-style roll to fit your tank. You can either tape one of these to the back of the tank or buy one that's self-sticking. I prefer the former because I like to have the option of changing my tastes. Many of these backgrounds are two-sided so that you can reverse them when you want a change of scenery.

Dioramas

The most elaborate background involves the construction of a diorama behind the tank. This is basically a box behind the tank that has natural aquarium decorations and lighting. It's an extension of the aquarium without water in it. This gives your aquarium a remarkable 3-D effect that looks very natural. Dioramas are usually custom built or result from do-it-yourself endeavors. For this reason, they tend to be more expensive than the average aquarium background.

Unraveling the Gravel

The best place to start when furnishing the inside of your aquarium is literally from the ground up. The ground in the aquarium is called the *substrate* and is generally composed of gravel. Some experts prefer not to use any substrate, but I don't subscribe to that method. There's substrate in the ocean, and I think it belongs in the aquarium, if you set it up right.

Unlike the gravel in a freshwater aquarium, the gravel in the saltwater tank must be of a specific type. If you use calcareous decorations in your marine aquarium, you're sticking to products made of calcium carbonate (just like many invertebrate skeletons), which acts to keep the alkalinity in the aquarium high. Your gravel should do the same. Calcareous gravel for the marine aquarium includes dolomite, calcite, aragonite, crushed coral, coral sand, and crushed shells.

Before using your gravel, make it a point to give it a rinse in fresh water. If possible, do this outside — it's easier. Simply place the gravel in a bucket and run water into it, mixing the gravel with your hands. The water will be cloudy gray for a while, then gradually clear up. The gravel doesn't have to be spotless, but this rinsing removes a lot of the dust and dirt.

Dolomite and aragonite are some of the most common substrates for the saltwater aquarium. Dolomite, which is named after the French mineralogist Deodat de Dolomieu, is found in massive beds several hundred feet thick throughout the world. Aragonite is similar to dolomite, but it lacks magnesium. It's named after the place where it was discovered: Aragon, Spain.

It's alive!

A close relative of live rock (see the "Long live rock" section in this chapter) is live sand. Of course, this doesn't mean that the sand is moving, but it's alive with literally millions of little critters, including helpful bacteria. Live sand is good to add to your saltwater aquarium because it brings important bacteria to the system. A layer of live sand over your gravel will help you establish a healthy aquarium. Be careful if you have an undergravel filter because the sand will eventually move through the gravel and will probably clog your filter.

Grain size

The grain size of your gravel is important and depends on a couple of factors. If you have an undergravel filter (see Chapter 3), your choice of gravel is critical. Remember, this substrate will also be working as your filter media, so it must be the right size. The name of the game is surface area, and gravel that's between ⅛ and ¼ inch has a lot of it. Grains that are any smaller will clog your filter, while grains much bigger will trap debris and also clog your filter.

If you don't have an undergravel filter, you can use finer gravel or sand. These finer substrates are great for invertebrate tanks and reef tanks because they allow these little critters to burrow, which actually helps keep the substrate clean.

Depth

How much gravel you use depends on whether or not you have an undergravel filter. The general rule for undergravel filters is one to two inches of gravel. Some aquarists recommend the use of two sizes of gravel (fine gravel on top of coarse) separated by a plastic mesh or *gravel tidy.* This may allow for filtration while minimizing the amount of substrate that can become clogged. The gravel tidy also protects the filter from burrowing tank inhabitants.

If you're setting up a reef tank without an undergravel filter, you'll find a couple of schools of thought as to how much gravel you should use. It was once thought that a minimal amount of gravel would minimize the amount of dead space in the gravel. Now, a thick layer of two inches or more of gravel or sand is preferred. The deepest layers do become *anoxic* (without oxygen), but the bacteria that live there break down nitrates and help filter the aquarium.

Determining how much gravel to buy depends, of course, on the size and shape of your aquarium. A good place to start is about one to two pounds per gallon.

Buy a bit of extra gravel so that when you aquascape your tank, you have sufficient amounts to sculpture the bottom and provide some contouring.

Getting Rocked

After you've done the groundwork, it's time to get creative. Your choices at this point depend on the kind of marine aquarium you're planning. For example, the typical fish-only aquarium doesn't lend itself to live rock, not only because fish will eat the inhabitants of the rock, but also because standard fish medications will kill it. Therefore, a fish-only aquarium typically has dead coral, tufa rock, or lava rock.

On the other hand, a reef tank, by definition, has live invertebrates, including live corals and live rocks. This doesn't mean that you can't use other kinds of rocks. Oh, to the contrary, other rocks are usually used to build a foundation for the reef. You don't want to pile live rocks on top of live rocks if you're building a nice terrace. There are other rocks for that! (See Chapter 1 for more on fish-only and reef tanks.)

Dead rock

Some people think they can go outside, dig around, and find some rocks for the aquarium. Not true! Please don't do this. Depending on where you live, the rocks around your house may be high in metals and, therefore, dangerous for your tank.

Plus, a chunk of granite is not exactly what I call a natural-looking saltwater decoration, — on earth, at least. Some people find slate attractive in the aquarium, but it's heavy and should rest on the aquarium bottom and not just on top of the gravel.

Tufa

Tufa is a natural addition to your aquarium that's composed of calcium carbonate and, therefore, good for your water chemistry. Tufa is calcareous rock that's soft, porous, and easy to mold. It's ideal for a fish-only or reef tank because you can shape it, and algae and invertebrates will readily colonize it. It's lightweight and porous, so it doesn't displace a lot of water. Tufa is a nice addition to any tank.

Lava rock

This is not real lava rock, and that's good because volcanic lava is high in metals and toxic to your aquarium. Instead, lava rock is an attractive man-made material that, like the tufa, is light with low volume displacement and becomes readily colonized by algae, invertebrates, and other beneficial critters (like bacteria). Although it can be expensive, lava rock is easy to handle and stacks well if you decide to build a centerpiece or terrace.

Long live rock

When I say "Long live rock," I'm not talking about a classic song by The Who; I'm referring to live rock for your aquarium. This is really not the best name for this type of rock because it's not alive. Live rock does, however, provide a home for all kinds of small living sea life, from bacteria to starfish. So it could be called "rock with living things on it," but that would be tough to market.

Live rock is coral rubble or reef rock that's carpeted with living material. It's either collected from wild areas, like Fiji and Tonga in the Pacific, or cultivated in Florida or other areas. In the United States, it's illegal to harvest live rocks from U.S. waters, but it can be cultured. The cultured live rock is less damaging to natural reef systems, but some consider wild Pacific rock to be higher quality because it's lighter, is typically over 80 percent covered with algae, is commonly sold as branches or slabs, and its color ranges from orange to purple.

What's alive?

A lot of people, including me, talk about live rock and say "oh, it's covered with a lot of critters." What does that mean? In Chapters 11 and 15, I discuss invertebrates and algae in more detail, but here's a small list of the kinds of life that can be found on live rock: bacteria, many kinds of algae, corals, sponges, snails, clams, bryozoans, sea squirts, crabs, barnacles, shrimps, starfish, and worms. While most of these critters are great for the tank, a couple, like mantis shrimp and bristle worms, can be a problem. I discuss solutions to these problems in Chapter 11.

Fancy or just the base-ics

Live rock is sold in a couple of different forms based on its quality. Less expensive live rock is often referred to as *base rock* and as the name implies, it's used as the foundation or bottom layer of the mini-reef in your aquarium. Base rock looks pretty barren, but it has a lot of helpful bacteria.

Decorative live rock is the expensive stuff. This is the live rock that has the most life (critters) on it. Depending on who is marketing it, higher quality live rock may be called *fancy rock, decorator rock, algae rock, premium rock,* or *reef rock.*

Cured and uncured

You can purchase live rock that's either cured or uncured, and the definition of this sometimes depends on the source. When live rock is harvested from the wild or from a cultivator, it's handled in many ways and many times before it gets to you. During this process, some of the life on the rock is going to die, and this simply can't be avoided. When a piece of live rock is cured, it's held in a facility at some point until dead and dying critters are cleared away by natural and man-made processes. Uncured live rock is harvested and shipped without this process.

Many live rock dealers sell both cured and uncured products, but the extent to which the live rock is cured differs among dealers. For example, some claim to cure the rock for six weeks in a holding pen, while others do so with salt spray. All claim to have the best method for removing dead or harmful critters.

My recommendations are as follows:

- ✔ Place in your aquarium only live rock that has been cured at some point.

- ✔ Live rock that has been cured at your local trustworthy dealer for several weeks is best.

- ✔ If you're going to have cured live rock shipped to you directly by a dealer, don't add it to an established aquarium without curing it again in a separate tank (see the following section for details).

- ✔ If you just set up your aquarium for the first time, add cured live rock from the dealer and essentially cure it again in your aquarium.

- ✔ Live rock should only be added a little at a time, no more than ten pounds at a time. The amount of live rock should not exceed 1 to 1.5 pounds per gallon, so the aquarium isn't overwhelmed.

Is there a cure?

If you didn't buy your live rock from a local dealer that had time to cure it, you're going to have to cure it yourself. Some people call this *cycling* or *seeding* the live rock. I recommend that you do so in a tank separate from your main display aquarium. Many aquarists have another isolation or quarantine tank for dealing with isolating new fish and invertebrates, treating animals that are sick, and curing live rock. This doesn't need to be a complicated setup, but the separate tank should have basic filtration, a protein skimmer, and some lighting. If you're establishing your main aquarium for the first time, new live rock can be cured right in the main aquarium.

As with most topics in an ever-changing aquarium hobby, how to cure your live rock is a matter of debate. The traditional method involves first removing dead critters with a small brush, and then isolating the rock for two to four weeks in a separate tank with no lighting. Monitor the water chemistry, aerate the water, and frequently clean the protein skimmer. This traditional method may allow dead organisms to cycle through the tank, but the conditions will stress the living organisms.

The more advanced method of curing live rock involves exposing the rock to low levels of actinic light and slowly increasing the amount of light. The actinic lighting allows photosynthetic organisms to thrive but doesn't provide enough light to promote the overgrowth of algae. This method requires a protein skimmer, other filtration, and regular water changes (20 to 50 percent every day). Start the light at six hours per day and increase by an hour every two days until 12 hours is reached. Monitor water chemistry daily by conducting standard water tests (see Chapter 13) and slowly introduce regular lighting when ammonia and nitrite levels are undetectable. When the rock is adapted to normal lighting, the curing process is complete, and you can transfer the live rock to the main tank, if not already there. This process still takes 2 to 4 weeks, but your rock will emerge much healthier.

Supplying Coral

By far, the most popular decoration for a tropical marine aquarium is coral and artificial coral replicas. These structures give the aquarium a natural look, providing excellent shelter for tank inhabitants and ideal substrate for algae (see Chapter 15). Real coral and other calcareous objects like shells also provide the added benefit of buffering the water for pH maintenance (see Chapter 14).

Coral is an animal with a calcium carbonate skeleton that lives in a colony of millions, forming large reefs. In a natural coral reef ecosystem, the outermost layer of the reef is the living coral colony. As the reef grows, layers are added extremely slowly, taking hundreds of years to establish. Because of this, efforts must be made to protect coral reef systems, and live reefs shouldn't be harvested without care and concern for nature.

Dead heads

The skeletal remains of coral are ideal for both fish-only and reef aquariums. These can be purchased at many aquarium dealers or collected at the shore of many tropical areas. Dead coral collected at the shore is perfectly suitable for the aquarium after it has been properly cleaned.

I recommend that you boil all dead coral regardless of where you get it before putting it your aquarium.

Most coral that you purchase will be bleached white. In a natural setting and in a well balanced aquarium, this will not last. Colonization by algae will add green and brown to the coral, diminishing its sterile look. While some beginners find this "dirty" look unappealing, be assured that it is more natural looking (see Chapter 15 for more about algae). In fact, coral that's bleached white in the wild is unhealthy and it should be avoided.

The occasional removal of algae by boiling is recommended if growth becomes excessive and unsightly.

Not real, but cool

One of the alternatives to dead coral is the artificial coral replica. These are becoming increasingly popular and readily available as coral reef protection is increasing worldwide. These natural-looking synthetics are safe for the aquarium, come in a variety of colors, and provide the same benefits as real coral with the exception of water buffering. Many large commercial aquariums utilize artificial corals to mimic the natural reef system. After the coral is overgrown with algae, the artificial coral is virtually indistinguishable from the real thing. Most importantly, fish can't tell the difference. The coral replica is clearly the best choice for the environment.

Some say that replica coral fixtures are expensive. When you compare them to both live and dead coral, you'll find that they actually cost less. Besides, coral replicas can't die.

Live coral

You've likely seen beautiful photos of saltwater aquariums teeming with life including live coral. These are reef tanks, and live corals are very common aquarium inhabitants that act as both pets and decorations. Because live coral is an invertebrate, I discuss it extensively in Chapter 11.

Adding Invertebrates

Many other invertebrate species act as natural decorations for a reef aquarium. Like coral, they are pets and furnishings at the same time. Clams, sponges, anemones, and sea cucumbers are just a few examples of invertebrates that add a lot of beauty to a reef aquarium. I talk more about these animals in Chapter 11 because they're more like pets than decoration.

Shells are popular natural additions to the saltwater aquarium. Be sure to boil shells before using them in your tank, however. Sea fans and sea whips provide plant-like decoration to the aquarium but must be soaked to expose the black skeleton before use.

Providing Plants

While real plants are pretty common in the freshwater aquarium, they are somewhat rare in saltwater tanks. This is because with few exceptions, most of the ocean's plant life can be classified in the primitive group known as *algae*. The term *seaweed* actually refers to the many-celled forms of algae called *macro-algae*. Macro-algae are common in reef tanks and generally come with live rock. In a fish-only tank, macro-algae are consumed by the fish and may not last long. I discuss algae in more detail in Chapter 15.

Plastic seaweed is available, and some marine hobbyists like their plant-like appearance. Many of these fixtures are realistic and attractive. They have the added advantage of not being something that can die and cause problems in the tank.

Offering Ornaments

Aquarium dealers sell a variety of tank decorations that can enhance your aquarium. Many come in the form of plastic, ceramic, or resin creations. By purchasing these tank decorations from the dealer, you're buying a product made for the aquarium, thereby avoiding the potential of adding toxic substances to your tank. Castles, mermaids, divers, and shipwrecks are common shapes that you or your child may want to add to the aquarium. Air can be pumped to some of these fixtures, producing interesting effects and providing aeration. My nephew Nathan has a sunken battleship in his aquarium. Not for me, but I'm not eight.

Chapter 7

Final Ingredients

You know that your new pets need clean water, oxygen, heat, light, and housing. I discussed most of these topics in the preceding chapters. But there are a few loose odds and ends to buy in order to get your new aquarium up and running. In this chapter, I discuss the basics of what you need to get your aquarium up and running and keep it running. That includes little things that you need on a daily basis to keep your aquarium clean and to take care of your new pets.

Salt Water

There's not a lot you can do at this point if you don't have salt water. I don't know about you, but if I turn on my faucet I get fresh water. And I don't need to remind you that this is not a freshwater aquarium book! So you need to get you some salt water, but what exactly is it? Can you grab a bucket of water and add table salt? No!

Natural seawater

The chemical composition of seawater is extremely consistent throughout the world. Although it is 96 percent pure water (one atom of oxygen bonded with two atoms of hydrogen: H_2O), it also contains many dissolved minerals and salts. These are mainly sodium and chlorine (85 percent), but magnesium, sulphate, calcium, and potassium make up another 13 percent, and bicarbonate and 68 other elements make up the remainder in *trace quantities* (really small amounts).

You need to mimic natural seawater in the aquarium as closely as possible. The best way to do this is to buy a synthetic salt mixture at your dealer.

The natural inclination for any beginner is to try to obtain natural seawater from the local seashore. However, I strongly recommend that you don't do this unless you live very close to clean tropical seawater. I say this because

- If you don't live in the tropics and intend to maintain a tropical aquarium, your local seawater will be colder. The colder water will contain species of plankton (small critters) that are adapted to these temperatures. Elevating the temperature to tropical levels will cause these organisms to die or rapidly proliferate, yielding polluted or poor quality water.

- The logistics of moving large quantities of seawater from the seashore is impractical and will probably break your back. Oh, you may say "I won't have to do it often." Not true. Aquarium maintenance requires a steady supply of salt water. It would probably be easier to run a pipe from the beach!

- You have no guarantees that your water source is free of pollutants. Seemingly clean seawater may contain high levels of toxic compounds and metals. Even if you live in a pristine coastal area, the quality of the water can change with the tide, and natural toxins can also be a problem. Why take any chances?

You may be able to purchase filtered natural sea water from a public aquarium in your area. It can't hurt to ask.

Artificial seawater

The science of marine chemistry has produced sea salt mixes that mimic the marine environment without the potential toxins. These mixes are dissolved in ordinary tap water when you set up the aquarium. While most of these mixes are similar, you want to be sure that they are nitrate- and phosphate-free. Not all are created equal, so it wouldn't hurt to talk to your dealer. In addition, some manufacturers claim that their mixes will help detoxify tap water or add essential vitamins and minerals. This is always an added bonus.

Sea salt mixes are sold in a variety of sizes relative to the volume of salt water that they can produce. Be aware that the actual volume of water in the tank will be less than the tank volume because of gravel, aquarium equipment, and ornamentation. So a 50-gallon mix will work for a 55-gallon aquarium because the actual volume of the tank is less. However, it doesn't hurt to have extra salt around for water changes.

You can prepare your salt water in a couple of different ways, and each has its own merits. Regardless of the mixing technique, you must follow the instructions on the package. These mixes don't all use the same fresh-water-to-salt-water ratio, so I can't tell you how much to add per gallon — only the people who make it can. Read the package carefully.

The simplest technique is to add the salt directly to the aquarium after you fill it up. This works fine as long as you don't put in too much salt. The best way to avoid oversalting is to measure the amount of water that you're adding as you fill the tank. Add a little less salt than the manufacturer recommends for that volume of water. So, if you put 27 gallons into your 30-gallon tank, add enough salt for 25 gallons, let it sit overnight so that all the salt dissolves, measure the salinity or specific gravity (see below), and slowly add more salt until the mix is right.

The other method involves premixing your salt water in a separate container. This method involves a little more work, but may be more accurate. It also allows you to have some salt water on the shelf for water changes. To do this, you get a large 5-gallon plastic bucket, preferably a food-safe bucket, and slowly mix a batch of salt water just as you would in the aquarium. Make note only of the exact amount of water and salt mix used to get the chemistry just right. Always allow the water to sit overnight so all the salt mix has time to fully dissolve. When the salinity is right on, you can mix up salt water as needed by using the bucket with the known amounts of water and salt mix.

Regardless of the method used, always mix up additional properly balanced salt water for water changes and emergencies. Store batches of seawater in non-metallic containers in cool, dark places until needed.

Conditioning tap water

To make salt water, you're going to need fresh water. Most people use water straight from the tap. This is the way to go. Forget the idea of filling your tank with bottled water — it's too costly and not feasible unless your tank is ten gallons (and it shouldn't be that small).

Now, I hate to tell you this, but the water out of your tap isn't pure water. In most places, the local water municipality chemically treats the water for health reasons. The typical treatment includes chlorine or chloramine, which can be toxic to fish. In addition, tap water can contain nitrates, sulphates, phosphates, and heavy metals, which are also harmful to fish and invertebrates.

Call your local water company and ask them how they treat the water and what the concentrations of these substances are, because most companies routinely test their water.

To remove these chemicals, you have to condition your tap water. This can be done in several ways. One of the easiest methods for removing chlorine and chloramines is to let the water sit for 48 hours and let these chemicals percolate out. However, this may not do much in the way of removing high levels of heavy metals or other compounds.

The more efficient way to condition your tap water is to purchase a chemical water conditioner and dechlorinator. Your dealer will offer a variety of water conditioners and, if he or she is local, will probably know the best one for the water in your area. These conditioners can be added to your water to remove chlorine, chloramine, and heavy metals.

A number of water-purification units are available to the aquarist as well and these are used to remove high levels of phosphates and nitrates from your tap water. These are called reverse osmosis and deionization units and they come in a variety of capabilities. This equipment attaches to your faucet and removes a number of substances like nitrates, phosphates, toxins, heavy metals, and chlorine, depending on the unit that you buy. I'll warn you that these units can be expensive, but if your water supply is known to have high levels of these toxins, you will probably need to buy one.

Adding reef supplements

While you're in the chemical section of your aquarium dealer, you'll probably want to pick up a couple of other supplements if you plan on having a reef tank. These are generally referred to as *reef supplements* and include important elements like iodine and calcium. These are essential elements for your invertebrates that you need to add to your aquarium water. Also buy a solution of calcium hydroxide, commonly referred to as *kalkwasser,* which is German for lime water. This product helps maintain calcium levels in your reef tank. I discuss this in more detail in Chapter14. Fish-only tanks don't require these kinds of supplements.

If you're really in the mood to spend money, you can also buy a dosing pump for dispensing reef supplements into the aquarium. This means that these supplements are added accurately and automatically, without human error. These can be as simple as one that works with gravity like a hospital intravenous unit or one that has a built-in pump, which is much more expensive.

Water Exams

As part of the proper care and maintenance of your aquarium, you have to routinely test the water chemistry. Believe me, this sounds a lot worse than it is. If your water passes the exams, your fish will be healthy. If not, you're going to have to make some corrections. (If this a bit confusing, don't worry, because in Chapters 13 and 14 it all becomes much clearer.) But because you're putting together the equipment for your aquarium, now is the time to buy all the essentials, which includes test kits.

Hydrometer

Have you ever been swimming in the ocean, tasted salt water, and wondered how much salt is in the sea? Well, science has developed a couple of ways to measure the amount of dissolved salts in seawater. One measure is called *salinity* and another is called *specific gravity.* Although these measurements aren't the same, either can be used to determine the correct level of salt in your aquarium. In Chapter 14, I discuss these terms in greater detail. For now, you need to make sure that you have just the right amount of salt in your aquarium. To do this, you're going to measure the specific gravity with a hydrometer. There are basically two kinds of inexpensive hydrometers on the market: floater and swinger.

Specific gravity should be established in the range of 1.021 to 1.024, but more importantly, it should be maintained at a very specific level within this range. Even minor fluctuations can cause problems for your tank inhabitants. More on this in Chapter 14.

Floater

The most common hydrometer in my early aquarium days was the floating hydrometer. This model looks like a large floating thermometer (see Figure 7-1) and may actually have one inside it. It consists of a long-necked tube with a scale inside. The level at which the tube floats depends on how much salt is in the water. You read the scale at the point where the water's surface meets the hydrometer and, bingo, the specific gravity. However, water movement makes the floating hydrometer difficult to read accurately.

Swinger

The *swing-needle hydrometer* is easier to read. This is basically a small plastic box with a needle in it that pivots when the box is filled with aquarium water. When the needle settles, it points to a scale that tells you the specific gravity. Swinger hydrometers often need to be calibrated before they will give an accurate reading, so be sure to read the instructions. Also, needle can sometimes stick, so tap the hydrometer to make sure it hasn't. This hydrometer is also known as a *pointer hydrometer* or *floating-needle hydrometer.*

Fancy equipment

You can purchase more expensive pieces of equipment to measure salinity and specific gravity. These are electronic monitors and refractometers that give very accurate measurements. However, unless you plan on opening an aquarium dealership, you really don't need to make the investment.

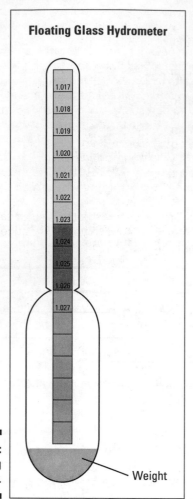

Floating Glass Hydrometer

1.017
1.018
1.019
1.020
1.021
1.022
1.023
1.024
1.025
1.026
1.027

Weight

Figure 7-1:
A floating
hydrometer.

Water chemistry test kits

You're going to have to closely monitor the water chemistry of your aquarium in order to maintain a healthy home for your pets. Sorry, there is no way around it. The number of tests you conduct depends on whether you have a reef tank or a fish-only tank (see Chapter 1). The latter isn't as complicated and its inhabitants really don't care about the levels of certain elements.

Throughout the rest of this section, I give you a simple shopping list of the test kits I think you should buy, depending on the kind of aquarium that you set up. You may see some terms that don't make a lot of sense to you, but don't worry about that. Chapters 13 and 14 go into great detail about water chemistry, and you'll be brought right up to speed in no time.

The following test kits are the ones you need to set up and maintain your aquarium: pH, ammonia, nitrite, and nitrate. These four tests will tell you how well your biological filtration is working.

Other tests include alkalinity, calcium, copper, phosphate, dissolved oxygen, iodine, and a number of others that have been introduced into the hobby recently. Most of these are optional for the fish-only tank but required for the mini-reef tank. Because test kits are used to tell you the quantities of various substances in your aquarium, how much testing you do depends on how much you need to know. The more you test, the more you know — and the more you can monitor the quality of your aquarium environment and make corrections. Newer aquarists have a tendency to test the water more frequently than seasoned veterans, and there's nothing wrong with that.

Use Table 7-1 as a general guide for purchasing test kits. As your tank becomes more complicated, you can always add to your test kit collection.

Table 7-1	Test Kits for Your New Aquarium	
Test Kit	*Fish-Only Tank*	*Reef Tank*
pH	Yes	Yes
Ammonia	Yes	Yes
Nitrite	Yes	Yes
Nitrate	Yes	Yes
Alkalinity	Optional	Yes
Dissolved oxygen	Optional	Optional
Copper	Optional	No
Phosphate	Optional	Yes
Calcium	No	Optional

Test kits are made so that you don't have to be a chemist to use them. While a couple of methods have been developed, the most common involves adding drops of a test chemical to an aquarium sample that changes the color of the water. You then match the water color with that on a color chart, which tells you the correct level of what you're testing.

Be sure to follow the instructions that come with the test kit so that you get accurate results.

Test probes

As society becomes more and more electronically oriented, aquarium-testing monitors will become more widespread and less expensive. In addition to the salinity and specific gravity meters, there are also pH and dissolved oxygen probes available. These provide fast, reliable, and accurate measurements without test chemicals, but they're much more expensive than the average test kit.

Quarantine Tank

The *quarantine tank* is really just another small aquarium that you use to isolate a fish or an invertebrate. That's why it's also called an *isolation tank,* but I think that sounds too lonely.

A quarantine tank is a piece of equipment that you may eventually use to isolate new fish and new invertebrates to make sure that they're healthy before putting them into your well established aquarium (see Chapter 12). More importantly, a quarantine tank is used to isolate diseased fish for treatment (see Chapter 19). This is particularly true for reef tanks because you can't treat fish with invertebrates.

A quarantine tank is a straightforward setup that includes a small tank with simple filtration, a heater, and minimal ornamentation. So a ten-gallon tank with a sponge or box filter, a clamp-on heater, and a couple of plastic plants will do the trick.

Frankly, the quarantine tank is a nice idea, but if your budget is limited, you can delay the purchase of this setup until your main aquarium is fully established.

Nets

All aquaria should be well equipped to handle fish and other tank occupants. This means that you will definitely need a fishnet or two — see Figure 7-2. You will likely use a net more than you think. It will come in very handy when you need to remove a fish that is ill or dead, one that's too aggressive, or one that you simply want to get rid of.

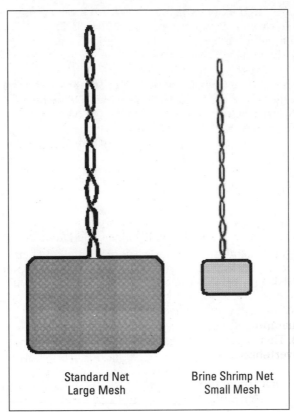

Figure 7-2:
Nets for the
aquarium.

Standard Net
Large Mesh

Brine Shrimp Net
Small Mesh

Size

Nets for the aquarium come in variety of sizes, from a couple of inches across to ten inches wide. Too small a net will be difficult to use to corner a fish, while too large a net will be difficult to maneuver in the tank. Match the size of the net with the size of the fish and the size of the tank. Trying to catch a six-inch fish in a 55-gallon tank with a four-inch net is pretty entertaining to watch.

Meshing around

The netting itself is called the *mesh,* and it can be either fine or coarse. Fine mesh tends to be softer and less abrasive to the fish, but it moves slower in the water. On the other hand, coarse mesh may scrape the fish, but you'll probably catch it faster. You have to strike the right balance. The more you chase your fish around the tank, the more stressed it becomes, and the more you disrupt the aquarium and its other inhabitants. So I tend to buy a larger net with mesh that allows me to move the net quickly and effectively through the water to bag the fish.

Consider keeping a couple of sizes handy. For example, a fish that's ill is probably not moving much and needs to be handled with care, so a fine-meshed soft net is best for this critter. But that irascible wrasse that has been terrorizing the tank needs to be removed quickly, and a coarse-meshed fast net will do it with minimal disturbance. Let's face it, a healthy fish doesn't want to be caught. Just ask my brother Paul, the fisherman!

Keepin' It Clean

As you develop your talents as an aquarist, you're going to accumulate many accessories for your tank that make your job easier and help you maintain a well-balanced aquarium. This section shares a few items that will give you a head start.

When I talk about cleaning your aquarium, it doesn't in any way, shape, or form mean that you use any kind of soap. Household detergents leave residues that are toxic to your pets. Glass cleaners are fine for the outside of the tank, but make sure that you apply them to a cloth without spraying the tank. Spray goes everywhere, including inside the tank, which means bye, bye, fishy.

You can purchase special nontoxic chemical cleaners for your aquarium. These include disinfectants, fungicides, and sanitizers that leave no residues.

Bucket, please

You may laugh at this, but I think one of the most important pieces of standard aquarium equipment is the common bucket. I really don't need to fully explain why because you're going to find out soon enough. Right from the get-go, you should have at least one (or many) bucket(s) committed to your aquarium, and only to your aquarium. Going into the cabinet under the sink or into the broom closet for a bucket isn't a good idea because you know what those buckets are used for: cleaning the house. And what did I just say about soaps and detergents?

You use a bucket to fill your tank, hold tank inhabitants, empty your tank, hold aquarium fixtures and decorations, transport new water, transport old water, hold aquarium equipment, sit on, store conditioned water, and on and on. Go for a bucket that is considered food safe and holds at least five gallons.

Write in big letters on the side: FOR AQUARIUM USE ONLY or LENORE'S AQUARIUM or whatever, but mark it in some way to keep brother Bernie from changing his car's oil with it.

Sucking the substrate

Part of your maintenance routine will include cleaning the gravel. This doesn't mean scooping it out of the tank and washing it — no way. In the old days, we used to use just a short piece of hose to suck the debris off the surface of the gravel. Now, the much simpler way involves the use of a gravel vacuum (shown in Figure 7-3), which lets you get into the gravel to clean it.

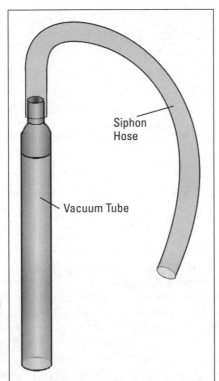

Siphon Hose

Vacuum Tube

Figure 7-3:
A typical
gravel
vacuum.

Gravel vacuums remove the debris that accumulates in the gravel, clogs your undergravel filter, and causes water-chemistry problems. Most gravel cleaning is done during water changes, which is a great time. So gravel vacuums are designed to remove water and debris at the same time. A number of models are available, from pump-, siphon-, or battery-powered to those that connect directly to the faucet for bucket-free cleaning.

Be aware that topping off evaporated water is different from changing the water. It's okay to add fresh water when topping the tank off, but you don't want to add fresh water to an established aquarium during partial water changes; this will mess up your salinity. Instead, add pre-mixed salt water of the same salinity. So, gravel vacuums that remove water, clean the gravel, and refill the aquarium are fine as long as they don't add water directly from the faucet.

In addition to your gravel vacuum, keep a short piece of hose available. It will come in handy for the occasional siphon job.

Rub a dub dub (algae scrubber)

Algae is an issue that I discuss in detail in Chapter 15, but suffice it to say that it will grow in your aquarium and on your aquarium. If it gets out of hand, you won't be able to see your fish! Hence, the algae scrubber.

A variety of styles are available, but the concept is pretty straightforward: Rub the algae off the glass. Aquarium pads, scrapers, scrubbers, and mitts are all available to do the job. I tend to favor the scrubbing pad on a stick with a head that angles so you can apply pressure to stubborn areas. The pads are usually made for acrylic or glass tanks because you don't want one that will scratch.

Some folks prefer to place their hands in the tank and use scrubbing pads or mitts. This is fine as long as you don't disturb your tank inhabitants too much. Every time you go into the tank, your pets are going to be disturbed, and any way you can minimize that, the better. A big hand with a scrubbing mitt in a small aquarium may drive the fish into hiding for days.

If you want to be completely hands off, use one of those magnet setups that has a scrubbing pad on a magnet inside the tank held by a magnet outside the tank. Moving the magnet on the outside moves the magnet on the inside and cleans the glass. However, these don't clean stubborn and tight areas very well and, inevitably, the inside magnet falls off and you have to reach in to get it.

Odds and ends

Tongs and grabbers let you work in your aquarium without having to place your whole hand and arm in the tank. This minimizes disturbances to your fish and invertebrates. Suppose you want to adjust the placement of a fixture or your nephew Camden dropped your car keys in the tank. Grab the tongs and take care of it without having to go swimming.

Another handy item is a tube brush. This is used to keep aquarium intake and output tubing clear and free of algae. The brush is round in diameter and flexible so it inserts into the tube. Standard scrubbers and brushes simply don't do the job. You do, however, have to size the brush to the tube, but that's no big deal.

Chapter 8

Setting Up Your Aquarium Step by Step

In This Chapter

▶ Setting up an aquarium step by step

▶ Getting it all together

▶ Understanding why you don't want to skip any steps

*P*erhaps, if I were a fly on the wall, I would see you scratching your head standing next to an empty aquarium (on a stand with a hood or glass canopy) with some lighting fixtures, a heater or two, one or two filters, filter media, a protein skimmer, a thermometer, a hydrometer, a bucket full of rinsed gravel, some aquarium decorations and fixtures, an aerating pump, air-stones, fishnets, water conditioners, a bag of artificial salts, a bucket or two, an aquarium background, test kits, and some algae scrubbers. (If that doesn't sound like the components you've put together, go over the other chapters in this part.)

Now you have to put them all together. In this chapter, I walk you step by step through the process of setting up your new saltwater aquarium. The aquarium components may differ from system to system, but the same general steps apply. For best results, follow this chapter in the order presented here.

Stand Placement

Place the aquarium stand in the appropriate location, taking into account floor stability, access to water and electricity, aesthetic value, visibility, and adequate distance from doors and windows. Make sure that the stand is level, stable, and doesn't rock. Leave enough room for air tubing, electrical cords, and equipment that hangs on the back of the tank (filter, protein skimmer, and heater).

Aquarium Rinse

Before you place the aquarium where it will sit for a very long time (I hope), move it to a place where you can give it a quick rinse. In the summer, you can do this outside with a garden hose, but in the winter you may not want to go outside, especially if you live where water freezes. In this case, rinse the tank in a bathroom tub or in the kitchen. This doesn't require thorough washing, just a simple rinse with fresh water and a clean sponge to remove dust and dirt. Remember, though, no soap or detergent.

Aquarium Placement

Place the aquarium on the stand so that it sits properly. That means that there is no overhang, and the tank sits perfectly flat on the stand. Double-check to make sure that you left enough room behind the aquarium for equipment.

Background

This is a good time to put your background on the back of the tank. Otherwise, it may be tough to do so after the filters and tubing are in place. Most backgrounds are affixed with regular tape.

Filters

Regardless of the type of filter you purchased, now is the time to set it up. But I mean only "set it up," not "turn it on," so don't plug it in or fill it with water. In Chapter 3, I discuss filters in great detail. In this section, I'll walk through how to set up the most common varieties. Please don't only take my word for it, read the instructions that come with the filter from beginning to end.

Undergravel

Place the undergravel filter into the aquarium and make sure it sits flat inside the tank. Make sure the lift tubes are at the back of the tank and put the powerheads in place, clipping them to the back of the aquarium. If your undergravel filter is powered by air, attach the airstones to the rigid tubing, place them in the lift tubes, and put the exhaust caps on the tubes. Attach the air lines to the tubes and run them to an air pump. Angle the powerheads or the exhaust ports toward the front center of the tank.

External power filter

Rinse the filter media and put it in the filter as recommended by the manufacturer. Hang the external power filter on the back of the tank, but don't fill it with water yet. Trim the filter so it hangs straight up and down on the back of the tank.

Canister filter

Follow the manufacturer's instructions and fill the canister with filter media that has been rinsed. Snap the top into place, paying particular attention to the O-ring, making sure that it's seated correctly. Check with the written directions to see whether the canister should be filled with water before closing it up. Place the canister in the desired position and run the intake and output lines to the aquarium, attaching them with suction cups, if supplied.

Trickle filter

Place the trickle filter into the appropriate position under the tank. Follow the instructions provided by the manufacturer to install the overflow system on the back of the tank, add the filter media, and set up the lines to and from the aquarium.

Fluidized bed filter

Most fluidized bed filters hang on the back of the tank and receive water from a powerhead or a separate pump. Follow the instructions supplied by the manufacturer to set up the plumbing to and from this unit.

Protein skimmer

With so many designs available on today's market, I can't tell you how to set up your particular brand. My best advice is to follow the instructions closely and seek assistance from your local dealer.

Substrate

After rinsing your gravel or sand (see Chapter 6), add it to the tank. Feel free to provide a little depth to the aquarium by sloping it gently to the front of the tank. The depth of the gravel should be about two inches.

Don't place live sand in the tank at this time because it requires water to stay alive, and you haven't gotten that far yet.

Ornamentation

Add the rocks, coral, and other decorations in the pattern you've planned. Now's the time to pull out that piece of paper with your design on it and see how it looks. Don't forget to place really heavy rocks down through the gravel and close to the bottom of the tank for stability. This is a good time to add plastic plants as well, even though you may want to adjust them later.

Don't put live rocks or live corals in at this time, because they really need water!

Aeration

Place airstones or run air lines to aerating ornaments in the aquarium. They should be placed near the substrate. Use suction cups, if provided, to secure the airstones. Run air lines to the air valves or directly to the air pump.

Heater

Clip the hanging heater on the back of your aquarium or place the submersible heater in the tank. Put the submersible heater near the bottom of the aquarium at the back and use suction cups if you have them. Make sure you position it so you can see the indicator light. See Chapter 4 for more on heaters.

Don't plug the heater in.

Water

Place a large saucer or bowl on the gravel in your aquarium. This will buffer the force of water and keep it from upsetting your gravel and decorations. Using a bucket, fill your aquarium with tap water or pre-mixed salt water. Use your thermometer to make sure that the temperature of the water you're adding is between 75° and 78°. After the tank is filled to within an inch of the top, remove the saucer or bowl.

At this point, make sure that your tank has no leaks. Dry the entire outside of the tank with paper towels and closely inspect the seams for drops of water. If you see a leak, empty the tank and return it to the dealer.

Water Conditioner and Salt

If you haven't pre-mixed your salt water (see Chapter 7), add your water conditioner, following the instructions on the bottle. Then add your artificial salt mix, following the instructions of the manufacturer. Test the water with your hydrometer to check the specific gravity, which should be in the range of 1.021 to 1.024.

Hood

Now that all the equipment is in place, but not started, place the hood or glass canopy on the tank to fit it properly. You may have to adjust not only the hood, but also other aquarium equipment, like the heater or protein skimmer, to make the hood sit correctly. Now is the time to move equipment before it's up and running. Some hoods need to be fitted by adjusting and trimming, so follow the instructions that came with your hood to make sure you do it right. You may need to remove the hood to complete the aquarium setup, but now you know that components are where they should be and replacing the hood is easy.

Thermometer and Heater

Place your thermometer in or on the aquarium, depending on the model that you purchased. Check your temperature and make sure the temperature is between 75° and 78°. Plug your heater in and adjust it accordingly to set the temperature in this range. If you need to calibrate your heater, flip to Chapter 4 and review how.

Filters, Again

After your aquarium is full of water, fire-up your filter systems to get the ball rolling. How you do this depends heavily on the type of filter that you have — they're discussed in the following sections.

Undergravel filter

This is pretty simple. Start the powerheads or plug in the air pump if you have an air-driven system. You should see bubbles pouring out of the exhaust ports.

External power filter

Fill the filter box with water from the tank and plug it in. Make sure that water is flowing out of the filter. It will expel bubbles at first, but this will end shortly, and the filter should run smoothly.

Canister filter

Follow the manufacturer's instructions to start the canister filter. Some need to be primed with water before plugging them in. This filter will also spit bubbles until the air is driven out of the system. You may need to fill the intake hose with water to get it going. If you have an undergravel filter with a powerhead, use it to fill the intake line. Otherwise, you can draw water into the output line from the tank end.

Trickle filter

My best recommendation for firing up the trickle filter is to follow closely the instructions of the manufacturer. That's because with so many models out there, what works for one doesn't apply to another. These filters provide excellent filtration, but they can be a bit complicated to get going properly. Don't be afraid to go to the source and talk to the dealer who sold it to you.

Fluidized bed filter

This simply involves plugging in the pump or powerhead that drives the water into the filter. Make sure all connections are tight.

Protein skimmer

Follow the instructions that came with your protein skimmer to get it going. You will need to adjust the flow of air to make sure that the unit is working properly.

Aeration, Again

Start your air pump and check your air lines and connections for air leaks. Make sure the airstones are positioned properly.

Lighting

After your filters are running and the hood or glass canopy is in place, you can set up the lighting fixtures. Strip lights are placed on top of the tank, while hanging lamps and pendants need to be suspended from the ceiling attached to a ceiling hook. After all the lighting is in place, plug everything in and turn your lights on.

Twenty-Four-Hour Adjustments

Your filters are running, heater is working, and lights are on. What do you see? Foggy water. Don't worry, this will clear up pretty rapidly, usually overnight. Over the next 24 hours, carefully monitor water temperature and salinity (specific gravity) and adjust your heater and add salt as needed. If your specific gravity is too high, you may need to take water out and add fresh water.

Live Sand and Rocks

If your first 24 hours went smoothly, the aquarium is well balanced with salt and heat, your filters are running smoothly, and the water has cleared. Now you can add some live sand to introduce bacteria into the tank and start to build the biological filtration. You can add some live rock, as well. This, too, will start the tank-maturation process and get your aquarium into the nitrogen cycle, which I talk about in Chapter 13.

Make sure you don't add too much live rock at this point, particularly if it's not properly cured. Also, be sure to remove some water before adding the rock so the tank doesn't overflow.

Maturity

Your aquarium needs to mature before you add fish and invertebrates. What do I mean by mature? Well, in Chapter 13, I discuss this thoroughly, but it means that a healthy bacterial colony needs to be established and the tank needs to be cycled. So don't run out and buy fish and invertebrates until you read that chapter. At this point, though, you can run some water chemistry tests for pH and ammonia. Start a chemistry log and write down the results you get, because they're going to change, and you want to follow these changes.

Adding Fish

When your aquarium has matured, you can add fish slowly. Which fish you add is the next big decision, and I discuss that in Part II of this book.

Part II
Fish and Invertebrates

The 5th Wave   By Rich Tennant

"Of course being clownfish, we supplement their feed with a little cotton candy, ice cream and a corn dog now and then."

In this part . . .

It's time to enter the world of marine biology. The chapters in this part give you an overview of life in the sea. At the end of this part, I show you how to bring that life into your home.

Chapter 9

Fish Basics

*W*hat is it that made you want to set up an aquarium? The fancy equipment? The opportunity to learn water chemistry? The nitrogen cycle? I really don't think so. I'll bet it has a lot to do with your fascination with the beauty of the critters that live in the sea. I share that fascination with you — in this chapter, I share some basic information about fish.

Defining "Fish"

The group of aquatic animals that we call fishes has been around for over 400 million years and is the most numerous and diverse of the major vertebrate groups. (*Vertebrates* are different from *invertebrates* in that they have a *vertebral column,* which is really just another word for backbone.)

You have seen me use the words "fish" and "fishes," but you probably thought the plural of "fish" was "fish." Actually, when you're referring to more than one kind of fish, known as a *species,* the plural of "fish" is "fishes," as in "there are many kinds of fishes in the ocean." However, when you're talking about more than one fish of the same kind, then the plural is fish, like "these damsels are beautiful fish."

Fishes have permeated all the waters of the world, adapting an incredible variety of forms, lifestyles, and behaviors. From the seasonal freshwater streams, desert springs, and salty bays to the coral reefs, open oceans, and deep abyss, these incredible animals have found suitable homes. Well over 20,000 species of fish currently inhabit the earth and many more are being discovered every year.

Because salt water covers over 70 percent of the earth's surface and fresh water only 1 percent, you may expect to find many more marine (saltwater) species than freshwater species of fish. Surprisingly, though, only 58 percent of the world's fish species live exclusively in salt water. By far, the most kinds of fish (46 percent) live in the narrow band of water less than 700 feet deep along the coastline. As you move into warmer tropical waters where coral reefs are, the number of species dramatically increases. Fishes that live in the warm waters of the coral reef are usually the most sought after for aquariums because of their incredible beauty.

Acquainting Yourself with Anatomy

Because there are no less than 11,000 kinds of marine fish, the "typical" fish is difficult to describe. However, for the most part, all fishes have some common characteristics. Water is 800 times denser than air, so fish have developed a variety of ways to move easier, breath, and feed in a dense medium. These involve the body shape, fins, scales, and swim bladder (see Figure 9-1).

Body shape

You can learn a great deal about a species of fish by looking at its body shape. Fishes that are streamlined or bullet-shaped are specially adapted to open waters. A couple of examples of these fishes include tunas and sharks. Flat or deep-bodied fish are well adapted for living on or close to the bottom of the ocean. Just look at a flounder and you'll see a fish perfectly adapted for life on the bottom.

Fins

Almost all species of fish have fins in one form or another. The fins are critically important appendages that allow the fish to propel, stabilize, maneuver, and stop. In some cases, fins have developed to protect the fish, as well. Lionfish, for example, have developed fins that are long, protective, poisonous spines.

Depending on the type of fish and where it lives, the fins take on many shapes and functions. Bottom, sedentary, and slower-moving fishes possess rounded fins, while faster open-water fishes generally have longer, pointed fins.

In general, the supporting structures of fish fins are hard spines and soft rays. Anyone who has handled a fish knows that the spines of the fins can be sharp. These bony structures provide protection against predators, which can include humans, of course.

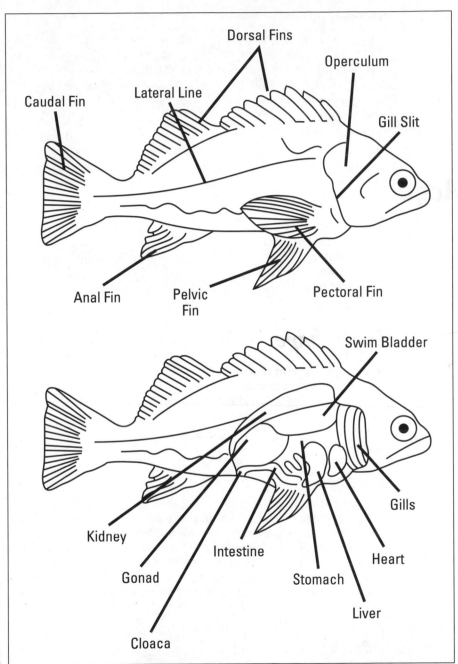

Figure 9-1: The anatomy of a fish.

Fins come in ones or twos, so they're either paired or unpaired. Paired fins include the pectorals and pelvics, while unpaired fins are the dorsal fins, caudal fin, and anal fin.

Pectoral fins

These are the most forward fins, and if fish had arms, these would be them. These fins act to help the fish stabilize, turn, maneuver, hover, and swim backwards. The pectoral fins are generally found just behind or below the gills on each side of the fish, under the midline of the body.

Pelvic fins

These are the leg fins, so to speak. They are also paired and are the most variable in position. In some fishes, the pelvics lie under the fish toward the rear. In others, like many tropical fishes, the pelvics are closer to the head under the pectorals. In general, the pelvic fins act as brakes while helping to stabilize and turn the fish.

Dorsal fin

This unpaired fin is found protruding from the top of the fish. The dorsal fin helps to stabilize the fish and keep it moving straight. Dorsal fins may be long or short, elaborate or simple, singular or multiple. The spines of the dorsal fin can be sharp, and this makes handling some fish difficult. I've been "spined" by a few fish, and it's not a pleasant experience. The dorsal fins of most fish fold down to help streamline the fish while its moving through the water. However, the dorsal fins of sharks are rigid and don't fold down, which gives sharks their classic look as they move through the water. Some species of fish, like goldfish, don't have a dorsal fin.

Anal fin

This is another unpaired fin that helps stabilize the fish when it swims. This fin is located on the underside of the fish behind the anal vent and before the tail fin.

Caudal fin

The caudal or tail fin is an unpaired fin that's largely responsible for propelling the fish forward. This fin is the source of forward momentum for most fishes and can also assist in turning and braking. The shape of the tail can tell you a lot about the lifestyle of a fish. Faster fishes, like tuna and sharks, have deeply forked tails, while many slower, deep-bodied, bottom fishes have square or rounded tails. The tail of the eel is pointed, and this fish moves along the bottom like a snake moves through the grass.

Scales

The bodies of most fish are covered with scales. The scales are composed of a hard, bony substance and serve to protect the fish, reducing the chance of injuries and infection. Covering the scales is a very thin layer of *epidermal* (skin) tissue that contains mucous cells. These cells produce that slimy texture you feel when you pick up a fish. This mucous coating not only protects the fish against injury and infection but also helps the fish swim more easily in the water, reducing the friction between the body and the denser water.

The scales of a fish are actually translucent and lack color. The vibrant colors of tropical fishes come from specialized pigment cells, called _chromatophores,_ in the deeper dermal layer of the skin. Fish that are clear, like the freshwater glassfish, lack these pigments. The color of a fish depends on the types of chromatophores present. There are generally three types of chromatophores in fish: melanophores, xanthophores, and iridophores. _Melanophores_ give fish the darker colors of black, brown, and blue; _xanthophores_ produce the colors of red, yellow, and orange; and _iridophores_ reflect light, producing a silvery shine that's common to many fish.

The bodies of sharks and rays are covered with specialized scales called _denticles_. These actually look like tiny teeth that are pointed toward the tail of the shark. The denticles have the texture of sandpaper and give the shark that rough feeling, but only when you rub the shark toward its head. Not that a lot of people have the opportunity to pet a shark!

Swim bladder

Living in the dense medium of water presents a few problems for fish, and one of these is buoyancy. Maintaining a certain level in the water column without having to expend a lot of energy is important to fish. Therefore, most species have special organs called _swim bladders_. This gas-filled sac, located in the abdominal cavity of the fish, acts as a life vest that keeps the fish at the correct level in the water column.

Fishes have many types of swim bladders, ranging from the simple single-chambered sac of the trout to the three-chambered bladder of the codfish. Fish may also have two types of mechanisms to fill the swim bladder with air. Some fish have direct connections between the esophagus and the bladder and simply swallow air to fill it. Others must rely on gas exchange from specialized blood vessels in the circulatory system to fill the bladder.

In addition to its role in buoyancy control, the swim bladder also helps to amplify sound for better hearing in certain species of fish.

Not all species of marine fish have swim bladders. For example, the sharks and their close relatives, the rays, have large fatty livers instead of swim bladders to help maintain buoyancy. Their skeleton is composed of cartilage, which also reduces their density in water. Many of the tunas also lack swim bladders; their streamlined bodies and forward speed help them maintain buoyancy.

Feeding

Just as the body form of a fish can tell you a lot about its swimming habits, the mouth can tell you something about its feeding habits. Bottomfeeders have downward pointing mouths while surface feeders have mouths that are upward-pointing. However, for most fishes, the mouth is at the end of the snout.

The size of the mouth is usually related to the size of the fish's preferred food. For example, large predatory fish, like sharks and barracuda, have large mouths armed with teeth for consuming other fish. On the other hand, fishes that normally feed on small invertebrates, like butterflyfish, have smaller mouths. Some tropical marine fishes have specialized mouths for specialized feeding strategies. The sharp "beak" of the parrotfish aids this fish when feeding on the coral reef. The basking shark, which feeds on microscopic planktonic creatures, has a mouth that opens very wide and specialized gills that allow it to sift the water.

Most marine fish have a relatively straightforward digestive system that can vary a little from species to species. In general, food passes from the mouth, down the esophagus, to the stomach, through the intestine, and out the anal vent. However, several species of fish lack true stomachs and have elongated, supercoiled intestines. Sharks and rays are different in that they possess a specialized large intestine called the *spiral valve*.

Respiration

One of the most basic needs of fish is oxygen. Like land animals, fish are living creatures that require oxygen to live. However, fish must breathe oxygen from the water and they have specialized organs called gills that allow them to do so. The gills of a fish are similar to human lungs: They provide oxygen to and remove carbon dioxide from the blood of the fish. This oxygen is then transported by the blood to the tissues, where it is utilized to produce energy in a series of chemical reactions called *respiration*.

Although a few kinds of fish can breathe air from the water's surface, without gills, fish would certainly die. In addition, water contains much less oxygen than air, and fish must breath ten to thirty times more water to get the same amount of oxygen than a land animal would get from air.

Most fish have four gills on each side of the head, and they are protected by a singular gill flap or operculum. Sharks and their relatives possess five to seven gills, each with its own gillslit.

When a fish breathes, water is taken into the mouth and passed over the gills and out the *operculum* or *gillslits*. As water passes over the membranes and filaments of the gills, oxygen is removed, and carbon dioxide is excreted. To accomplish this, the gills have a high number of blood vessels that deliver the oxygen to the rest of the fish via the blood. Oxygen and carbon dioxide aren't the only substances exchanged by the gills. Large amounts of ammonia are also excreted by the gills, and as Chapter 13 discusses, ammonia is something that you have to be concerned with in your home aquarium.

Other organs

Fish typically possess general circulatory, digestive, respiratory, and nervous system features common to most vertebrates. If you're interested in learning more, examine the suggested reading list in Appendix A for more detailed descriptions of the unique anatomy of fishes.

Senses

With few exceptions, fish have no less than five senses that they use to feed, avoid predators, communicate, and reproduce.

Sight

The eyes of most fishes are similar to those of humans, except that they lack eyelids, and their irises work much slower. Some species of sharks, however, have special eyelid-type structures, called *nictitating membranes,* that protect the eyes. Fish eye lenses are spherical, which helps to focus light on the retina underwater. The location of the lens in fish eyes makes most fish nearsighted. Fish are generally thought to be able to detect color, although this varies from species to species.

Rapid changes in light intensity tend to shock a fish, so provide gradual changes in light to allow the fish to accommodate and avoid temporary blindness.

Sound

Water is a much more efficient conductor of sound than air is. Therefore, sound carries much farther and faster in water. Most fish don't posses external ears, but they do have an inner ear not noticeable on the outside of the fish. The auditory component of the inner ear consists of the *sacculus* and the *lagena,* which house the sensory components of hearing, the *otoliths*. Sound vibrations pass through the water, through the fish's body, and reverberate off the otoliths in the inner ear. In some cases, the swim bladder articulates with the ear to amplify sound.

Hearing is an important sense for the fish. Although sharks and rays don't possess otoliths, their inner ear structure allows for the directional detection of low-frequency sounds.

Smell

Fish have external nostrils, called *nares,* that draw water into and out of the olfactory organ located above its mouth and below its eyes. Water flows through the nares and into the olfactory pits, where odors are perceived and communicated to the brain via a large nerve.

The olfactory system of the fish isn't attached to the respiratory system like it is in humans, but remains isolated from the mouth and gills. Smell is particularly important in prey and mate detection in fishes.

Taste

This is generally a close-range sense in fishes and is especially helpful in the identification of both food and noxious substances. While taste buds are only found in our mouths, those of fish aren't only in the mouth but also on the external surfaces of the skin, lips, and fins. Catfishes have special *barbels* that have taste buds and help the fish detect food items in murky waters.

Touch

Fish have specialized organs called the *lateral line system* that allows them to detect water movements. Sensory receptors lying along the surface of the fish's body in low pits or grooves detect water displacement and, therefore, give the fish the sensation of touch. The lateral line is easily visible along the sides of most fish. This unique system helps the fish detect other fishes, sense water movement and currents, and avoid obstacles.

In addition to the lateral line system, sharks and rays possess sophisticated sensory organs called the *ampullae of Lorenzini,* which allow them to detect weak electrical fields.

Grasping the Difference between Fresh and Salted

Just what are the differences between saltwater and freshwater fishes? Why can't you just move a saltwater fish into fresh water and vice-versa? Put simply, it's because these fish would die, and in this section, I explain why.

In general, the freshwater species of fish are hardier than their marine counterparts, having evolved to withstand the rapid and dramatic changes in water conditions that occur inland. On the other hand, most marine species have lived in constant and stable environmental conditions. Therefore, they don't have the ability to deal with sudden changes, such as those that may occur in the home aquarium. This, of course, makes saltwater fish more difficult to maintain in captivity.

As the name implies, salt water contains much higher concentrations of dissolved salt (sodium chloride) than fresh water. Although salt is the major constituent, there are many other dissolved elements in higher concentrations than found in fresh water. The amount of these dissolved "salts" in water is referred to as its salinity or specific gravity. In Chapter 14, I discuss the chemistry of salt water in great detail, so I won't bore you with it here.

Osmosis

Because fish live in water, they are surrounded by the chemistry of the water they live in. Also, keep in mind that a fish has water and dissolved salts in its body, as well. So a fish surrounded by fresh water has more salts in its body than outside its body, and a fish surrounded by salt water has fewer salts in its body than outside.

Both of these situations can create real problems for the fish because the process called *osmosis* causes water to flow through cell membranes from areas of low salts (salinity) to areas of high salts. This means that fish in fresh water are constantly subjected to an influx of water because their cells are more saline than their environment. On the other hand, marine fish are always threatened by the loss of water from their cells because their environment is more saline.

Osmoregulation

Although anatomically the two groups of fishes are similar in appearance, they have evolved two very different ways of living in these chemically different environments. As a means of maintaining their internal salinity, freshwater fish drink little water and produce large quantities of dilute urine. On the other hand, most marine fishes drink large quantities of water and eliminate salts in small amounts of highly concentrated urine and feces, as well as at the gills. So the kidneys of these groups are very different.

Sharks and their close relatives, the rays, are exceptions to this pattern in marine fish. These species concentrate urea in their tissues and blood to offset the loss of water.

This aspect of water balance in the fish is called *osmoregulation*. It's important to understand the basic principles of osmoregulation because it has large implications for fish held in captivity. Why?

- Now you understand why freshwater fish can't be kept in salt water and vice-versa. Their bodies simply can't adapt to the change.

- Marine fish must burn a lot of energy to prevent the loss of water and excrete salt, so they require good nutrition and good health.

- Because marine fish drink large amounts of water, the quality of water must be excellent.

- Abrupt changes in salinity disturb the internal chemistry of marine fishes.

Therefore, marine fishkeeping can be more difficult than the maintenance of a freshwater system, but with a little extra effort, it can also be more rewarding.

What's in a name

As you know, humans have a tendency to name living things and this is called *taxonomy,* but this can be a problem because humans speak many different languages. So, for example, what we call a shark is called a tiburon in Spanish. To get around the confusion associated with language differences, a scientific naming scheme was set up many years ago. The language that was chosen for scientific naming is Latin. But don't worry, you don't need to learn the entire language!

At the simplest level, all fish and other living creatures are classified into species. So, when I say that there are over 11,000 kinds of marine fish, I mean that there are that many species. A bluefish is one species, and a grouper is another. When a species is scientifically classified, it is given a scientific name that is composed of two parts called the *genus* and the *species*. For example, the scientific name of the threadfin butterflyfish is *Chaetodon auriga* and that of the spotfin butterflyfish is *Chaetodon ocellatus*. The first name refers to the genus to which both species belong. A genus is a scientific grouping of similar species. If you look at these two fish, you can see that they are

extremely similar. The second name refers only to that species and no other.

This classification scheme continues as you group similar *genera* (plural for genus) into families. Then you group similar families into *orders,* similar orders into *classes,* and similar classes into *phyla* (singular is phylum). All the different phyla make up the kingdom that we call *Animalia,* for the animals. There are also subdivisions of these categories, like *suborder* and *infraclass.* It gets pretty complicated.

So, at the risk of boring you to tears, I'll give you an example: the Great White Shark has the genus and species name of *Carcharodon carcharias*. It belongs to the family Lamnidae, the order Lamniformes, the superorder Selachimorpha, the subclass Elasmobranchii, the class Chondrichthyes, the superclass Gnathostomata, the subphylum Vertebrata, and the phylum Chordata. Whew!

For the purposes of this book, I'm going to stick with the most common names and the genus, species, and family, so don't worry about all this classification stuff right now.

Identifying Common Tropical Marine Fish Families

In this section, I touch upon the various families of fish that commonly inhabit coral reefs and whose members may be available for your tropical marine aquarium. The diversity of these fishes is daunting. They are found throughout the world along the band of warm water near the earth's lower latitudes. By no means is this a complete list of tropical marine fish families, however, because there are literally thousands of species and hundreds of families. I strongly recommend that you consult with the references listed in Appendix A for more comprehensive information about fish species. You can see pictures of specific fish species in Chapter 10.

Angelfishes

The angelfishes are often confused with the butterflyfishes, having ornate colors and deep, flattened bodies. The angels, however, belong to the family Pomacanthidae and can be readily distinguished from the butterflies by the presence of a spine on the gill cover. Angelfishes are popular aquarium fish originating from coral reefs throughout the world. Some grow quite large, exceeding 24 inches, while others rarely exceed a few inches. Angels come in a variety of colors and patterns, sometimes changing as the fish matures from juvenile to adult. In general, angelfish can be offered a variety of foods, but some large adults can be somewhat finicky, preferring sponges and corals, which means they can't be kept in the reef tank. The pygmy or dwarf angels are well suited for a home aquarium while other species of angelfish grow larger, are prone to being territorial, and do better in larger public displays.

Blennies

These long, slender, very active fishes belong to the family Blenniidae, which includes about 345 species. They generally live near, on, or in the bottom and have comb-like teeth for cropping algae. One blenny, the false cleanerfish, is known to mimic the cleaner wrasse, but when the host fish approaches, it will bite off a piece of fin instead of cleaning the fish. It's best to avoid this critter. Blennies generally eat a variety of foods, from algae to flake foods, and prefer hiding places, like caves and crevices. Most are less than four inches long and make peaceful additions to a fish-only or reef aquarium.

Boxfishes and trunkfishes

The fish of the family Ostraciidae possess box-shaped bodies covered with bony plates, and they have no pelvic fins. These fish release poisons into the water when threatened and are, therefore, poorly suited for the average aquarium. Boxfishes are generally bottomfeeders that can be intolerant of their own kind.

Butterflyfishes

These are popular aquarium fish belonging to the family Chaetodontidae that have oval, flattened bodies; terminal mouths; and stunning color patterns. The butterflies are well adapted to life on the coral reef, feeding on the reef itself while seeking algae, sponges, and corals. Although among the most beautiful, these aren't the hardiest of marine tropicals because they're sensitive to changes in water quality. Feeding in captivity can be difficult, and some species can be territorial. These fishes aren't recommended for the inexperienced fish hobbyist and should not be kept in the reef tank because they consume invertebrates.

Cardinalfishes

This group of fish of the family Apogonidae includes almost 200 species of slow-moving peaceful fishes. Large eyes, two separate erect dorsal fins, and a large head are characteristic of these fish. Although nocturnal, cardinals can be acclimated to daytime feeding and activity. When kept with other tranquil species in a community tank, these fish are well suited for both fish-only and the reef tanks.

Catfishes

Although there are about 34 families of catfishes, only two have species that live in salt water. The most common marine aquarium catfishes belong to the family Plotosidae. These fish prefer to live in schools so they are best kept in groups. They do, however, have highly venomous spines, so take care when handling them.

Clownfishes and damselfishes

These fishes are popular in the aquarium trade for all levels of experience. Although comprising one family, the Pomacentridae, this group contains 315 species and is usually divided into the clownfishes and the damselfishes. The clownfishes are also called anemonefishes because in the wild, these small ornate fish are able to live unharmed among the stinging tentacles of anemones, which are soft invertebrates related to corals (see Chapter 11). The clowns and anemones live in harmony and both receive protection from the relationship. This relationship can be mimicked in the aquarium as well, but clownfishes don't need anemones to survive in the aquarium. Clownfishes are one of the few groups of marine species reared in captivity, and they do well in both reef and fish-only tanks.

Damselfishes are considered by many to be the hardiest of the marine aquarium species and are, therefore, usually the first to be introduced into the new aquarium. These fish, however, can be territorial and aggressive, and if introduced too early to a new tank, less tolerant of new tankmates. Nonetheless, some of the damsels can be exciting additions to your tank, particularly when introduced in *shoals* (schools). They will harm invertebrates, so they don't belong in the reef tank.

Dottybacks

These fish of the family Pseudochromidae are very similar to the fairy basslets in size and appearance, yet they are distributed in the Indo-West Pacific, while the latter are confined to the Caribbean. This family contains the large genus *Pseudochromis,* comprised of about 40 species. Unfortunately, some of the dottybacks can be highly territorial and must be kept alone. Use care when choosing the right species for a peaceful marine aquarium. They adapt well to a reef tank with a lot of hiding places.

Dragonets

The family Callionymidae has 130 species of small, shallow water fishes that live in the Indo-Pacific. Some species are drab colored and live over sand, while others can be very colorful. Sometimes called mandarinfish, these fishes eat tiny invertebrates and, therefore, thrive only in a reef tank.

Fairy basslets

There are only three species of basslets of the family Grammatidae. These somewhat shy fish from the Caribbean prefer a lot of shelter, which they will defend from other tank inhabitants. Although a beautiful addition to any tank, the basslet's finicky habits are best suited for the fish-only or reef tank of the experienced hobbyist.

Filefishes

Like their close relatives the triggerfishes, filefishes of the family Monocanthidae have a modified dorsal spine that locks into place. Unlike the triggers, these fish are more peaceful, less active, and generally smaller, making them better suited to a tropical community tank. However, you may have difficulty getting these fish to feed in captivity because they normally feed on coral and algae.

Gobies

Somewhat similar in body shape to the blennies, the gobies belong to the family Gobiidae. Gobies have modified pelvic fins that are united to form a sucking disk. This family is the largest of the marine fishes with over 200 genera and 1,875 species. Some are able to live out of water for extended periods, returning to water to wet their gills. Others live on sand or in close association with invertebrates, like sea urchins, sponges, hard and soft corals, and shrimps. Like the blennies, gobies prefer hiding places and shelters. Some reef-dwelling gobies act as "cleaner fish," removing parasites from other reef fishes at specified cleaner stations on the reef. Most gobies are brightly colored, peaceful, and relatively small in size, eating a wide variety of foods. They do well in fish-only tanks and are excellent additions to a reef tank.

Groupers and sea basses

Similar to the grunts and snappers, this group of fishes of the family Serranidae is comprised of fast-growing, large, predatory fishes. Most, therefore, require larger fish-only aquaria if they are to be kept for any length of time. Nonetheless, with over 450 species belonging to this family, there are a few smaller species that are suitable for the peaceful aquarium of the beginner. Many of the groupers are nocturnal, spending most of their daytime hiding or laying on the bottom.

Grunts

These fast-growing, hardy fish are so named for the grunting noises they make when their swim bladders amplify the sound generated by the grinding of their teeth. Belonging to the family Haemulidae, the grunts accept a wide variety of foods but require a lot of space. It is best to keep only small juveniles in small schools. This family also contains the sweetlips fishes, which is some researchers consider to have their own family known as the Plectorhynchidae. Originating in the Indo-Pacific, sweetlips fishes can be active like grunts, but are excellent aquarium inhabitants as juveniles. They are generally brightly colored as juveniles, becoming more drab as they get older. These fish have a quiet disposition, preferring a peaceful fish-only tank without aggressive tankmates.

Hawkfishes

So named for their habit of perching themselves on a rock waiting to ambush prey, the 32 species of hawkfishes belong to the family Cirrhitidae. With the exception of one or two species that are suitable for the home aquarium, most hawkfishes are highly predatory and get too large in the peaceful marine aquarium.

Lionfishes and scorpionfishes

No aquarium book is complete without mention of these unusual fishes of the family Scorpaenidae. This family is comprised of over 300 species of fish with stocky spiny heads and spiny fins armed with venom glands. They are generally predators that hover or lie in wait for their prey, suddenly lunging at and engulfing it. Their often-camouflaged coloration aids them in doing so. For obvious reasons, these fish must be handled with great care. In captivity, they are generally peaceful but will readily consume smaller tankmates. For now, I suggest avoiding them. They don't belong in a reef tank.

Moray eels

These well known, unique fish belong to the family Muraenidae. The morays lack pectoral fins but possess small gill openings and long, fang-like teeth. Morays are generally nocturnal fish, feeding on other fish and invertebrates at night, spending most of their daytime hours in holes and crevices. In the wild, these fish will easily attain lengths in excess of five feet, but this size is not common in the average aquarium. Although moray eels readily accept a variety of foods, they are carnivorous and will consume smaller fish in the aquarium. These fish are recommended for the fish-only aquarium.

Parrotfishes

Belonging to the same suborder as the wrasses, the parrotfishes belong to the family Scaridae, which includes 83 species. These fishes are best known for their fused teeth that form bird-like beaks, hence the name. The beak is used for biting off pieces of dead coral to get at the algae living within it. For this reason, parrotfishes aren't well suited for a reef aquarium. In general, these fish get relatively large, which makes them a poor choice for the average fish-only aquarium as well.

Porcupinefishes

These oddities of the marine aquarium belong to the family Diodontidae. These fish, whose scales possess spines, have the ability to inflate their bodies with water to ward off danger. Although relatively easy to keep in captivity, they generally attain too large a size for the average aquarist.

Puffers

Although the puffers look very much like porcupinefishes without spines, these fish belong to a different family called the Tetraodontidae. They are smaller than the porcupines and have fused, beak-like jaws. These fish will also inflate as a defense mechanism to avoid being eaten. Their flesh is poisonous when consumed. These fish are vigorous feeders in the aquarium, and some species can be aggressive.

Rabbitfishes

The family Siganidae originates from the Indo-Pacific and contains two genera and about a dozen species. Their flattened, oval bodies and small mouths are similar to those of surgeonfishes. Like rabbits, they prefer to browse on vegetative matter, in the wild, and in the aquarium they will consume algae and can be lured into taking vegetable foods as well. These fish possess venom glands in their dorsal and anal spines, so use care when handling them. Many rabbitfish grow fast, so adequate swimming space is required in either a fish-only or reef tank.

Seahorses and pipefishes

These exotic fishes of the family Syngnathidae are no strangers to the aquarium trade. The pipefishes lack the prehensile (wrapping and folding) tail, vertical swimming position, and angled head that are characteristic of the seahorse. Unfortunately, their feeding and water quality requirements make them difficult for a beginner to maintain in an aquarium for any length of time. They don't compete well with other species for food. These fish are peaceful and do best in a quiet aquarium by themselves. The group is characterized by unusual reproductive behavior where the female deposits eggs into an abdominal pouch on the male. They are then fertilized and incubated by the male in this pouch.

Sharks

Scientists have identified at least 31 families and over 350 species of sharks in the world, most of which have never been kept in aquaria. Sharks and their relatives, the rays, are different from the rest of the fish in this chapter. Their skeletons are composed of cartilage, they have teeth-like scales, and they have five to seven gillslits. Therefore, they belong to a completely different class of fish known as Chondrichthyes. Sharks in general grow too large for the home aquarium, can be very aggressive, and are sensitive to water quality. For these reasons alone, sharks aren't recommended for the average saltwater aquarium.

Snappers

These fish of the family Lutjanidae with over 200 species are another group of fast-growing, highly active fishes that aren't suitable as adults for the average marine aquarium. Several species in this family are commercially exploited for food throughout the world. These fish are predatory by nature, require a lot of space, and will quickly dominate an aquarium.

Squirrelfishes

These red fishes of the family Holocentridae are normally nocturnal creatures in the wild, using their large eyes to feed at night. The family also includes the big eyes and soldierfish. In the aquarium, they can be conditioned to feed during the day. Their long bodies have two dorsal fins: a longer fin of spines and a shorter soft-rayed fin close to the tail. Squirrelfish need a lot of space to accommodate their highly active nature and may be disruptive to a peaceful tank. In addition, they may consume smaller fish as they get larger. They prefer to live in schools and do well in a fish-only tank.

Surgeonfishes and tangs

These common aquarium fish belong to the family Acanthuridae. They are characterized by high-profile, flattened, oval bodies. Their name is derived from the presence of two scalpel-like spines at the base of the caudal fin (tail). These are used in defense or during territorial disputes, so it's best to keep them alone. These schooling fish are algal grazers (feeding on algae) in the wild as well as in captivity, but can be trained to take other kinds of food, as well. In the wild, they reach sizes in excess of 15 inches, but rarely reach half this size in captivity, depending on the species. Surgeonfish and tangs can be kept in both fish-only and reef aquariums.

Triggerfishes

So named for their first dorsal fin that locks into place, triggerfishes belong to the family Balistidae, which includes over 130 species. Sound production in this group is common, produced by grinding the teeth or vibrating the swim bladder. The legendary Hawaiian name for the triggers is *humahuma nukunuku apua'a*, which means "the fish that sews with a needle and grunts like a pig." I'll stick to triggerfish! They can also rotate their eyes independently. The triggerfishes can be quite aggressive, having sharp teeth that are ideal for feeding on invertebrates in the wild. They readily accept any food in captivity, but their aggressive nature makes them unsuitable for the reef tank. These fish move primarily using their dorsal and anal fins, saving the tail for emergencies.

Wormfishes

At one time included with the blennies and gobies, the family Microdesmidae contains 60 species of fishes that inhabit mostly tropical seas. Also called firefishes, the wormfishes have an eel-like body with an extended first dorsal ray. In the wild, these fish hover in groups close to the reef feeding on small planktonic animals. They rapidly retreat to nooks in the reef when startled. These fishes can be kept in small groups, but they require plenty of hiding spaces into which they can retreat.

Wrasses

The family Labridae has over 500 species all over the world, not only in tropical waters. This group can be quite diverse with its members having a variety of body shapes, behaviors, and sizes. Many wrasse species are capable of changing sex as needed for reproductive purposes. Some are substrate burrowers that require sand, while others rest in crevices at night. Some members perform cleaning services similar to those provided by a few species of gobies. The more active species of wrasses can be disruptive to a peaceful tank, aggressive toward smaller fishes, or too large for the average tank. Most wrasses have special jaw plates, called *pharyngeal jaws,* that allow them to grind crabs, clams, snails, and sea urchins. Hence, keep them out of the reef tank.

Chapter 10

Choosing the Right Fish

*I*n Chapter 9, I discuss the anatomy of fish and the general types (families) that are available to you. Now it's time to narrow your choices. To do so, you need a little more information about your options.

By far, the majority of marine fishes sold by pet dealers come from warm, tropical coral reefs. Brilliant colors, unique body shapes, and animated behavior make these fish preferred saltwater tank inhabitants. The coral reef system is a diverse community of algae, invertebrates, and vertebrate animals that function as a whole — it's the foundation upon which the community is built. For many species of fish, the coral reef is their home, providing food, protection, and companionship.

A number of fishes are well suited for the community marine aquarium. The important thing to do is to balance the types of fishes in your tank. Species of fish have varying lifestyles and different behaviors. Therefore, some fish live throughout the tank, some in the middle, and some on the bottom. Some are active in the daytime; some thrive at night. In your aquarium, you want to recreate the natural coral reef community by having fish at all activity levels, thereby minimizing competition, utilizing the entire aquarium, and creating a well-balanced community.

Determining Whether Fish Are Best at Night or Day

Fish, like most organisms, respond to changing light levels. This means that their activity patterns are tuned to day and night. Most of these activity patterns involve feeding or reproduction.

Fishes that are more active and feed during the day are called *diurnal* and those that feed at night are called *nocturnal*. Because most of the fishes available for your aquarium are caught in the wild, they will exhibit similar patterns in your home.

While some species may adapt to a diurnal lifestyle, you want to make sure that you don't stock your tank with fishes that are all nocturnal. I've put together a list of nocturnal and diurnal species in Table 10-1, which you can use as a general guide when you purchase your fish.

Table 10-1	Activity Levels for Common Aquarium Fishes	
Activity Level	*Common Name*	*Family*
Diurnal	Surgeonfishes	Acanthuridae
	Butterflyfishes	Chaetodontidae
	Gobies	Gobiidae
	Wrasses	Labridae
	Angelfishes	Pomacanthidae
	Damselfishes	Pomacentridae
	Parrotfishes	Scaridae
	Rabbitfishes	Siganidae
Nocturnal	Cardinalfishes	Apogonidae
	Porcupinefishes	Diodontidae
	Grunts	Haemulidae
	Squirrelfishes	Holocentridae
	Snappers	Lutjanidae
	Catfishes	Plotosidae
Both	Groupers	Serranidae
	Moray eels	Muraenidae
	Scorpionfishes	Scorpaenidae

School Days

Many species of fish form natural groups that we refer to as *schools*. Fishes swim in schools not to get smarter, but to increase feeding success and to avoid predators. As many as half of all fish species form schools at some point in their lives. Some species, like herrings, school for their entire lives and others, like puffers, school only as juveniles.

Many authors use the terms shoals and schools interchangeably, but this is not correct. Technically, *shoals* are groups of fish that are unorganized, and schools are groups of fish that are synchronized and polarized.

Schooling fish are an attractive addition to the aquarium. They add action to the tank because they rarely stop moving.

Of course, if you add schooling fish to your aquarium, don't try to mimic the numbers that occur in the wild. Your tank is simply too small, no matter how big it is. Keep the size of your school small, no more than five or six fish, taking into account the capacity of your aquarium. Also, it's not a good idea to buy a schooling fish and keep it alone. Imagine what that would feel like.

Why Everybody Can't Get Along

Fish, like all animals, interact with each other in a variety of ways. This can occur with individuals of the same species, as well as between species.

Aggressive interactions are referred to as *agonistic*. Agonistic behavior between fish can be due to defending a territory, a predatory attack, competition for food, or defense of mates, eggs, or young. This usually results in a pecking order forming, in which some fish are subordinate to others. This is particularly true for coral reef fishes.

Of course, fish in the wild have a higher probability of avoiding each other. But when you bring fish into your home, they're forced to deal with each other in the confined space of your aquarium. Does this mean that they're always going to get along? No way! Take care to choose fish that are compatible, considering the elements discussed in the three following sections when selecting your new pets.

Size

One aspect of choosing fish that the novice will sometimes overlook is the maximum size of a particular species. A fish will grow continuously throughout its life, and some species grow faster than others. You don't want to put in your tank a fish that will grow to 12 inches in less than a year. This will not only disrupt your aquarium capacity, but the larger fish will also undoubtedly dominate the tank. Some species are compatible with other species when they are smaller juveniles but become solitary and aggressive as adults. These fish don't belong in the peaceful reef or fish-only tank.

Keep in mind that in the wild, bigger fish usually eat smaller fish and invertebrates. This will also happen in your aquarium. This is just one more reason to keep large fishes out of the average aquarium.

To be safe and avoid the event of one fish becoming the dinner of another, keep fishes of similar size in the fish-only and reef aquarium.

Attitude

Have you ever met somebody who always seems to have a bad attitude? Well, I have, and I've met a few fish like that, as well. Some species simply have an surly disposition. Whether it's because they're territorial, defensive, or just plain hungry, these fish are not for the reef tank and don't fit into most peaceful fish-only aquaria.

The best advice I can give you is to avoid aggressive fishes. Use the guides in both Chapter 9 and in this chapter to determine whether the species that you want is a problem child. Also, just because this book, another book, or a dealer tells you that a species isn't normally aggressive doesn't mean that your fish will be docile. Many species that are considered peaceful have been known to have a few bad seeds. Take the time to discuss your options with your dealer and keep a watchful eye on any new tank addition. If one of his fish is aggressive, he should tell you (at least, you hope he will), or you will undoubtedly find out one way or another. This is a good reason to establish a good rapport with a dealer.

Diet

In addition to size and attitude, always consider the diet of your tank inhabitants. In Chapter 17, I discuss feeding in greater detail, but in the "Finding Good Choices" section in this chapter, I offer some recommended fishes with their food preferences. Fish definitely have a variety of food preferences. Be wary of predatory fish (called *carnivores*), because they eat other fish and invertebrates.

You really don't want to add large predators to your reef tank or fish-only tank: It's a bad mix (at least for the prey). In addition, don't choose fish that are going to be difficult to feed. For example, it's hard to feed fish with specialized diets, like those that eat only corals. Use the guide to fishes in this chapter (in the "Finding Good Choices" section) and always consult with your dealer.

Appreciating Habitat

Without a doubt, fish have preferred habitats. The term *habitat* really just refers to the type of environment that a fish inhabits. For example, flounders prefer to live in a sandy bottom habitat, and you're not likely to see one swimming at the surface. The best saltwater aquarium is well balanced with fishes that inhabit all levels of the tank. A couple of bottom dwellers, a couple of top-water fellas, and a few mid-water critters presents the most natural pleasing appearance. It keeps any one part of the tank from getting overcrowded and helps to avoid agonistic interactions.

Know where your fish come from. This way you can not only impress your friends but also keep a region-specific natural aquarium with fishes from only one region of the world, if you so choose.

The distributions of tropical marine fishes indicate four major regions of the world. In the "Finding Good Choices" section, I tell you where specific fish come from and refer to the following regions for the fish that I recommend:

- **Indo-West Pacific:** From South Africa and the Red Sea east through Indonesia and Australia to Hawaii and the South Pacific Islands to Easter Island. About 3,000 species live in this region, the most of any region.

- **Eastern Pacific:** This region extends from the western coast of North America south along the tropical shores of Central America to the tropical and temperate shores of western South America. This region is separated from the Indo-West Pacific region by a huge expanse of ocean, and it contains fewer than 1,000 species.

- **Western Atlantic:** This region includes the temperate shores of eastern North America, the Gulf of Mexico, the Caribbean Sea, and the tropical and temperate shores of eastern South America. It contains about 1,200 species.

- **Eastern Atlantic:** Tropical species of fish are limited to the Gulf of Guinea, a small area along the western coast of Africa. This region contains only about 500 species of tropical shore fishes.

Good Choices

When your tank is fully established, the water chemistry is balanced, and you're ready to stock your aquarium, I thoroughly recommend that you have a game plan in mind. Don't blindly go to your pet dealer and look for fish for your tank. This can result in fish incompatibility.

Instead, pre-select the kind of fish you want to start with, keeping in mind my suggestions in this section. (Also consult with some of the fish encyclopedias listed in Appendix A.) In other words, establish a good list of potential fish that you want to introduce into your aquarium. Remember to choose a variety of species that will live throughout the water column, from the top to the bottom.

This section gives you a list of tropical marine species that are relatively easy to care for. They are well suited for the beginner's peaceful tank where pH ranges from 8.1 to 8.3 and temperature is maintained between 75 and 79°F. I've listed both the common and scientific names and tried to include common representatives of each of the families reviewed in Chapter 9. Also included is information on the level of the tank that the fish is most likely to inhabit, where it comes from, and its feeding preference. The size that I have listed for each fish is usually attained in the home aquarium, which may be less than in the wild. In addition, for some species, I've included close relatives that are similar and equally suited for the aquarium.

Bear in mind that every aquarium book has specific recommendations for fish that vary among authors. There are literally thousands of fish species kept by aquarium hobbyists, and no one author has a perfect list. The following sections include the species that I prefer, but others may be equally suitable.

Surgeonfishes and tangs (Acanthuridae)

The common names surgeonfish and tang both refer to members of this family, but these fishes have more in common than doctors and breakfast drinks. The family is typically called the surgeonfishes, but the *acanthurids* that I recommend happen to be tangs.

Goldrim tang (Acanthurus glaucopareius)

The goldrim's oval body and steeply sloping forehead that you see in Figure 10-1 are typical of the tangs. This species, like other tangs, prefers a vegetarian diet, so tank algae and vegetables are essential. This species is safe with small fishes, but is best kept as a single specimen in a large aquarium.

- **Distribution:** Indo-West Pacific
- **Size:** Six inches
- **Food:** Herbivorous
- **Tank level:** All levels

Figure 10-1:
The goldrim
tang.

Lipstick tang (Naso lituratus)

This species is another peaceful tang that's an attractive addition to a larger aquarium. The common name refers to the well-defined facial markings (see Figure 10-2) and red around the mouth of this fish. Remember that tangs and surgeons have two scalpels on each side of the tail, so care must be taken when handling these fish. Although the lipstick tang and other tangs are listed as herbivorous, they can be acclimated to other protein foods and flake foods.

- **Distribution:** Indo-West Pacific
- **Size:** Eight inches
- **Food:** Herbivorous
- **Tank level:** All levels

Figure 10-2:
This tang
has lipstick.

Regal tang (Paracanthus hepatus)

The deep royal blue body and bright yellow tail of this tang shown in Figure 10-3 are distinctive and have made this fish a popular aquarium choice. Unfortunately, some of this coloring is lost as the fish gets older. Although some feel that the regal can be kept with members of the same species, it is best to limit your tank to one unless you have a very large tank. These vegetarians will also accept brine shrimp most of the time.

- ✔ **Distribution:** Indo-West Pacific
- ✔ **Size:** Six inches
- ✔ **Food:** Herbivorous
- ✔ **Tank level:** All levels

Figure 10-3:
A truly
regal tang.

Cardinalfishes (Apogonidae)

If you're looking for a calm, cool, and collected species of fish that blends with other mellow species and many invertebrates, keep your eyes open for a cardinalfish. This critter is the Ghandi of fish.

Flamefish (Apogon maculatus)

The flamefish is one of the tranquil cardinalfishes that's well suited for the aquarium of the beginner. This fish has a striking red coloration which isn't done justice in the grayscale rendition in Figure 10-4, prefers a peaceful aquarium, and takes all kinds of aquarium foods provided they will fit into its mouth. Because cardinalfishes are nocturnal by nature, they may be a bit shy at first. Feed these fish in the evening.

- ✔ **Distribution:** Western Atlantic
- ✔ **Size:** Three inches
- ✔ **Food:** Omnivorous
- ✔ **Tank level:** Middle and lower levels

Figure 10-4:
The flamefish is on fire.

Pajama cardinalfish (Sphaeramia nematopterus)

This species of cardinalfish is wearing those pajamas that my father refuses to throw out. It has three distinct color patterns on its body, each completely different as shown in Figure 10-5. Like other cardinalfishes, the pajama has large eyes for nocturnal feeding and can be kept in groups. Care must be taken not to introduce boisterous fishes with cardinalfish because doing so will disrupt their quiet lifestyle. Cardinalfishes are ideal for the invertebrate reef tank.

- ✔ **Distribution:** Indo-West Pacific
- ✔ **Size:** Three inches
- ✔ **Food:** Omnivorous
- ✔ **Tank level:** Middle and lower levels

Figure 10-5:
It's bedtime
for the
pajama
cardinalfish.

Triggerfishes (Balistidae)

The black-finned triggerfish *(Melichthys ringens)* is one of the few species of triggerfishes recommended for inclusion in a peaceful fish-only tank. By looking at Figure 10-6, you can tell that whoever named this fish lacked a little creativity. The black-finned trigger is a gentle fish that readily accepts all kinds of foods that are offered. It is generally safe with small fishes and is considered relatively easy to keep in captivity. It may, however, be difficult to obtain.

- ✔ **Distribution:** Indo-West Pacific
- ✔ **Size:** Ten inches
- ✔ **Food:** Omnivorous
- ✔ **Tank level:** All levels

Figure 10-6:
The black-
finned
triggerfish
has black
fins.

Blennies (Blenniidae)

The lovely little blennies are the all-around nice guys of the peaceful aquarium. They're cute, intelligent, and fun to hang with. Everybody wants to know the blenny!

Midas blenny (Ecsenius midas)

Like most blennies, this fish needs plenty of nooks and caves to hide in. After they're acclimated, the midas blenny is quite animated, perching itself on rocks to observe the rest of the aquarium. This yellow-hued fish shown in Figure 10-7 swims like an eel, and its healthy appetite for all types of food makes it an ideal beginner's fish for the fish-only and reef tank.

- ✔ **Distribution:** Indian Ocean, Red Sea
- ✔ **Size:** Three inches
- ✔ **Food:** Omnivorous
- ✔ **Tank level:** Lower level

Figure 10-7: The midas blenny is cute.

Bicolor blenny (Ecsenius bicolor)

This blenny shown in Figure 10-8 has a front *(anterior)* half that is brown and a rear *(posterior)* half that is orange, hence the name, which means "two color". The bicolor is a shy species of fish that lives in small holes and caves. It is a pleasure to watch. When feeding, it darts from its home to catch food, quickly returning to the safety of its den by backing in. Like the midas blenny, the bicolor will readily accept a variety of foods and is compatible with invertebrates.

- ✔ **Distribution:** Indo-West Pacific
- ✔ **Size:** Three inches
- ✔ **Food:** Omnivorous
- ✔ **Tank level:** Lower level

Figure 10-8:
The two
colored
bicolor
blenny.

Butterflyfishes (Chaetodontidae)

The butterflyfishes in general are not suitable for the inexperienced aquarist because they can be difficult to maintain. However, a couple of species are popular in the aquarium trade and can fare quite well if water quality is properly maintained.

Threadfin butterflyfish (Chaetodon auriga)

The threadfin butterflyfish shown in Figure 10-9 is named for the threadlike extension that develops on the dorsal fin of the adults. It will consume a variety of aquarium foods and particularly enjoys live brine shrimp. Similar species include pearlscale butterflyfish *(Chaetodon chrysurus)*, vagabond butterflyfish *(Chaetodon vagabundus)*, Klein's butterflyfish *(Chaetodon kleini)*, and racoon butterflyfish *(Chaetodon lunula)*.

✔ **Distribution:** Indo-West Pacific, Red Sea

✔ **Size:** Four inches

✔ **Food:** Omnivorous

✔ **Tank level:** Middle and lower levels

Figure 10-9:
The
threadfin
butterflyfish
and its
cousins are
pretty and
peaceful.

Wimplefish (Heniochus acuminatus)

This peaceful butterflyfish is easy to keep, easy to feed, and may be kept in groups of two or three if your aquarium is large enough. The front rays of the dorsal fin on the wimplefish are extended and grow with age, as shown in Figure 10-10. The wimplefish is often called the *Heniochus butterflyfish, bannerfish,* or *poor man's moorish idol.* Young of this species have been known to act as cleaner fish (see Chapter 9).

- ✔ **Distribution:** Indo-West Pacific, Red Sea
- ✔ **Size:** Six inches
- ✔ **Food:** Omnivorous
- ✔ **Tank level:** Middle and lower levels

Figure 10-10: The wimpy wimplefish likes safety in numbers.

Gobies (Gobiidae)

The gobies remind me of the blennies, except their heads are little bit bigger. They too are animated, which makes them fun to watch. These are the proverbial worker bees of the fish world, cleaning the substrate, the rocks, and even the other fishes.

Lemon goby (Gobiodon citrinus)

The lemon goby typically spends much of its time perched on aquarium decorations, quietly observing the rest of the tank. Its beautiful yellow coloration with blue streaks (see Figure 10-11) is a nice addition to any tank. This peaceful fish shouldn't be kept with large fishes because of its size, but it does well in a reef tank. After they've settled, the lemon goby will accept most foods and has a particular fondness for live brine shrimp.

✔ **Distribution:** Indo-West Pacific

✔ **Size:** One and a half inches

✔ **Food:** Carnivorous

✔ **Tank Level:** Lower level

Figure 10-11:
The lemon goby will garnish your aquarium.

Neon goby (Gobiosoma oceanops)

The neon goby, shown in Figure 10-12, is a popular fish both in the wild and in the aquarium. It is well known for the cleaning services (removing parasites) that it offers to other fish. This species can be kept in a shoal of five or six as long as no larger predators are present. The neon goby is one of the few marine aquarium fishes that breeds in captivity. Unfortunately, it is short-lived, lasting only between one and two years in the average aquarium.

✔ **Distribution**: Western Atlantic, Caribbean Sea

✔ **Size:** One inch

✔ **Food:** Omnivorous

✔ **Tank level:** Lower level

Figure 10-12:
The neon goby is a cleaner fish.

Orange-spotted goby (Valenciennea puellaris)

The orange-spotted goby is a hardy, colorful fish that will readily accept a variety of foods of suitable size, including frozen and flake foods. This goby is pictured in Figure 10-13. It likes to dig into the substrate, so a sandy bottom is required. Like many gobies, the orange-spotted goby makes a nice addition to a reef tank.

- ✔ **Distribution:** Indo-West Pacific
- ✔ **Size:** Four inches
- ✔ **Food:** Omnivorous
- ✔ **Tank level:** Lower level

Figure 10-13: This orange-spotted goby is a hardy fish.

Blue-cheek goby (Valenciennea strigata)

This is an easy-to-keep, peaceful goby that will spend much of its time sifting through the substrate for food. This will enhance your filter bed by keeping it free of detritus and waste. The blue-cheek goby is happy with members of its own kind and can be kept in pairs, as well. This colorful addition to the aquarium pictured in Figure 10-14 thrives on all types of marine foods.

- ✔ **Distribution:** Indo-West Pacific
- ✔ **Size:** Three inches
- ✔ **Food:** Omnivorous
- ✔ **Tank level:** Lower level

Figure 10-14: The blue-cheek goby.

Grunts and sweetlips (Haemulidae)

In general, the sweetlips are hardy but shy fishes that feed on meaty marine foods. The colors on the yellow sweetlips *(Plectorhynchus albovittatus)* change with age, as well, and they tend to become more drab with size. The beautiful yellow stripes of the yellow sweetlips, as shown in Figure 10-15, fades, and the fish become browner as its gets larger. This species can be reclusive if kept with boisterous tank mates, but it's ideal for a peaceful fish-only or reef tank.

- **Distribution:** Indo-West Pacific, Red Sea
- **Size:** Four inches
- **Food:** Carnivorous
- **Tank level:** Middle and lower levels

Figure 10-15: The yellow sweetlips is a real sweetie.

The grunts are the boisterous cousins of the sweetlips that tend to require a lot of space to party. Therefore, I don't readily recommend any of the grunts for your first saltwater aquarium.

Wrasses (Labridae)

Many of the wrasses grow quite large, something to take into account before you purchase one. In general, juveniles are peaceful, hardy fish that accept a variety of marine foods, but they do grow up so be careful.

Spanish hogfish (Bodianus rufus)

Hogfish, like the one pictured in Figure 10-16, are colorful wrasses with a funny name. Young Spanish hogfish are known to clean other fish. As the fish matures, depending on the locality of capture, the coloration changes and red becomes more predominant. Larger hogfish will make a meal of smaller aquarium inhabitants, so you may need to remove them when they grow too large. In other words, you may need to kick out some wrasse! Similar species include the Cuban hogfish *(Bodianus pulchellus).*

- ✔ **Distribution:** Western Atlantic
- ✔ **Size:** Eight inches
- ✔ **Food:** Omnivorous
- ✔ **Tank level:** All levels

Figure 10-16:
The Spanish hogfish can become a pig when it grows too large.

African clown wrasse (Coris formosa)

This wrasse shown in Figure 10-17 also changes colors as it matures, with its white stripes changing to blue-green. The African clown wrasse is a bottom-feeder that prefers live marine invertebrates, like brine shrimp, as well as other meaty foods. Keep this wrasse as a single specimen in your tank, because there is a tendency for these fish to quarrel among themselves. The African clown wrasse is generally safe with small fishes while a juvenile but may become more aggressive as it ages. This and other wrasses aren't well suited for the reef tank. Similar species include the clown wrasse *(Coris gaimardi).*

- ✔ **Distribution:** Indo-West Pacific, Red Sea
- ✔ **Size:** Eight inches
- ✔ **Food:** Carnivorous
- ✔ **Tank level:** Lower level

Figure 10-17:
Is the circus in town or just the African clown wrasse?

Cleaner wrasse (Labroides dimidiatus)

The cleaner wrasse shown in Figure 10-18 is a popular fish in the marine aquarium and well suited for the beginner. As the name implies, this fish is indispensable at feeding on the parasites of other tank inhabitants, working around the body, gills, and mouth of its client. It not only provides a useful service for the tank but also feeds in a natural manner. Meaty marine foods can augment the fish's diet. More than one cleaner can be kept in the same tank, as well. Similar species include the *Labroides phthirophagus*.

- ✔ **Distribution:** Indo-West Pacific
- ✔ **Size:** Two inches
- ✔ **Food:** Carnivorous
- ✔ **Tank level:** All levels

Figure 10-18:
Every aquarium needs a cleaner wrasse.

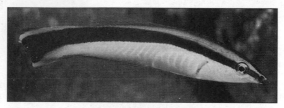

Four-spot wrasse (Halichoeres trispilus)

With its bright yellow body and characteristic four black spots, this wrasse pictured in Figure 10-19 is a beautiful addition to the beginner's aquarium. It's a hardy peaceful fish that readily accepts a variety of frozen and live marine foods. Similar species include the banana wrasse (*Halichoeres chrysus*).

- ✔ **Distribution:** Indian Ocean
- ✔ **Size:** Four inches
- ✔ **Food:** Carnivorous
- ✔ **Tank level:** All levels

Figure 10-19:
This wrasse has four spots, trust me.

Angelfishes (Pomacanthidae)

Angelfishes can grow to large sizes, and they have a tendency to become aggressive and territorial as they get older. Unless you plan on keeping large boisterous fishes in a high-capacity aquarium, the dwarf angelfishes of the genus *Centropyge* shown in Figure 10-20 are the right angelfish for the beginner. Specifically, this group includes the African pygmy angel *(C. acanthops),* the coral beauty *(C. bispinosus),* the lemonpeel angel *(C. flavissimus),* Herald's angel *(C. heraldi),* the flame angel *(C. loriculus),* the resplendent angel *(C. resplendens),* and the cherubfish *(C. argi).* Unlike the larger species of angelfish, many of these angels associate in pairs and can be kept with members of the same species. These fishes enjoy a variety of marine foods. An added advantage of these angelfish is that they are compatible with many marine invertebrates, should you decide to establish a reef tank. Provide many aquarium decorations in which these species can seek refuge.

- **Distribution:** Western Atlantic, Indo-West Pacific
- **Size:** Three inches
- **Food:** Omnivorous
- **Tank level:** All levels

Figure 10-20: Touched by an angelfish.

Damselfishes (Pomocentridae)

The damselfishes, or damsels for short, comprise a charismatic group of aquarium fishes. This bunch has a lot of personality and, in some cases, too much. Damsels can be like party guests that don't know that the party ended two hours ago, but some can be nice.

Common clownfish (Amphiprion ocellaris)

The common clownfish pictured in Figure 10-21 is the most popular anemone-fish in the aquarium trade. This species doesn't live well when alone and should be maintained in pairs. It will readily accept a variety of finely chopped frozen foods and can be coaxed into accepting flake. Clownfish are adapted to living with an anemone (see Chapter 11), so they are well suited for the reef tank. The anemone is not mandatory, though, so they can be kept in the fish-only tank, as well.

- **Distribution:** Indo-West Pacific
- **Size:** Two inches
- **Food:** Omnivorous
- **Tank level:** Middle and lower levels

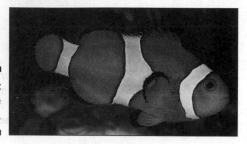

Figure 10-21: Send in the clownfish.

Clark's anemonefish (Amphiprion clarkii)

These hardy, peaceful community fish shown in Figure 10-22 can live happily without an anemone, but more than one may not get along. Its coloration can vary according to locality of capture, and it will eat a variety of foods including flake, live foods, and green foods. Similar species include the tomato clownfish (Amphiprion frenatus).

- **Distribution:** Indo-West Pacific
- **Size:** Three inches
- **Food:** Omnivorous
- **Tank level:** Middle and lower levels

Figure 10-22:
The colors of Clark's anemone-fish vary by locality.

Sergeant major (Abudefduf saxatilis)

This damselfish is named after its black and yellow banding pattern that looks like military epaulettes, as shown in Figure 10-23. This is an active shoaling species that should be kept in groups of four or more. The sergeant major is considered an ideal marine tropical for the beginner because it is hardy and accepts a wide variety of marine foods. In addition, the sergeant major is less territorial and pugnacious than other damsels. Other damsels, including the blue damselfish *(Abudefdul cyaneus),* the humbud damselfish *(Dascyllus carneus),* the yellow-tailed damselfish *(Chromis xanthurus),* and the beau gregory *(Stegastes leucostictus,)* are also considered excellent fish for the beginner because they are extremely hardy and easy to feed. However, these fish can be quite territorial and may create problems for the other fishes in your tank.

- ✔ **Distribution:** Indo-West Pacific, western Atlantic
- ✔ **Size:** Two inches
- ✔ **Food:** Omnivorous
- ✔ **Tank level:** All levels

Figure 10-23:
The sergeant major will command your attention.

Green chromis (Chromis caerulea)

This is another peaceful, colorful damselfish that should be kept in a shoal of four or more. The green chromis shown in Figure 10-24 is an active fish that may be finicky at the start but will consume a variety of chopped meaty foods after it has acclimated to the aquarium. Its bright green coloration looks like green tinted chrome, hence the name.

- **Distribution:** Indo-West Pacific, Red Sea
- **Size:** Two inches
- **Food:** Omnivorous
- **Tank level:** Middle levels

Figure 10-24:
The green chromis doesn't need to be polished.

Dottybacks (Pseudochromidae)

The strawberry gramma (Pseudochromis porphyreus) shown in Figure 10-25 is a brilliant purple dottyback that's easy to feed and hardy in captivity. Like many dottybacks, however, it can be aggressive toward similar species or similar-looking species. Therefore, it is best kept singly. It will accept most marine frozen, live, and flake foods. Similar species include the flash-back gramma (Pseudochromis diadema).

- **Distribution:** Indo-West Pacific
- **Size:** Two inches
- **Food:** Omnivorous
- **Tank level:** Lower levels

Figure 10-25:
The strawberry gramma can be fresh towards its own kind.

Sea basses (Serranidae)

Belonging to the family of sea basses, the wreckfish *(Anthias squamipinnis)* shown in Figure 10-26 is unlike many of its relatives in that it is a shoaling species that doesn't become overly large and predatory. It is best kept in shoals of four or more, and it adapts well to a peaceful fish-only tank. It is carnivorous, so it requires live or meaty foods. A shoal of these colorful fish is an attractive addition to the aquarium that can also be kept with invertebrates.

- **Distribution:** Indo-West Pacific
- **Size:** Four inches
- **Food:** Carnivorous
- **Tank level:** All levels

Figure 10-26:
You don't need a wreck to have a wreckfish.

Rabbitfishes (Siganidae)

The foxface *(Lo vuplinus)* is the most common rabbitfish kept in captivity. It is sometimes called the badgerfish because of its facial markings, which highly contrast its bright yellow body, as shown in Figure 10-27. This fish is an algae eater, so an aquarium with lush algal growth is preferred. It will, however, accept a variety of foods as long as vegetable matter is presented. The foxface can be aggressive toward its own kind, so it should be kept singly. This fish is not recommended for the reef tank.

✔ **Distribution:** Pacific Ocean

✔ **Size:** Six inches

✔ **Food:** Herbivorous

✔ **Tank level:** Middle and lower levels

Figure 10-27:
A foxy
foxface.

Pufferfishes (Tetraodontidae)

The sharp-nosed pufferfish *(Canthigaster solandri)* shown in Figure 10-28 is the smallest and most beautiful of common pufferfishes. This species differs from the others in that it's a small fish that will not outgrow the tank. It is a peaceful fish that should be kept away from its own kind and will accept a variety of finely chopped seafood. It is not recommended for the invertebrate tank.

✔ **Distribution:** Indo-West Pacific, Red Sea

✔ **Size:** Two inches

✔ **Food:** Carnivorous

✔ **Tank level:** Middle and lower levels

Figure 10-28:
The sharp-
nosed
pufferfish is
one of the
smaller
puffers.

Identifying the Wrong Fish for the Beginner

Many species of fish aren't well suited for the beginner's aquarium for a number of reasons.

- ✔ Some may be highly sensitive to fluctuating water quality conditions characteristic of the new aquarium.

- ✔ Others may have special needs, like special water or lighting conditions. The beginner should not try to provide this type of habitat without acquiring some experience.

- ✔ A number of species aren't socially compatible with the peaceful tank. This group includes large carnivorous fish that eat smaller fish, territorial fish that don't tolerate trespassing and mature fish that display aggression and combative behavior.

- ✔ Some species of marine fishes exude poison when threatened. In a closed aquarium, this poison can have deadly consequences.

Many of the aggressive species are offered by the pet store and may even be promoted by pet dealers because the fish are smaller juveniles that they consider harmless. Don't be fooled by this argument: Large predatory fish generally grow fast and develop aggressive behavior early in life.

Also, don't be convinced to buy fish without doing a little homework. You may end up with a pet that requires special aquarium conditions. Oh, it may live for days or weeks in your tank, but chronic stress will set in, its immune response will fail, and the fish will ultimately die due to disease.

Don't rush into a purchase. As you develop your talents as an aquarist, you will expand your capabilities and be able to keep some of the more sensitive species of fish. You may even want to establish an aquarium of compatible aggressive species. However, at this stage of your aquarium keeping career, concentrate on maintaining water quality with a few compatible and rugged species of fish.

The following sections list those species that you should avoid in your tropical marine aquarium when you're first getting started. These fish are those that you're most likely to encounter in the aquarium store. I've included some basic reasons why these fish are not suitable for the beginner.

Surgeons and tangs (Acanthuridae)

Sometimes it's best not to have a surgeon (or a tang) in the house! While not a lot of surgeons are available to the average aquarist, your dealer may carry the following tangs that may prove difficult to keep.

- **Achilles tang** *(Acanthurus achilles):* Delicate; not compatible
- **Blue tang** *(Acanthurus coeruleus):* Aggressive as juveniles
- **Yellow tang** *(Zebrasoma flavescens):* Highly territorial

Triggerfishes (Balistidae)

Many species of triggerfishes are beautiful and fun to watch, but don't let that fool you! They can be predatory and aggressive and nobody needs a hairpin triggerfish in their aquarium.

- **Undulate triggerfish** *(Balistapus undulatus):* Large; very aggressive
- **White-lined triggerfish** *(Balistes bursa):* Aggressive
- **Queen triggerfish** *(Balistes vetula):* Large predator; aggressive
- **Clown triggerfish** *(Balistoides conspicillum):* Large predator; aggressive

Blennies (Blenniidae)

The blenniidae may be a peaceful family, but every family has a few bad seeds. These bad seeds shouldn't be planted in your tank!

- **False cleanerfish** *(Aspidontus taeniatus):* Predatory fish biter
- **Redlip blenny** *(Ophioblennius atlanticus):* Territorial; harasses other fish

Butterflyfishes (Chaetodontidae)

Believe me, many new aquarists want to include butterflyfish in their aquarium. They are simply too beautiful to resist. But their beauty is a two-edged sword because they are also delicate and difficult to feed. What follows are a few examples. As you become a seasoned veteran of aquarium-keeping, butterflyfishes will become part of your pet repertoire.

- **Yellow long-nosed butterflyfish *(Forcipiger flavissimus):*** Delicate; needs very high water quality

- **Pakistani butterflyfish *(Chaetodon collare):*** Difficult to feed

- **Saddleback butterflyfish *(Chaetodon ephipippium):*** Difficult to feed; incompatible with others

- **Banded butterflyfish *(Chaetodon striatus):*** Delicate; incompatible

- **Copper-band butterflyfish *(Chelmon rostratus):*** Delicate; difficult to feed; needs very high water quality

- **Four-eyed butterflyfish *(Chaetodon capistratus):*** Delicate

- **Red-headed butterflyfish *(Chaetodon larvatus):*** Delicate

- **Chevron butterflyfish *(Chaetodon trifascialis):*** Delicate

Porcupinefishes (Diodontidae)

The porcupinefishes are oddities that many aquarists are drawn to. But these fish outgrow their homes very quickly, and their predatory nature will quickly disrupt your tank. Also, if you have a large one and it gets spooked and inflates — well, you get the picture.

- **Spiny boxfish *(Chilomycterus schoepfi):*** Large; predatory

- **Long-spined porcupinefish *(Diodon holacanthus):*** Large; predatory

- **Common porcupinefish *(Diodon hystrix):*** Large; messy eater

Fairy basslets (Grammatidae)

One would think that with a name like fairy basslet, this fish is ideal for the new aquarium. Not really. Put away those images of Snow White and wait until you have a little more experience before buying one of these critters.

- **Black-cap gramma *(Gramma melacara):*** Highly territorial

- **Royal gramma *(Gramma loreto):*** Highly territorial

Squirrelfishes (Holocentridae)

Although an attractive fish, the common squirrelfish *(Holocentrus diadema)* is predatory and boisterous and will quickly outgrow your aquarium.

Wrasses (Labridae)

While many species of wrasses are very attractive, some can be disruptive to a peaceful tank, aggressive toward smaller fishes, or too large for the average aquarium.

- Dwarf parrot wrasse *(Cirrhilabrus rubriventralis):* Delicate
- Twin-spot wrasse *(Coris angulata):* Grows too large
- Birdmouth wrasse *(Gomphosus caeruleus):* Boisterous
- Harlequin tuskfish *(Lienardella fasciata):* Large; predatory
- Moon wrasse *(Thalassoma lunare):* Boisterous; large; aggressive

Snappers (Lutjanidae)

Like many of its fellow family members, the emperor snapper *(Lutjanus sebae)* grows too large for the average home aquarium.

Filefish (Monocanthidae)

The long-nosed filefish *(Oxymonocanthus longirostris)* is a delicate fish.

Moray Eels (Muraenidae)

It's a simple fact that moray eels are cool. One of my first fishes was a moray eel. Huge mistake! These snakes of the sea grow large and eat fish, enough said.

- Snowflake moray *(Echnida nebulosa):* Large; predatory
- Reticulated moray *(Gymnothorax tesselatus):* Large; predatory

Boxfishes (Ostraciidae)

This group includes the spotted boxfish *(Ostracion meleagris),* which is delicate and secretes poison. Living in poisonous water tends to make life difficult for other critters in the aquarium.

Angelfishes (Pomacanthidae)

Like the butterflyfishes, the angels are delicate, beautiful, and attractive to the new aquarist. Many species are offered by your dealer, but allow your aquarium keeping talents to develop before you become the guardian of an angelfish.

- ✔ **Three-spot angelfish** *(Apolemichthys trimaculatus):* Delicate; territorial; difficult to acclimate
- ✔ **Purple moon angelfish** *(Arusetta asfur):* Aggressive; territorial
- ✔ **Bicolor cherub** *(Centropyge bicolor):* Delicate
- ✔ **Blue-faced angelfish** *(Euxiphipops xanthometapon):* Delicate
- ✔ **Queen angelfish** *(Holocanthus ciliaris):* Aggressive; territorial; grows large
- ✔ **King angelfish** *(Holocanthus passer):* Very aggressive; grows large
- ✔ **Rock beauty** *(Holocanthus tricolor):* Very aggressive; finicky
- ✔ **French angelfish** *(Pomacanthus paru):* Nippy when young; grows large
- ✔ **Koran angelfish** *(Pomacanthus semicirculatus):* Grows large; territorial
- ✔ **Regal angelfish** *(Pygoplites diacanthus):* Delicate; shy; difficult to acclimate

Damselfishes (Pomacentridae)

Although it sounds funny, on more than one occasion I've been nipped by a damsel while diving in the tropics. That's because these little bullies are territorial and the size of the intruder does not matter when it comes to defending their turf.

- ✔ **Blue devil** *(Pomacentrus coeruleus):* Aggressive
- ✔ *Dascyllus* **species:** Territorial; aggressive

Dottybacks (Pseudochromidae)

Like many dottybacks, the false gramma *(Pseudochromis paccagnellae)* can be aggressive.

Lionfishes (Scorpaenidae)

When you're tired of looking at all those beautiful small fish in your aquarium, introduce a lionfish and the balance of power will quickly shift. You will then have an aquarium with only one fish. Oh, another neat feature of this critter: It has venomous spines! Get the point?

- **Turkeyfish** *(Dendrochirus brachypterus):* Predatory; poisonous
- **Lionfish** *(Pterois species):* Predatory; poisonous

Sea basses (Serranidae)

If you want to keep a pet that you will eventually fillet and serve for dinner, buy one of these basses and groupers. Simply stated, they grow big and they do so by eating small fish.

- **Marine betta** *(Calloplesiops altivelis):* Predatory
- **Coral trout** *(Cephalopholis miniatus):* Large; predatory
- **Golden-stripe grouper** *(Grammistes sexlineatus):* Large; predatory

Seahorses and pipefish (Syngnathidae)

There is no doubt about it, the seahorses and their cousins, the pipefishes, are beautiful and graceful. But please don't run out and stock your new tank with them. These fishes belong in a specialty aquarium where their special needs can be tended to.

- **Banded pipefish** *(Dunkerocampus dactyliophorus):* Delicate
- **Florida seahorse** *(Hippocampus erectus):* Delicate
- **Yellow seahorse** *(Hippocampus kuda):* Delicate

Pufferfishes (Tetraodontidae)

The spotted puffer *(Arothron meleagris)* is a large, messy eater.

Chapter 11

Identifying Invertebrates

*I*n Chapter 10, I discuss only the smallest portion of what makes up a natural coral reef: the fishes. Although the number of fish species is in the thousands, this is nothing compared to the number of invertebrates. Did you know that biologists have described over a million species of animals, but only about five percent are vertebrates? The others are all invertebrates. While many of these species live in the ocean, only a few, discussed in this chapter, are available to the marine aquarist.

In Chapter 1, I discuss living reef tanks and invertebrate tanks. Here's a quick overview: Aquariums with invertebrates are becoming more common because of better filtration systems, more sophisticated technology, and the availability of healthy invertebrate species. Invertebrates require special lighting and water of high quality. In Chapters 3 and 5, I discuss this equipment as it pertains to invertebrate tanks. In this chapter, I am more specific about what exactly an invertebrate is, and I highlight species that are typically available to the home aquarist.

Understanding Invertebrates

As the name implies, *invertebrates* are animals that are not vertebrates. The single unifying feature of invertebrates is that they lack a backbone.

However, while animals with a backbone are all lumped into the phylum Chordata, the invertebrates are so diverse that they comprise many different phyla. For example, insects are invertebrates and snails are invertebrates, as are jellyfish. But you know by looking at these critters that they are not even remotely related, except for the fact that they are invertebrates.

It's difficult to describe the typical invertebrate because of the great diversity among the groups. However, in general, invertebrates do have special needs when compared to fishes. (In Chapter 1, I discuss these needs in more detail.) These animals are extremely sensitive to water quality, so advanced filtration systems are required. Other equipment, including protein skimmers and specialized lighting, is also essential. Chapter 3 helps you understand why a protein skimmer is important, but why would invertebrates need more light? Some invertebrates, like corals and anemones, have tiny organisms in their bodies that capture light the way that plants do, providing energy for their hosts. Without intense light, these organisms and their hosts will die.

So the bottom line is that if you're going to keep invertebrates, make sure that you have the right equipment, discussed in Part I of this book.

Comprehending Classification

Like all living creatures, invertebrates are classified into species. Similar species are grouped into families, similar families into orders, similar orders into classes, and classes into phyla.

With so many families of invertebrates, I could write several textbooks to cover all of them. In fact, each phylum of the invertebrates would require a textbook of its own. For our purposes, it isn't necessary to cover all invertebrate phyla. Instead, I simply tell you about those that are available to the typical marine aquarium. Individual species will vary with availability, so I highlight the most common.

Recognizing Common Aquarium Invertebrates

In the following sections, I've arranged common invertebrates, starting with the most primitive and ending with the most complex.

Phylum Porifera

Members of the phylum Porifera are commonly known to us as *sponges*. The sponges are the most primitive of the multicellular organisms, lacking true tissues and organs. The fact that these critters don't even have a mouth led many early biologists to think they were plants.

The sponge in your kitchen sink is synthetic. However, for centuries, the sponges used by man were the porous skeletons of animals harvested from the ocean and, in some parts of the world, they still are. Most of the 5,000 species of sponges are marine, found wherever there are rocks, shells, or coral to provide a suitable place for attachment.

The bodies of sponges are organized around a system of water canals and chambers lined with hairs, called *flagella,* that move to create the flow of sea-water through the sponge. Feeding, gas exchange, and waste removal are dependent on the flow of water through the sponge. Hence, sponges are filters.

More important to the aquarist, sponges are rarely drab colored. They typically exhibit bright colors of green, yellow, red, orange, or purple. They also come in a variety of interesting shapes, ranging from flat to heavily branched.

If you decide to add sponges to your aquarium, realize that they require high water quality and adequate flow that allows them to maintain healthy clean open canals and chambers. Also try to keep them out of direct lighting, which will enhance algal growth on their surfaces and literally choke them. Lastly, never remove sponges from the water: This will kill them as air pockets form inside.

A sponge that dies after being inadequately maintained can cause a significant toxic reaction, perhaps wiping out everything in the tank. Know this before considering them for your aquarium.

Common aquarium varieties include the orange cup sponge (*Axinellid* spp), the blue tubular sponge (*Adocia* spp), and the red tree sponge (*Haliclona* spp).

Phylum Cnidaria

This large group of invertebrates includes the jellyfish, hard and soft corals, sea anemones, sea whips, and sea fans. When you impress your friends with the funny name that these animals are called, make sure that you don't pronounce the "c": nie-DARE-ee-ah.

These critters are all united by their *radial symmetry;* that is, their bodies are cylindrical. Unlike the sponges, cnidarians have a digestive cavity and a mouth surrounded by a circle of tentacles with stinging capsules, which aid in the capture and ingestion of food. These stinging capsules are referred to as *nematocysts,* a common feature of all cnidarians.

This phylum is composed of about 9,000 species and, with few exceptions, they are marine. Some cnidarians, like jellyfish, are free swimming, but most are *sessile;* that is, they are attached to the bottom.

Of all the invertebrates suited for the marine aquarium, cnidarians are the most popular. However, they are also the most delicate, requiring high water quality, optimal bright lighting conditions, and rigorous water flow.

There are three classes of cnidarians:

- The Hydrozoa includes the hydras and hydroids.
- The Scyphozoa are what people commonly call jellyfish.
- The Anthozoa comprise the soft and hard corals, sea anemones, and sea fans.

Because this is an aquarium book and not an invertebrate biology book, I don't discuss the hydras and jellyfish in great detail because you're not likely to find them at the typical aquarium dealership. However, this doesn't mean that you won't have them in your aquarium because the tiny stalked hydroids, which look like little plants, can be found on live rock with dozens of other invertebrate species.

On the other hand, the Anthozoans are the most popular invertebrates, and I want to highlight the groups that comprise this class.

Sea anemones

Pronounced ah-NEM-o-nee, these beautiful tank additions of the order Actiniaria are common in the marine aquarium. My first anemone was purchased to house my first clownfish, which seek refuge in a sea anemone's stinging tentacles. The sea anemone is one of the few invertebrates that may make its way into the fish-only tank for that sole purpose.

A sea anemone is a solitary animal known as a *polyp*. It differs from corals, which consist of a number of animals or polyps connected together to form a colony. Sea anemones are often brightly colored as white, green, orange, red, or combinations of these colors, which can be spectacular. They inhabit coastal waters throughout the world, and they live attached to rocks, shells, or other bottom features.

The body of the anemone consists of a column with a pedal disk that attaches to the substrate at one end and an oral disk with a slit-like mouth for feeding at the other. The latter is surrounded by one or more rows of tentacles, which vary greatly in size and number. The tentacles bear stinging cells that are used to stun prey and draw them to the mouth. Clownfish, *Amphiprion* species, are able to live among the tentacles of the sea anemone because something on their skin prevents the nematocysts from stinging. Other animals that are able to live on the anemone include cleaning shrimps, snapping shrimps, arrow crabs, and brittle stars.

The reaction of people to these stinging tentacles will depend on the species and the location of the sting, so care must be taken when handling a sea anemone.

Like many forms of coral, some species of anemones house photosynthetic algae called *zooxanthellae* and, therefore, require intense aquarium lighting. Although seemingly immobile, the anemone can move about the aquarium and will find a spot that provides protection and adequate lighting and current.

Sea anemones (a *Heteractis magnifica* is shown in Figure 11-1) are capable of retracting their tentacles and oral disk to rid their bodies of wastes. They will also display this behavior when disturbed or under stress. Pay attention to your anemone. If it remains retracted for an extended period of time, it may be unhealthy, or the water quality in the tank may be poor.

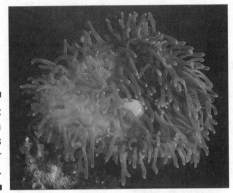

Figure 11-1:
The sea anemone is a popular cnidarian.

Although anemones house algae that supply much of their nutritional requirements, they should be fed regularly once or twice a week with small chunks of seafood, like fish, shrimps, clams, and scallops. Some aquarists prefer to feed inexpensive freshwater fish, like goldfish, to anemones on a regular basis. This practice should be discouraged because the fatty acid distribution in these fish is unlike that found in marine fish and can result in nutritional problems in the anemone.

Common aquarium anemones include the following:

✔ **Pink-tipped anemone *(Condylactis gigantea)*:** This long-tentacled anemone is the most common and inexpensive to keep. Its body is white, brown, or pink and the tentacles are white or pink with an intense pink tip. Originating in the tropical Atlantic Ocean and Caribbean Sea, the pink-tipped anemone doesn't typically house clownfish, which prefer Indo-Pacific anemones. In the wild, this species grows to 6 inches high and 12 inches across.

- **Pink malu anemone *(Heteractis aurorae)*:** This pinkish-purple anemone originates in the Indo-Pacific and is readily accepted by most clownfishes.

- **Clownfish host anemone *(Entacmaea quadricolor)*:** Also known as the *rose anemone, bubble tip anemone,* and *bulb anemone,* this pink and green species has swollen tips on its tentacles. As the name implies, clownfish are readily attracted to this species.

- **Long-tentacle anemone *(Macrodactyla doreensis)*:** This is another Indo-Pacific species that is readily accepted by clownfish. Its coloration is typically red or pink with pink or purple-tipped tentacles.

- **Gelam and Malu anemones *(Heteractis* spp.):** These closely related species are actually quite different in appearance. Gelam anemones typically have shorter tentacles with swollen tips. For this reason, they are also sometimes called bubble anemones. Their small size and vivid coloration make them nice additions to the aquarium. The Malu anemones, which come from Indonesia, are ideal for the invertebrate aquarium because they are readily available, attractive to clownfishes, and easy to maintain. They are typically larger than the Gelam anemones and have longer-tapered purple-tipped tentacles.

None of the Indo-Pacific anemones mentioned in the preceding list are suitable for the beginning aquarist. Experienced aquarists should read up on their species of interest before making the commitment.

Polyps

Members of the order Zoanthidea are small anemone-like animals that are sometimes referred to simply as *polyps.* These critters can be either solitary, like the anemone, or colonial, like coral. They are typically small, short, and button-like with a short fringe of tentacles surrounding a broad oral disk.

Species of the genus *Zoanthus* are the most common in the aquarium trade. These polyps are found in clusters and come in various shades of green and brown. Like all invertebrates, they require high water quality and excellent lighting, but they are easy to keep.

Mushroom anemones or polyps of the genera *Discosoma* and *Rhodactis* are sort of a cross between anemones and corals. They are clonal but lack the skeleton common to the corals. They, too, have photosynthetic algae and are popular with marine aquarium hobbyists. They are typically flat with broad oral disks. Coloration can be red, green, or brown with radiating stripes. Periodic feedings to supplement their algae are recommended.

Stony corals

Moving your way through the class Anthozoa, you come to the close relatives of the anemones, the animals in the order Scleractinia, called the *stony* or *hard corals.* The foundation of diversity and beauty of the natural coral reef community is the hard calcium carbonate skeleton of the coral animals.

Like anemones, coral animals are polyps with a columnar body and tentacles. However, individual coral polyps are connected to one another to form a colony of animals. Unlike anemones, stony corals are not only clonal, but they also produce a calcium carbonate skeleton. Individual coral polyps are usually small, averaging one to three millimeters, but coral reef colonies can become large, covering huge sections of the ocean floor.

Most people who are familiar with stony corals think of the hard skeleton that is left behind when the animals die. In fact, the shapes and structure of this skeleton are typically used to classify species. Some corals are highly branched, while others resemble large boulders. If you're familiar only with dead coral and want to know what the live animal looks like, imagine the coral skeleton covered with a fine layer of interconnected tiny anemones.

As coral colonies grow in the wild and, hence, reefs build, the animals add new layers of calcium carbonate skeleton on top of the old. To do so requires calcium, which is readily available in the ocean. However, in the closed system of the aquarium, stony corals can easily use up the calcium, so you must add supplements (see Chapter 14).

Most species of corals have tiny photosynthetic algae within them called *zooxanthellae*. These algae provide the coral with much of their nutritional needs, so corals don't have to be regularly fed. Supplement the coral every now and then, however, with tiny bits of seafood. Also, many species of corals can extend their tentacles and are capable of stinging and killing other corals, so keep corals separated.

Because it is illegal to harvest stony corals from the Caribbean, all of the corals available to you originate in the tropical areas of the Indo-Pacific. The following are those that you will find easy to maintain and are most likely to encounter:

- **Staghorn and elkhorn corals (*Acropora* spp.):** Corals of the genus *Acropora* are so named because of their distinctive shapes. These are relatively fast-growing stony corals that are heavily branched, ranging in coloration from yellowish or purplish brown to cream colored with paler tips.

- **Vase and frog spawn corals (*Euphyllia* spp.):** This genus of coral has pronounced tentacles that resemble those of sea anemones. Vase corals have round tentacles, while those of frog spawn coral resemble a mass of frog eggs.

- **Brain corals (*Leptoria* spp.):** These stony corals are familiar to most people because they are aptly named after that which they resemble, the brain. These corals can be massive, but stick with smaller specimens for your home aquarium. Coloration can vary depending on species from shades of brown to vivid green to purple and pink.

- **Plate corals (*Fungia* and *Heliofungia* spp.):** These flat corals with long tentacles are readily confused with anemones. Like anemones, some species are solitary animals that are mobile, moving about the aquarium. These species fend well when placed directly on the substrate, where lighting is good and flow is moderate. The tentacles of these corals make them easy to feed.

✔ **Bubble corals (*Plerogyra* spp.):** This genus is aptly named after the bubble-like sacs that cover the mouths and tentacles of the colony. These tan or pearl colored corals are loaded with zooxanthellae algae but should be fed pieces of seafood once a week.

✔ **Sun corals (*Tubestrea* spp.):** This vivid orange genus of coral, shown in Figure 11-2, is a beautiful addition to the marine aquarium, although it may be more difficult to maintain. Unlike other species of corals, sun corals don't possess photosynthetic algae and must rely on trapping food with their tentacles. Therefore, you must regularly feed these corals and typically have to tease them with seafood juice to get the polyps to open for feeding. After they're well acclimated, sun corals will readily accept small pieces of seafood neatly tucked into their tentacles.

Figure 11-2: Stony corals have a calcareous skeleton.

Soft corals

Not all corals have calcium carbonate skeletons. Those belonging to the order Alcyonacea are called soft corals because they have a soft skeleton comprised of calcareous spicules. These animals form soft fleshy or leathery colonies that are irregularly shaped and quite large. The colonies of soft coral can have finger-like projections, as well. Soft corals are generally more hardy than their stony counterparts.

✔ **Colt corals (*Alcyonium* spp.):** These tree-like branched soft corals are easy to maintain in captivity and are ideally suited for a beginning invertebrate aquarist. Coloration is brown to soft white. These fast growing corals can be trimmed when they become overgrown.

✔ **Leather corals (*Sarcophyton* spp.):** Widespread throughout the Indo-Pacific, the leather corals are so named after their texture and brown coloration (see Figure 11-3). Leather corals can be mushroom-like in shape, but other forms can be finger-like, as well. The polyps of these species are conspicuous when the animal is feeding, but retract when disturbed. This is a hardy group of soft corals that grows rapidly and is well suited for the beginner.

✔ **Pulse corals (*Anthelia* and *Xenia* spp.):** So named after the rhythmic pulsing of their polyps, the pulse corals appreciate a good current in your aquarium. Pulse corals consist of a cluster of feathery or branch-like polyps that join at the base like a tree trunk and anchor the coral to the substrate. These corals are easy to keep, growing rapidly in the marine aquarium of even the most inexperienced aquarist.

Figure 11-3:
Soft corals lack the calcium of their cousins.

Sea fans and sea whips

Sometimes referred to as the horny corals, the sea fans and sea plumes belong to the order Gorgonacea. The gorgonians differ from the stony and soft corals by having a body that contains a central axial rod composed of an inorganic substance called gorgonin. In addition, the living tissue has embedded calcareous spicules of different shapes and colors of yellow, orange, or lavender.

Like some other corals, gorgonians possess photosynthetic algae. These colonial animals are flexible, swaying gently in the currents of your aquarium.

Gorgonians can be anchored in your aquarium with marine epoxy that's designed for aquarium use.

✔ **Sea fans (*Gorgonia* spp.):** As the name implies, sea fans grow in a flat plane that resembles a fan. Although their lacy appearance is attractive, they require a strong current and can be difficult for the beginner to maintain. Most species come from the Caribbean.

✔ **Sea whips (*Muricea* spp.):** The sea whips are similar to the sea fans, but possess finger-like projections that extend in all directions. Like sea fans, sea whips require plenty of circulation and may be best suited for the advanced aquarist.

Phylum Platyhelminthes

Commonly referred to as *flatworms,* members of the phylum Platyhelminthes are aptly named because they are flat. Although there are three major classes of flatworms, only one, the Turbellaria, is not parasitic. Turbellarians range in size from microscopic forms to species that are more than two feet long. They are primarily aquatic, and most are marine bottom-dwellers that live in sand and mud. Flatworms are considered the most primitive animals that posses bilateral symmetry, that is, two sides that are identical.

Flatworms are not common in the aquarium trade, but some kinds may be imported as hitchhikers on live rock. Only one species is occasionally offered for sale, the red-rim flatworm (*Pseudoceros splendidus*).

Phylum Mollusca

The group of invertebrates called mollusks is one of the most familiar because we like to eat them! Clams, oysters, scallops, mussels, squids, snails, and octopi all belong to this group and have been part of the human diet for centuries. There are over 100,000 known living species of mollusks.

Mollusks are much more complex than the other invertebrates in the preceding sections. Members of this group are united by several anatomical features. The body consists of three regions: a head with sense organs, a mouth, and a brain; a visceral mass surrounded by a body wall and containing most of the internal organs; and a foot, the muscular lower part of the body on which the animal creeps. In addition, mollusks secrete a calcareous shell and possess a feeding organ called a radula. In some mollusks, like snails, these parts are pretty obvious, but in others, like squids, some of these features are reduced or absent.

Some species of mollusks, like snails, adapt well to the marine aquarium, and their scavenging habits make them easy to feed. However, many species of mollusks are filter feeders. That is, they actually filter food particles and small critters from the water when they feed. You probably already know that your aquarium should be well filtered in order to maintain healthy animals, so, you may have a problem with filter feeding critters. In general, the water in your aquarium is too clean for them. Therefore, filter feeding invertebrates are difficult to maintain in captivity, and I don't recommend them for the beginner.

There are seven classes of living mollusks and the following are some of those that are most suitable for the marine aquarium.

Snails

The class Gastropoda consists of over 75,000 species of mollusks that we call snails. These critters live not only in fresh and salt water, but they have adapted to life on land, as well. You probably remember finding what I called slugs under rocks in the garden. Snails, in general, have a shell and a muscular foot that they use to move about. However, some species have lost their shells, like the terrestrial slugs that I just mentioned.

With so many different kinds of snails, it is difficult to single out a few species for the marine aquarium. However, in general, snails are scavengers that will consume algae, grazing it from the fixtures and glass. And that is a good thing.

Some species of snails aren't suitable for your aquarium because they grow too large, like queen conches, or they are predatory of other invertebrates, like whelks.

Here are some common snails:

- **Cowries (*Cypraea* spp.):** These gastropods have a highly polished domed shell with decorative patterns, but the shell is often concealed by a fleshy mantle that's drab in coloration. Some feed on algae, a few are omnivores, and some are predatory with feeding preferences toward soft corals and other invertebrates. Read up on the particular species you plan to obtain.

- **Top snails (*Astraea* spp.):** These snails are also excellent algae grazers and are considered excellent additions to the reef aquarium.

- **Nudibranchs (*Aplysia* and *Chromodoris* spp.):** Sometimes called sea slugs or sea hares, these are snails without shells (see Figure 11-4). While many nudibranchs are brightly colored, they are very tough to maintain in captivity because many are predatory and difficult to feed. Avoid them. The common sea hare (*Aplysia* spp.), however, readily grazes on algae and does well in captivity.

Figure 11-4: A nudibranch: It's pretty but not worth the trouble.

Clams, scallops, mussels, and oysters

These animals belong to the class Bivalvia because their bodies are housed in two shells that close like valves to protect them. There are about 15,000 species of bivalves and more than 80 percent of them live in the sea.

These invertebrates are well adapted to burrowing in the substrate with their wedge-like shape, but many species also live on top of the bottom (if that makes any sense?). Most bivalves are filter feeders and they can be difficult to keep in the average aquarium. It is possible to purchase liquid food preparations that are specifically designed for filter feeders, but this is best left to the experienced aquarist.

Most species of clams, scallops, mussels, and oysters shouldn't be kept by the beginner because of their specialized feeding mode.

Nonetheless, the most common bivalve in the marine aquarium is the giant clam of the genus *Tridacna* (see Figure 11-5). Although these species are known to grow to over 200 pounds, smaller specimens are farm raised for the aquarium trade. Despite what you may have heard, these clams don't trap people in their shells in an attempt to eat them. In fact, these clams harbor photosynthetic algae that help sustain them (but they still need to be fed live or cryogenically preserved phytoplankton). And they must be provided with excellent lighting.

Figure 11-5:
The giant clam is not likely to eat your fish.

Squids and octopi

As I move through the phylum Mollusca, the complexity of the animals has been increasing and the general body plan has been changing from the standard molluscan form. The squid and octopus belong to the class called Cephalopoda, which is the most specialized and complex group of mollusks. In fact, these critters are considered the most intelligent invertebrates, as well.

Cephalopods have moved away from the substrate, and the body is adapted to a mobile life in the water column. The head of cephalopods bears a crown of arms and tentacles that squids and octopi use for movement and feeding. In addition, feeding is aided by the presence of a parrot-like beak, which is used to tear apart and kill its prey. Unlike their cousins the snails and bivalves, most cephalopods have no hard external shell.

There are only about 650 living species of cephalopods, and they are among the largest of the mollusks, ranging from just a couple of inches to over forty feet in length.

It will be tempting to keep squids and octopi in your new marine aquarium because they are so beautiful and intriguing. But these invertebrates are best left for advanced aquarists that are able to properly care for them. Cephalopods are sensitive to water quality, they are expensive, and they typically require their own space. I don't recommend them for a beginner.

Phylum Annelida

This group is commonly known as the segmented worms, which includes the most popular worm on earth, the earthworm. But not all worms live on or in land. In fact, of the 9,000 species of segmented worms, nearly two-thirds live in the marine environment and belong to the class Polychaeta.

In general, segmented worms have a more advanced body plan than the mollusks that I discuss in the "Phylum Mollusca" section of this chapter. As the name implies, they all have an elongated body that's segmented. In addition, most annelids have well-developed circulatory, nervous, and excretory systems. Some forms have gills for respiration.

The marine polychaetes come in two forms: those that move about and those that are sedentary, inhabiting tubes or borrows. The former worms can be predators, grazers, or bottom-dwelling detritus feeders, whereas the sedentary forms typically have large gills and tentacles for filter feeding.

Although these worms come in a variety of colors and sizes, not all are suitable for the typical aquarium. Some smaller forms may find their way into your aquarium on live rock, but you will hardly know that they are there scavenging marine detritus. The most common segmented worms kept in the home aquarium are the sedentary tubeworms of the following species:

✔ **Fanworms (*Sebellastarte* spp.):** Also known as featherduster worms, these sedentary worms are imported from the Indo-Pacific for the aquarium trade. These worms live in a parchment tube that's buried in the substrate. The feathery head is typically colorful and it is extended for feeding (see Figure 11-6). When startled, the feathery tentacles are withdrawn within a fraction of a second back into the safety of the tube. These invertebrates are not particular about lighting and can be fed brine shrimp. If your fanworms lose their feathers, it can be a sign that they aren't being fed well enough.

✔ **Christmas tree worms (*Spirobranchus* spp.):** Like featherduster worms, these creatures live in a tube, but the tube is calcareous and typically embedded in coral. In addition, these colorful worms with heads of yellow, red, blue, or white have two sets of spiraling tentacles.

Figure 11-6:
A fanworm.

Phylum Arthropoda

The phylum Arthropoda is by far the largest group of animals on the planet. There are over one million species of arthropods, but over 900,000 of these are insects, which I don't include here.

Instead, I direct my attention to the class of marine insects called Crustacea. This group comprises over 31,000 species and includes many familiar creatures, like shrimps, crabs, and lobsters, that you encounter not only in the aquarium but also in the kitchen.

Being arthropods, crustaceans have a hard encasement called an *exoskeleton,* which provides protection. Like the annelids, arthropods are segmented with joints in the exoskeleton that permit movement. It's tough to grow with a hard exoskeleton, so arthropods must periodically shed or molt their exoskeleton for growth.

Unlike the annelids, the segments of arthropods are not alike, and the body is divided into parts called the head, thorax, and abdomen. In the order Decapoda, which includes the shrimps, crabs, and lobsters, the head and thorax are fused to form the *carapace*.

The order Decapoda, which means ten feet, is named after the five pairs of legs that these critters all have. Many species of crustaceans are scavengers, but some can be predatory, as well. This means that not all crabs, shrimp, and lobsters are right for the marine aquarium.

Crabs

The crabs are decapod crustaceans that are more flattened than the others, have heavier legs, and have an abdomen or tail that's folded under the body. So, take a lobster and flatten it, shrink its tail, and fold it under the body, and you have a crab.

Some crabs can be crabby, so it's best to choose smaller species like the following:

- **Horseshoe crab *(Limulus polyphemus)*:** This common species, shown in Figure 11-7, is not a crustacean and actually belongs to its own class, known as the Merostomata. I include it here because it is typically marketed as a crab. Although this species grows to over 20 inches, smaller specimens can be entertaining. Much of their time is spent half buried in the bottom, and they can be fed small pieces of seafood. They require deep sand beds and tend to do a lot of digging, so they aren't suited for beginning aquarists.

- **Arrow crab *(Stenorhynchus seticornis)*:** With its triangular head and body and long legs, this odd-looking crab is a neat addition to any tank. The arrow crab is easily maintained and is a carnivore that can be fed bits of seafood. They will also consume the noxious bristleworm, which is good. Unfortunately, arrow crabs also eat tubeworms and other small invertebrates, so take care when choosing tankmates.

- **Anemone crab *(Neopetrolisthes* spp.):** Clownfish are not the only critters that can make a home out of an anemone — so can the anemone crab. This small (one inch) crab will gladly accept any kind of anemone. This genus has a number of species that come in a variety of spotted color patterns.

- **Hermit crabs:** There are hermit crab genera from all over the world that make nice additions to your aquarium. Unlike their cousins, hermit crabs have a soft abdomen that's protected by a snail shell that the crab steals or finds uninhabited. They can be ideal scavengers in the aquarium and excellent algae grazers. However, some species are large and predatory, causing damage to the average invertebrate aquarium. Take care when choosing a hermit crab for your tank. Smaller species, like the blue-legged hermit *(Clibanarius tricolor)* and the scarlet hermit *(Paguristes cadenanti),* are preferred.

Figure 11-7:
A
horseshoe
crab.

Lobsters

In general, lobsters are not recommended additions to the invertebrate tank. One is shown in Figure 11-8. They are boisterous, aggressive scavengers that are well known for rearranging and disrupting the tank. They can be predatory of other invertebrates and even fish, so they should be kept only with larger fish.

Figure 11-8:
The lobster,
like this
regal
slipper, can
disrupt your
aquarium.

Nonetheless, there are exceptions to this generalization, and the smaller species of lobsters are less noxious.

- ✔ **Purple spiny lobster** *(Panulirus versicolor)***:** This is one of the spiny lobsters, which means that it lacks large claws, but has two long antennae. These small colorful lobsters are typically less than five inches long and are efficient scavengers that readily feed on small pieces of seafood.

- ✔ **Slipper lobster** *(Scyllarides* **spp.)****:** This is an odd-looking lobster that actually looks like a slipper. Instead of claws and elaborate antennae, slipper lobsters have flattened plates for slipping under the substrate for food. Although relatively drab colored, this is a peaceful lobster.

Shrimps

The shrimps are the close cousins of the lobsters, without the attitude. They are much smaller and more delicate than lobsters, as well, which makes them attractive additions to the invertebrate and mixed species tank. Figure 11-9 shows a blood shrimp.

Figure 11-9:
Shrimps are like lobsters without the attitude.

The following shrimp species are best for the beginner. Most come from the Indo-Pacific, but some Caribbean species are also available. Take care to avoid aggressive shrimp, like mantis shrimp, which are predatory with powerful arms that can spear their prey.

- **Cleaner shrimp (*Lysmata* spp.):** These are by far the most popular shrimps for the marine aquarium. As you can imagine, these critters are named after their propensity to clean parasites and damaged skin from many species of fish. For this reason, fish will generally not feed on them. Cleaner shrimp are colorful, with various combinations of red and white stripes and long white antennae. They can also be kept in groups of four or five, as well.

- **Blood shrimp (*Lysmata debelius*):** Also called the *fire shrimp,* this beautiful decapod is vivid red with white spots. Although considered by some to be shy, they aren't really. They're just nocturnal.

- **Anemone shrimp (*Periclimenes* spp.):** If you know that the cleaner shrimp are like cleaner fish, and you guessed that anemone shrimp are like anemone fish, you're right! They live among the stinging tentacles of the anemone, which provides them with protection. These are generally small shrimp, rarely larger than one inch, and are almost clear in coloration with white, brown, or purple spots. Obviously, unless you're keeping an anemone, you shouldn't keep anemone shrimp.

- **Banded coral shrimp** *(Stenopus hispidus)*: Another common aquarium shrimp, this species has bands of white and red, as well as a pair of long claws. This larger species, which grows to over two inches, should be kept singly, although it is compatible with other shrimps. This shrimp is also called the boxing shrimp or the coral-banded shrimp. A number of other species of this genus are also available.

- **Candy shrimp** *(Rhynchocinetes* **spp.)**: Sometimes called the camel shrimp because of the hump on its tail, the candy shrimp is also named for its red and white striped coloration. These shrimp grow to just over an inch. They are a common species in the aquarium trade, readily available but not necessarily great for the beginner. They eat an awful lot of polyps from various species and thus are only safe for the largest reef tanks.

Phylum Echinodermata

This is a group of invertebrates that includes the familiar starfish, as well as sea urchins, brittle stars, sand dollars, sea cucumbers, and sea lilies. The group is characterized by *pentamerous radial symmetry,* which is a fancy way of saying that the average echinoderm has a body divided into five parts arranged around a central axis like a wheel. Look at a starfish, and you will see this clearly.

There are over 6,000 species of echinoderms, and all of them live in the marine environment. These critters have a unique water vascular system that operates numerous tiny tube feet that they use for locomotion and feeding. Some echinoderms, like starfish, have little suction cups at the end of the tube feet that help them cling to the substrate.

There are four classes of echinoderms, but not all of them have members suitable for the marine aquarium. The following are the most common.

Echinoderms are extremely sensitive to water salinity and under no circumstances should be exposed to a salinity lower 1.024.

Sea stars

Generally referred to as starfish, these echinoderms belong to the class Stelleroidea. Sea stars, like the peppered red shown in Figure 11-10, have a central mouth on their underside and, in some cases, they extend part of their stomach to digest their prey. Many sea stars are carnivorous, eating other invertebrates, like clams, using their tube feet to pry them open.

The tube feet and vascular system of the starfish are sensitive and easily damaged. Take care when purchasing a starfish to be sure that the animal is in good condition. Also, rapid changes in salinity may damage the vascular system.

Figure 11-10:
Shoot
for the
sea stars.

- **Orange starfish *(Fromia monilis)*:** Imported from Indonesia, this colorful orange and red species is a common addition to the invertebrate aquarium. The orange starfish is not a large species, rarely growing to more than three inches. It will feed readily on small pieces of seafood. It also needs to eat live sponges and tunicate, so it is not a species that a beginning aquarist should be keeping.

- **Blue starfish *(Linckia laevigata)*:** This species is another popular and colorful addition to the marine aquarium. So named for brilliant blue coloration, this species is readily available and easy to maintain.

- **Red starfish *(Fromia elegans)*:** As you can imagine, the red starfish is red. The species grows to only three inches and smaller specimens have black tips on their arms. Take care not to expose small sea stars to aggressive tankmates.

- **Brittle stars (*Ophiomastix* and *Ophiocoma* spp.):** These are not your typical starfish. Like most sea stars, they have a central disk, but their arms are long and thin and help them move quickly around the aquarium. Brittle stars are imported from the Caribbean, as well as the Indo-Pacific region. Although they tend to be drab colored and nocturnal, they are excellent scavengers and are easy to maintain.

Sea stars are well known for their ability to regenerate their limbs when they are damaged or lost. In some species, not only does the star regenerate the limb, but the limb can regenerate the star!

Sea urchins

Although related to the sea stars, sea urchins and their cousins the sand dollars belong to a different class of echinoderms called the Echinoidea. Like the sea stars, they are radially symmetrical, but they lack arms. Instead, sea urchins have a calcium carbonate skeleton, called a *test,* with movable spines, which you can see in Figure 11-11. If you've ever been to a tropical beach, it's not unusual to find the dried tests of sea urchins.

Figure 11-11:
Sea urchins
are
attractive
but difficult
to handle.

Like sea stars, sea urchins have a mouth on their underside and tube feet. However, the mouths of sea urchins have a toothed beak-like organ called *Aristotle's lantern*. This is used to gnaw algae and scavenge organic matter off the reef. In the aquarium, sea urchins will scavenge, as well.

Some sea urchins are also equipped with poison glands, which makes handling them a bit of a problem. The venom is not likely to cause death, but it will cause pain and infection.

- **Long-spined sea urchin (*Diadema* spp.):** Found throughout tropical seas, members of this genus are favored by many aquarists. They have long, thin spines that are extremely sharp and sometimes poisonous, but they are easy to maintain. Coloration is generally black, but some species and smaller sea urchins may have banded spines.

- **Common sea urchin (*Echinometra* spp.):** Members of this genus are sometimes called *black sea urchins* because of their coloration. They typically have shorter and blunter spines that can still penetrate your skin. Growing to about four inches, these sea urchins are easy to maintain.

- **Pencil urchin (*Heterocentrotus* spp.):** These species of sea urchins have thick blunt spines that don't pose a threat. Unlike most sea urchins, which are typically drab colored, the pencil urchin can be more colorful and, therefore, a more attractive addition to the aquarium. Although readily available, they tend to be expensive.

Sea cucumbers

Members of the class Holothuroidea are generally called sea cucumbers because of their shape. These echinoderms are elongated, with a mouth at one end and an anus at the other. They are related to sea stars and sea urchins because they have tube feet.

The mouth of the sea cucumber is surrounded by tentacles, which may be fingerlike, stalked with a button-like tip, or branched. The tentacles are actually modified tube feet: parts of the water vascular system that are used for feeding. While some sea cucumbers filter feed, most scavenge organic matter from the bottom, gobbling up the substrate and straining it through their bodies.

In general, sea cucumbers aren't recommended for the new marine aquarist because some species can extrude toxins, when disturbed, that will poison your aquarium.

Nonetheless, a couple of species are readily available and relatively easy to maintain in captivity.

- ✔ **Sea apple *(Pseudocolochirus axiologus)*:** Don't let the name fool you, this is indeed a sea cucumber and not a sea fruit. This is one of the most popular aquarium species because of its striking pink, orange, yellow, and red coloration. One is shown in Figure 11-12. With feathery tentacles, the sea apple is a filter feeder that will position itself in the current of your tank. Small pieces of seafood, brine shrimp, and rotifers will satisfy this critter. This is a species not to be kept with fish.

- ✔ **Black cucumber *(Stichopus chloronotus)*:** Although aptly named for its dark drab coloration, the black cucumber is enjoyed by some aquarists because it swallows mouthfuls of unfiltered substrate, scavenging detritus and providing a useful service.

Figure 11-12:
The sea cucumber will not pickle in your aquarium.

Chapter 12

From the Dealer to Your Home

As I indicate in Chapter 10, your new tropical marine fish and invertebrates come from the farthest reaches of the world. (The Indo-Pacific is probably not around the corner for you!) Fish and invertebrates are collected, double-bagged, and boxed for shipment, which can take days. While that's a long trip, professional collectors and importers are good at what they do. They don't stay in business long if they deliver dead fish, so they take great care to ensure that a healthy marine animal is delivered to your dealer.

Stress and Quarantine

Any time a living creature is abruptly removed from its natural environment and introduced into a new one after making a trip of several thousand miles, the creature is going to experience a little stress. How many times, after all, have you stressed just commuting to work? Stress in any animal can lead to disease and death (see Chapter 18), whether it's an anemone or an anemonefish. So, after that long trip from the tropics, your pets need to acclimate to their new home and settle down a bit. This settling down period is often referred to as the *quarantine period*.

In general, your new pets will have two quarantine periods: when they get to your dealer and when they get to your home.

Don't let the concept of a quarantine tank spook you. This is a simple aquarium, usually about 10 gallons, with an internal box or sponge filter and a heater (see Chapter 6). The water quality of the quarantine tank must be tested routinely because you don't want to add your new pets to an unhealthy environment. The quarantine tank should be set up at the same time as the main aquarium and well before you go to the dealer to purchase fish.

Choosing Healthy Fish

Your goal is to have happy healthy fish and invertebrates in your marine aquarium and the goal of your dealer is, you hope, to provide them to you. Chapter 1 discusses the importance of choosing the right dealer and tells you how to go about doing so. The right dealer has a consistent supply of healthy fish and invertebrates. The right dealer also lets you know where they come from, when they arrived, and how well they're doing in captivity.

If your dealer doesn't communicate, you need a different dealer.

When fishes arrive from distant places, they should be allowed to adjust to captivity and settle down from the trip in quarantine for at least a week before you consider buying them. You also want to make sure the fish is feeding before you purchase it.

Your first fish should be a hardy one that's easy to maintain (see Chapter 10). I recommend Floridian and Caribbean fish to start with because they have traveled the shortest distance and tend to be in better condition when they arrive. In addition, although few species are bred in captivity; some, like clownfishes, are, and these species tend to be healthier and better adapted to captivity than those imported from far off places.

Tropical marine fish are more costly than their freshwater counterparts. Spend wisely and walk before you run.

In Chapter 1, I discuss the importance of looking for healthy fish and invertebrates. Here are a few more tips for choosing healthy fish:

- ✔ Buy fish only from healthy-looking aquariums with clear water, a clean tank, and no dead fish in the tank.

- ✔ Make sure the fish you want is healthy looking. If the fish has any cuts, scrapes, or fin problems, don't buy it. Watch for possible symptoms of disease, such as white granular spots, cottony white patches, frayed fins, or dull skin. The stomach of the fish should be rounded and not pinched in, and the fish's eyes should be clear.

- ✔ Watch the behavior of the fish. Healthy fish swim horizontally in a lively manner and aren't shy.

- ✔ Watch the fish feed before you buy it to make sure it has recovered from the stress of shipping and has acclimated to life in an aquarium.

Heading Home

When you're satisfied with your choice, your dealer will net the fish or invertebrate and place them in a bag containing water from the aquarium. A properly bagged fish will have water in about two thirds of the bag and air in the remaining space. The air space is very important. It provides a supply of oxygen for the water in the bag.

If you have a particularly long trip home or you need to keep your new pet bagged longer than two hours, don't add more water and sacrifice air space. Instead, ask your dealer for a larger bag.

Some invertebrates, corals, live rock, and algae are bagged without water. Don't worry: This is how they are transported from distant seas, and they will be fine.

At the check-out counter, your bagged fish should be placed in a paper bag for the trip home. After you're in the car, make every effort to keep the bag from jostling too much and don't expose it to radical changes in temperature. Keep the fish away from direct exposure to sunlight and the car heater.

Water loses heat more slowly than you may think, so for a short trip home, you don't need to keep your car at 75 to 79°. On the other hand, a heavily air-conditioned car will slowly cool your fish if your trip home is too long.

Taking the Plunge

When you get home, take the time to acclimate your new pets to their new home. Don't unpack your groceries or take the dog for a walk; instead, tend to your fish immediately. This is a relatively simple process and one that I find to be one of the most exciting aspects of owning a new aquarium.

Serious aquarists establish a quarantine tank for their new fish to inhabit for a few days in order to evaluate the health of the fish. A quarantine tank is a much smaller and simpler aquarium set up. The quarantine tank needs to be properly filtered and tested routinely, however, just as the main aquarium. See Chapter 6 for more on quarantine tanks.

You can employ a number of methods to place the fish into your tank. The key is to minimize stress. The best way to accomplish this is to minimize handling and make the water in the bag similar to the water in the aquarium. I prefer to use a simple method that has worked for me for years:

1. **Float the unopened plastic bag (with your new fish inside) in your tank so that the temperature in the bag can acclimate to the temperature in the aquarium.**

   Let it sit in the tank for at least 10 to 15 minutes.

2. **Open the bag and let air in.**

   To ensure that the fish will not be shocked by the aquarium water, make sure that both have a temperature within a degree of each other. Add a cupful of water from your aquarium to the bag and let it sit for another 10 to 15 minutes.

3. **Add the fish to the tank by simply and gently inverting the bag and letting the fish out.**

This method can be used to add invertebrates to your tank, as well, but make sure the *salinity* (the amount of salt in your aquarium water) in the bag is similar to that in the aquarium for delicate species.

Keeping Your Eyes Peeled

Introduce your fish to the aquarium in batches, buying fish in lots every few weeks or a month. This is particularly important for your newly established aquarium because it allows fish to acclimate to each other and prevents aggressive behavior toward a single fish when it is introduced.

Be sure not to stock a marine aquarium too rapidly. Also, follow the tank capacity guidelines outlined in Chapter 2.

Your new tank inhabitants are definitely worth watching. Their behavior will probably not be normal in the beginning as they acclimate to their new surroundings and new tank mates. You may see aggression between the new arrivals and the tank inhabitants, which have set up territories. This is to be expected, so don't let a little nipping bother you. However, if it persists for several days, you may want to reconsider your choice of tank mates.

New arrivals typically require several hours to acclimate to their surroundings, and I don't recommend that you feed them during this period. They aren't likely to feed, so the food will only burden your filtration and pollute your aquarium.

Part III
Caring for Your Aquarium

The 5th Wave By Rich Tennant

"Honey! I think the angelfish have outgrown the neon tetras!"

In this part . . .

1 show you how to keep your aquarium system healthy. I concentrate on the chemical aspects of the aquarium, which involve maintaining water quality and thus a healthy environment for your fish.

Chapter 13

The Cycle of Nitrogen

*T*his chapter gets into the nuts and bolts of water chemistry. You're probably thinking, "Chemistry . . . ugh!" Don't worry, I stick to the basics and limit my discussion to what you really need to know to maintain a healthy saltwater aquarium. While some of the concepts may seem complex at first, they really aren't too bad.

When I established my first aquarium over 25 years ago, I was excited and antsy to have a fully stocked beautiful aquarium. And my family knew it! So, just a week after setting it up, my brothers, sisters, and parents loaded me up with some nice tropical fishes, including angels, butterflies, triggers, and even a lionfish. Well, you guessed it, within days, my fish started dying and, by the end of a week, I had literally flushed hundreds of dollars down the drain. Why? Overstocking too fast without a well-established nitrogen cycle! That was a tough lesson to learn, but this chapter helps you avoid a similar experience.

Nitrogen In, Nitrogen Out

In Chapter 3, I discuss filtration and the basic concepts of keeping your aquarium water clean. In that chapter, you discover that fish and invertebrates are living creatures that require food for energy, burning it with the help of oxygen that they respire (breathe) from the water. However, these processes produce waste products that are returned to the environment through the gills and in the urine and feces. These wastes are primarily carbon dioxide and nitrogenous compounds (like ammonia), which are extremely toxic to fish.

In the aquarium, these wastes must be removed. Carbon dioxide generally leaves the water through aeration at the surface or through photosynthesis by aquarium algae. Ammonia, on the other hand, must be converted to nitrite, which is then converted to nitrate, a less toxic compound. This is the *nitrogen cycle.*

Your marine animals aren't the only source of nitrogenous wastes. Every time that you feed your pets, excess food will decompose into harmful compounds, including ammonia. That is why you need to make every effort to feed your fish carefully so as not to leave excess food in the aquarium.

Understanding the Cycle

This conversion of harmful ammonia into nitrite and then nitrate is referred to as the nitrogen cycle (see Figure 13-1). Why do you need to know about the nitrogen cycle? Because it is the basis of biological filtration, and your filters will use biological filtration to keep your aquarium clean.

Before you can fully stock an aquarium, you need to establish the nitrogen cycle.

The role of bacteria

Biological filtration is actually bacteriological filtration. Believe it or not, the nitrogen cycle is driven by bacteria. Now, there are good bacteria and bad bacteria. The good bacteria that convert ammonia (NH_4) into nitrite (NO_2) belong to the genus *Nitrosomonas*. Nitrite, in turn, is converted into nitrate (NO_3) by bacteria of the genus *Nitrobacter*. These processes are referred to as *nitrification.*

A healthy aquarium depends greatly on the nitrogen cycle to reduce toxic ammonia into less-toxic nitrogen compounds. In your aquarium, ammonia will build slowly and will decrease as it is converted to nitrite. As the nitrite is converted to nitrate, it will decrease, and nitrate will slowly accumulate. Ultimately, your healthy aquarium will have consistently low levels of ammonia and nitrite, while nitrate slowly builds.

You may be wondering what happens to the nitrate. Well, nitrate may be assimilated by algae, or it may be converted to nitrogen gas by denitrifying bacteria. In most aquarium systems, however, nitrate slowly accumulates in the water because the amounts of algae and bacteria necessary to assimilate all the nitrate or convert it to nitrogen gas are lacking.

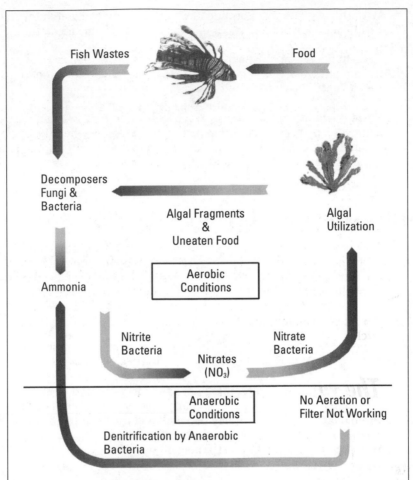

Figure 13-1:
The nitrogen
cycle.

Although nitrate is relatively harmless to fish, it must eventually be removed or diluted before toxic levels are reached. This is done with frequent water changes.

Testing the cycle

The nitrogen cycle will be properly established in a biological filter, which is a requirement for all marine aquariums. Even with a properly functioning biological filter, however, you want to monitor frequently the levels of ammonia, nitrite, and nitrate. This is done with commercial test kits that are available at your fish dealer.

With the test kits that I outline in Chapter 7, you can watch the cycle as it is established in your aquarium — you see your aquarium mature.

Keep in mind that most serious fish dealers provide free water testing. Take full advantage of this service, because it allows you to compare the dealer's results with those that you're getting at home.

Write down the results of your water testing so that you can follow the nitrogen cycle. By keeping these records, you will know when the cycle is firmly established in your aquarium. I even plot my results in a spreadsheet program, so I can see the rise and fall of ammonia and nitrite.

Watching the Maturation Process

When you complete the set-up steps in Chapter 8, you have a tank filled with salt water, but you don't have the working, well-balanced habitat for fish that I call an aquarium. To get to this, you need to let the tank mature. And I'm sorry to say, you have to be a little patient: It's going to take a few weeks.

The maturation process means simply that you're establishing a biological filter and, therefore, allowing the nitrogen cycle to get going. Nitrogen may not cycle only once, but you may see multiple cycles as the *bioload* in your aquarium is increased. That is, as you increase the number of animals, they produce more ammonia, which needs to be converted to nitrite, and then converted to nitrate. So, your aquarium will cycle again. The key is to stimulate bacteria growth without overwhelming the system.

You don't want to add more than a couple of fish to your tank without a working nitrogen cycle.

Taking the Next Step: Just Add Bacteria

Water circulation, temperature regulation, and filtration will help your water mature, but establishing bacterial colonies sufficient to drive the nitrogen cycle can take as long as four to five weeks.

After your aquarium is set up and the components are turned on, the water maturation process begins. There are a few proven methods for accelerating this process so that your aquarium doesn't remain empty for long. Which method you use depends on how fast ammonia and nitrite levels peak and then drop. Basically, to move the maturation process along and turn your infant aquarium into a teenager as fast as possible, you need to add bacteria, as discussed in the following sections. These methods aren't mutually exclusive and can be done in conjunction with each other.

Regardless of what method you use to mature your water and establish the nitrogen cycle, plan on the process taking a minimum of three to six weeks.

Seed it

I found that the most effective and inexpensive method to establish your nitrogen cycle is to seed the aquarium with bacteria from an established aquarium into your *substrate* (the gravel in your aquarium). After your aquarium is set up and filled with water, go to your local pet store and ask for a handful of gravel from one of their systems that has been well established. Mix the gravel in with your gravel. This will accelerate water conditioning by seeding the new system with the right bacteria.

Of course, make sure that the source of your bacteria-rich gravel has healthy fish and well maintained aquaria.

You can also seed your filters by adding material from the filter of an established aquarium. In fact, you will find that when you clean your filters during routine maintenance, you'll want to save some filter media to maintain the nitrogen cycle and biological filtration in that filter.

Start to stock

Another effective way to jump-start the maturation process is to add a couple of inexpensive, hardy fishes. The fishes will begin to excrete ammonia immediately, and this will provide fuel for the developing colony of bacteria. So, one or two days after your aquarium has stabilized in terms of temperature and salinity, go ahead and add a couple of hardy *damsels* (small fish of the family Pomacentridae).

When adding fish, start slowly and be conservative. Add the fish, let the aquarium cycle over a couple of weeks, add a couple more, and repeat the process. Don't overwhelm your bacteria with too much ammonia. Patience is a must!

Rock it!

A third approach to speeding up water maturation involves the use of live rock and live sand to seed a new aquarium. As you know from Chapter 6, live rock and live sand is loaded with helpful bacteria that are already nitrifying ammonia produced by the many critters living on the rock. You can add live sand and live rock after your tank has been running for about 24 hours, providing your salinity and temperature has stabilized.

Make sure you use only cured, live rock in your new aquarium. See Chapter 6 for details on cured rock.

Add accelerators

A number of products on the market today claim to accelerate the maturation process in your aquarium. These typically contain helpful bacteria that can be used to seed your aquarium. Your dealer will probably strongly recommend that you use one.

I may be old fashioned, but I prefer to use the more traditional methods outlined in the preceding sections instead of relying on one of these products.

Watch out for claims of super-accelerated water maturation from one of these acceleration products. Instead, suck it up, be patient, and let your water mature naturally.

The Final Steps to a Mature Tank

Test your water daily to monitor the nitrogen cycle and other water chemistry parameters that I discuss in Chapter 14. In general, after you've seeded the tank with bacteria, the sequence of events will proceed as follows:

1. **After seeding and waiting a couple of days, low values of ammonia begin to increase, peaking in about seven days.**

2. **As ammonia builds and the bacterial colony grows, the ammonia is converted to nitrite, and for about a week, the level of ammonia falls as nitrite increases.**

3. **As the bacterial population proliferates, ammonia drops out, and nitrite decreases as nitrification continues.**

   Nitrate slowly builds and stabilizes.

The filter bed will not be completely established for several weeks, so be sure to be conservative when you add your first fish. Start with a low number of peaceful, inexpensive fish. The introduction of territorial fish, like some of the damsels, may make it difficult to add more fish, because these fish will establish territories and may be aggressive toward new fishes.

In a healthy, mature, well-established marine aquarium, ammonia and nitrite levels in your water should be close to zero, and nitrate levels should be kept less than 20 mg/L.

What If Something Is Wrong

If something goes wrong and ammonia doesn't decrease within two weeks, don't panic! Your bioload may be too large, so that the bacteria in your tank are overwhelmed. The best thing is to just let the tank continue to mature. Eventually, the bacteria will catch up, and your tank will cycle. However, if your fish are stressed or dying, you probably need to physically get rid of the ammonia by conducting a partial water change (see Chapter 16) or using a commercial ammonia neutralizer available at your dealer.

Chapter 14

More Chemistry: Salt, Acidity, and Gases

Consider this chapter to be the second major part of your chemistry education. In Chapter 13, I discuss the nitrogen cycle thoroughly. In this chapter, I address some of the other water chemistry parameters that you use to monitor the quality of the water in your tank.

The quality of the water in your aquarium is the most important part of a healthy marine environment. That is why I emphasize the importance of proper filtration in Chapter 3. Fish can live for days without food, but they will certainly perish in minutes without high water quality.

But how do you determine whether the water in your aquarium is healthy? While cloudy or discolored water is a dead giveaway, in most cases you simply can't see whether your water is polluted. This is why you want to examine certain chemical aspects of the water.

Think of test kits as the only way your aquarium water can communicate with you if something is wrong. When you test the water, you're the doctor, and the tests will tell you whether your patient is healthy.

In Chapter 7, I tell you that test kits are important accessories to add to your equipment list and give you a summary of the kits you need. In this chapter, I explain what each of these kits actually does.

I try to keep the information in this chapter simple, so that you're not turned off by the water chemistry aspects of the hobby. Just the basics here, my friend. At this stage, you don't need to be a chemist to be an aquarist!

My friend Rick has the right idea: He set up his aquarium about a year ago. Allowing for water maturation, he stocked his tank slowly with the right number of compatible aquarium inhabitants. During this process, he religiously monitored his water quality on a weekly basis, all the while not allowing himself to be obsessed by the chemistry. Rick and his family enjoy their aquarium, which is well balanced and a picture of beauty. While you want to be cognizant of the chemical processes, use them to your advantage and think of them as a means of keeping your pets alive.

Checking Your Salt Level

As discussed in Chapter 7, the chemical composition of seawater is extremely consistent throughout the world. Although it is 96 percent pure water (one atom of oxygen bonded with two atoms of hydrogen: H_2O), it also contains many dissolved minerals and salts. These minerals and salts are mainly sodium and chlorine (85 percent), but magnesium, sulphate, calcium, and potassium make up another 13 percent, and bicarbonate and 68 other elements make up the remainder in small quantities.

You need to mimic natural seawater as closely as possible in your aquarium, which means that you need to make sure the amount of salt in your water is correct. Science has developed a couple of ways to measure the amount of dissolved salts in seawater. One measure is called salinity and another is called specific gravity. Although these measurements aren't the same, either can be used to determine the correct level of salt in your aquarium.

An affinity for salinity

Salinity refers to the actual concentration of major dissolved ions in the water, and it is not influenced by temperature. It is expressed as a ratio of parts-per-thousand (ppt). To directly measure salinity, you need special equipment, which can be expensive for the average aquarist. But if you choose to purchase one of these products, a salinity of 34-35 ppt is optimal for invertebrates, while fishes can tolerate lower salinities.

Heavy stuff: Specific gravity

An easier and more practical way to measure the salt level in your tank is to estimate specific gravity with a hydrometer (see Chapter 7).

Specific gravity refers to the ratio of densities of seawater to pure water at various temperatures. For example, a specific gravity of 1.021 means that a liquid is 1.021 times denser than seawater. However, because the specific gravity of a liquid is directly related to temperature, your *hydrometer* (an instrument used to measure specific gravity) may not be calibrated to the temperature in your aquarium. Most hydrometers are calibrated at 60°, so you need to use a conversion factor to adjust your hydrometer reading to true specific gravity. The conversion table should be included with the instructions that come with your hydrometer.

Under standard aquarium temperatures (75 to 79°), the conversion usually results in the addition of 0.002 to the hydrometer reading. For example, if your hydrometer reading is 1.023 and your water temperature is 77°, the actual specific gravity of your aquarium is 1.025.

Specific gravity should be established in the range of 1.021 and 1.024, but more importantly, it should be maintained at a specific level within this range. Even minor fluctuations can cause problems for your tank inhabitants.

Salty fluctuations

The greatest cause of salt level change is evaporation from the tank. When water evaporates in a marine aquarium, the salts remain in the solution, and the water becomes more concentrated, thereby increasing the salinity and specific gravity. You must monitor water levels in the aquarium to prevent these fluctuations. Evaporation is easily remedied by adding fresh water, not additional salt water, to the tank.

Don't wait until levels have dropped significantly before you top off the tank with fresh water; instead, do so regularly with small quantities.

Although water evaporation is the major source of fluctuating salt levels, you may also lose salt from the tank from the protein skimmer (see Chapter 3) and from crystallization on the hood and other fixtures. Keep an eye on the hydrometer.

Understanding Acid and pH

When I talk about acid, I'm referring to levels of hydrogen ions in solution. Ions are simply atoms with an electrical charge. These hydrogen ions are also called *hydrogen protons* because they have a positive charge. They look like this: H^+. You can measure the number of hydrogen atoms on a scale called pH. You may have heard the term pH for a number of solutions, ranging from blood to shampoo.

Scaling pH

The pH scale, shown in Figure 14-1, tells you how many hydrogen atoms are in a solution and, therefore, how acidic it is. It ranges from 0 to 14, with a pH of 7 being neutral, a pH of 1 being very acidic, and a pH of 14 being very alkaline, which is the opposite of acidic. The lower the number on the scale, the more hydrogen atoms are present, and the more acidic the solution is.

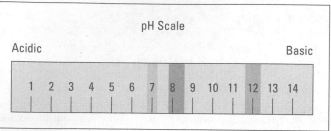

Figure 14-1: The pH scale.

The pH scale is *logarithmic,* which means that each number is ten times stronger than the preceding number. For example, a pH of 2 is ten times more acidic than a pH of 3 and 100 times more acidic than a pH of 4. Therefore, a single incremental change represents a huge change in the number of hydrogen protons in your water.

Salt water is more alkaline than fresh water. If you had a freshwater aquarium, you probably maintained the pH within the range of 6.5 to 7.5. On the other hand, the pH of seawater is about 8.2 and should be maintained in the aquarium between 8.1 and 8.3.

While maintaining the correct pH is important, it is even more critical that you avoid large changes in pH.

pH fluctuations

A number of factors influence the pH in your aquarium water. These include the amount of carbon dioxide and fish wastes in the water. The accumulation of either or both of these will cause the water to acidify and the pH to drop. In fact, the nitrogen cycle itself will often produce acids that will alter the pH of your aquarium.

Add a pH test kit to your repertoire of commercial test kits. The kit is simple to use and is an important step when monitoring the quality of your aquarium water. Monitor this water parameter every week to detect any changes. An abrupt drop in pH may be indicative of an increase of carbon dioxide or nitrogenous fish wastes. An increase in aeration and a partial water change (see Chapter 16) will be necessary to alleviate the problem before the lives of tank inhabitants are compromised.

The ability of a solution to resist changes in pH is called its *buffering capacity.* Most commercial salt mixes contain buffers that will keep pH from falling dramatically. However, over time, the buffering capacity of your water will diminish, and carbon dioxide or waste build-up will cause pH to drop.

pH solutions

Regular ten percent water changes (see Chapter 16) will maintain your pH at correct levels by replenishing your aquarium's buffering capacity. However, if your pH falls rapidly out of the acceptable range, you can restore it by doing the following:

✔ Using a commercially manufactured aquarium buffer. Available at most aquarium dealers, these chemicals buffer your aquarium when used properly. Be sure to follow the manufacturer's instructions carefully and use the buffers in conjunction with a waste-removing partial water change.

✔ Adding a solution of calcium hydroxide, commonly referred to as *kalkwasser* or *limewater.* This addition will help maintain calcium levels, thereby increasing pH.

Being Aware of Hardness and Alkalinity

The amount of dissolved minerals, namely calcium and magnesium, in the water is referred to as its *hardness.* Water with high concentrations of minerals is referred to as *hard,* while low levels would be indicative of *soft water.*

First, the good news

While general hardness is important for the typical freshwater aquarium, the salt in your marine aquarium dictates the water hardness. So, you really don't need to pay much attention to general hardness. However, you don't get off the hardness hook that easily! There is a specific kind of hardness — carbonate hardness — that you do need to measure.

Carbonate hardness

In the "Understanding Acid and pH" section, I mention the term "buffering capacity" relative to the ability of your aquarium water to resist changes in pH. Remember that pH is really just a measurement of the amount of positively charged hydrogen atoms in your water. The more positive charges, the more acidic the water, and the lower the pH.

You may think that the pH would increase if the number of hydrogen ions increases, but don't let this confuse you. All these hydrogen protons create a lot of positive charges in the water. The best way to counteract a positive charge is with a negative charge. So the water contains molecules and atoms that are negatively charged to buffer the positive charges. The amount of negative charges and, therefore, the ability of the water to resist the positive charges is the buffering capacity.

The negative molecules that are typically found in seawater and act as buffers are called *carbonates* and *bicarbonates*. Therefore, if you measure the amount of carbonates in your water, you're measuring the buffering capacity, and this is important. If buffering capacity diminishes, your pH will fall and problems can occur.

Checking carbonate hardness (alkalinity)

When you measure the amount of carbonates in your aquarium, you're measuring the carbonate hardness. This is often referred to as measuring the *alkalinity,* but don't get this confused with a pH measurement that is alkaline. Carbonate hardness will affect pH, but you're not measuring pH.

Carbonate hardness can be measured with a standard kit that's available from your dealer. Keep in mind that it may be called an *alkalinity test kit.* Carbonate hardness is usually reported in milliequivalents per liter (meq/L), and the level in your aquarium should be above 3.0 meq/L.

Adjusting carbonate hardness

If the carbonate hardness and, therefore, the buffering capacity of your aquarium water is below the recommended level, you need to make some adjustments. In all likelihood, your pH will probably be decreasing, as well. In fact, the methods you use to adjust your pH will also be used to increase your carbonate hardness.

 ✔ **Conduct a partial water change.** This will increase the buffering capacity of your water by removing old stale water with fresh buffered water (not fresh water!). This should be your first step. (See Chapter 16 for more on conducting a water change.) Wait a day, and then test the water again. If carbonate hardness is still low, try the next two tips.

✔ **Use a commercially manufactured aquarium buffer.** Available at most aquarium dealers, these chemicals, when used properly, buffer your aquarium. Be sure to carefully follow the manufacturer's instructions and use these in conjunction with a waste-removing partial water change.

✔ **Add a solution of calcium hydroxide or kalkwasser.** This increases the buffering capacity (alkalinity) of your water.

Use calcareous calcium-based substrates (gravels; see Chapter 6) in your saltwater aquarium because they interact with the carbon dioxide excreted by your pets, increasing the buffering capacity of the water.

Recognizing the Gases in Your Water

Through the process of *respiration,* we use oxygen and produce carbon dioxide when we breathe. These molecules are well known by most people simply because without them, we would certainly perish. Well, our marine friends are just like us in this respect.

Oxygen (O_2)

Like most living creatures, marine fish and invertebrates need oxygen to live. While humans can breathe oxygen from the air, marine critters must draw it from the water. Therefore, they need oxygen that's dissolved in water, called *dissolved oxygen.*

Most oxygen exchange occurs at your aquarium's surface where the water meets the air. You can increase the amount of dissolved oxygen in your aquarium by agitating the surface area of the tank through increased circulation. This process is called *aeration.* As I discuss in Chapter 3, aeration and circulation go hand in hand.

To maintain high levels of dissolved oxygen in your aquarium, you need to aerate the water. Despite what most people think, air delivered by airstones and diffusers help to increase circulation but don't contribute much oxygen directly to the water.

Test kits and electronic probes are available to measure the amount of dissolved oxygen in your aquarium, but only reef tank enthusiast may consider buying one. If you use a test kit, make sure that dissolved oxygen levels are maintained above 7.0 mg/L.

Carbon dioxide (CO_2)

Oxygen in, carbon dioxide out. That is how a living respiring system works. For every molecule of dissolved oxygen that you want in your tank, carbon dioxide will be produced when it is utilized by your critters.

In your aquarium, carbon dioxide will combine with water molecules and calcium in a dynamic equilibrium that produces hydrogen protons, bicarbonate ions, and calcium carbonate. Without going into great detail using chemical equations and lots of capital letters, realize that the levels of these compounds are influenced by the amount of carbon dioxide production (respiration) in your aquarium.

Carbon dioxide can profoundly affect your water quality. Excessive amounts will lower your pH; however, it will also affect the buffering capacity of your water to lower your carbonate hardness. Moreover, carbon dioxide will also affect calcium levels in your water, and as discussed in the "Calcium (Ca)" section, later in this chapter, you need high calcium levels for your invertebrates.

The bottom line: Carbon dioxide is a product of metabolism that needs to be removed from your aquarium. However, test kits for carbon dioxide are not common, and the best ways to keep carbon dioxide levels low are as follows:

- Maintain high levels of aeration and circulation so that carbon dioxide is removed from the water.
- Conduct regular partial water changes to physically remove carbon dioxide (see Chapter 16).
- To limit carbon dioxide production, don't overstock your aquarium with inhabitants.
- Maintain proper pH levels.
- Allow some growth of algae, which will remove some of the carbon dioxide (see Chapter 15).
- Don't overfeed your pets.

Tweaking Other Chemical Factors

A number of water tests are available to the average aquarist, so you may be a bit confused in the beginning. In Chapter 7, I list those tests that may be useful to you, depending on whether you have a fish-only or a reef tank. I discuss a few of these parameters throughout this chapter, but I cover a few more here.

Calcium (Ca)

You may recall from Chapter 11 that many invertebrate species, like corals and snails, possess calcium carbonate skeletons and shells. Therefore, for these animals to thrive and grow, they need to extract calcium from the water. As you can probably guess, the level of calcium in the water is important to you if you keep a reef tank. If you have a fish-only aquarium, the calcium levels in your water will be adequately maintained by your partial water changes.

Calcium test kits are available, and levels should be maintained at 375 to 475 ppm (parts per million) in the reef aquarium. If your testing indicates that you don't have enough calcium in the water; add calcium supplements, like limewater, to the aquarium. These supplements are commercially available and should be administered slowly.

Phosphate (PO$_4$)

Dissolved inorganic phosphorous, also called *phosphate,* enters your aquarium primarily through excretion by fishes, the breakdown of uneaten food, and tap water. These phosphates are readily incorporated by growing algae. In most cases, phosphate isn't a problem until excessive algal growth occurs on the live corals of a reef aquarium.

Therefore, take efforts to monitor levels of phosphate with a test kit. A phosphate level in excess of 0.10 ppm will cause an algal bloom, so reduce phosphate levels by increasing aeration and using a protein skimmer (see Chapter 3). Maintain a phosphate level less than 0.05 ppm.

Phosphate becomes bound to organic matter that binds to rising air bubbles. When the bubbles burst at the surface, the phosphates are lost to the atmosphere.

Copper (Cu)

Even though you make every effort to maintain a healthy aquarium, eventually one of your fish will need to be treated for disease (see Chapter 19). The most effective treatment for many parasitic infestations is copper. While I prefer to treat diseased fish in a separate hospital aquarium, some fishkeepers add copper directly to their aquariums.

In the aquarium, copper readily binds to calcium carbonates and becomes ineffective, so copper levels will need to be maintained continuously. At the same time, excessive copper is toxic to fish.

Copper levels in your aquarium should be tested during the treatment period to maintain adequate levels while avoiding excessive treatment.

Copper is toxic to invertebrates, so if you keep invertebrates, don't use copper. Many houses, particularly older ones, have copper pipes that may, on occasion, leach out enough copper to be toxic to many invertebrates. If your home has copper pipes, it is worthwhile to have a copper text kit to make sure your tap water is safe.

Chapter 15

Always Algae

Plants are an integral part of the freshwater aquarium but are somewhat rare in the saltwater tank. This is because with few exceptions, all of the ocean's plant life is classified in the primitive group known as *algae*. The term "seaweed" actually refers to the many-celled forms of algae.

Algae can be either good or bad for the marine aquarist, depending on whether or not the algae get out of control. In moderation, algae assimilate nitrates and other excess nutrients from the water, and they provide food for herbivorous fishes and invertebrates. This chapter explains the pros and cons of the algae in your aquarium. The latter part of the chapter reviews the types of algae, including those that you want to keep.

Defining Algae

Algae are photosynthetic organisms that occur throughout the world in many habitats ranging from fresh water to salt water and from the arctic to the equator. For many years, algae were grouped with the fungi into the class of plants known as Thallophyta. More recently, scientists have classified these plant-like organisms into their own kingdom, called the Protoctista. The term algae is used to describe a very diverse group of organisms that are difficult to define. Basically, they are aquatic organisms that utilize photosynthesis.

Algae are relatively simple organisms that range in size from the one-celled microscopic types to large seaweeds that grow to over 230 feet. Algae are also hardy organisms that have a tremendous reproductive capacity. They can enter your aquarium as algal spores borne by the air or carried by tank furnishings from another aquarium.

The term *alga* is singular, and more than one alga is called algae.

Algae have adapted to all kinds of water conditions. They are important as primary producers at the base of the food chain. They provide oxygen and food for aquatic life, but some forms can contribute to the mass mortality of other organisms. In tropical regions, coralline algae can be as important as corals in the formation of reefs.

Algae can be *planktonic,* meaning they float freely in the ocean, and when they do, they're called *microalgae.* The term seaweed refers to larger species of algae, called *macroalgae,* that live in the marine environment attached to the bottom. Despite their size, which can exceed 200 feet, seaweeds are simple organisms that aren't well understood. They don't have roots and shoots the way that plants do, but they do have root-like attachment structures and leaf-like fronds.

In your aquarium, algae can be found on the water's surface, suspended in the water, or on the surfaces of the aquarium glass, rocks, gravel, coral, and tank decorations. Many species are introduced on live rock or coral, but some enter your aquarium with water from other aquariums and as spores. You can also purchase seaweeds from your dealer to add plant-like décor to your aquarium.

Despite their diversity, all aquarium algae have one thing in common: They need light and nutrients to propagate.

Light and nutrients

Whether or not algae are plants, they act like them. They need light to grow and prosper just like your favorite backyard tree. And like that same tree, nutrients like nitrates and phosphates form the building blocks of algae. In your aquarium, these natural ingredients are well represented. Strong lighting and nitrate from the nitrogen cycle fuel the propagation of algae.

In addition, algae are photosynthetic, so they utilize carbon dioxide and convert it into oxygen. (Chapter 14 discusses that the reduction of carbon dioxide in your aquarium is a good thing.) However, this trait is a double-edged sword because algae need light to photosynthesize, and they respire at night, producing carbon dioxide.

Algae act as convenient organisms that can be used to remove excess nutrients from your aquarium. By routinely scraping some (not all!) of your algae from the tank, you will be physically getting nitrates, phosphates, and other nutrients out your tank.

So far, everything in this chapter shows that algae are good for the saltwater aquarium. So why do a lot of people think that algae are a nuisance?

The sterility syndrome

The primary reason that people find algae to be a problem is associated with what I call the *sterility syndrome*. Many new aquarists think that a sterile-looking aquarium is a clean and healthy aquarium, so they remove as much of the algae as they can at all times to keep it clean-looking. Well, this belief couldn't be further from the truth. Next time you go snorkeling or diving in the ocean, look closely at the rocks, coral, and sand: You'll see algae literally covering all the exposed surfaces.

Algae are an integral part of the natural coral reef ecosystem. Many species of fish and invertebrates feed exclusively on algae and some important species of algae actually live inside some invertebrates, providing them food (see Chapter 11).

Don't succumb to the sterility syndrome. Get used to seeing algae and promoting algal growth in your aquarium, yet routinely removing some of it to maintain a clear view of your pets and to get rid of excess nutrients.

Knowing When Algae Are Out of Control

At some point your aquarium algae may get out of control. Excessive algae will literally choke an aquarium by consuming oxygen during the night and covering live corals. It will clog your filter system and obscure your vision by covering the walls of your tank. You can physically remove the excess algae, but this will only remove the symptom and not solve the problem.

Go to the source

When the algae in your aquarium become a nuisance, consider this a sign that something is wrong in your aquarium. Algae need light and nutrients to propagate in your aquarium, so when algae become a nuisance, check these factors.

First, check your light levels: Is your aquarium too close to a window, allowing for excess sunlight? Is your light being kept on too long? Are you using the correct kind of lighting? How old is your light source? The quality of a light will degrade as it ages, and this may contribute to your algae problem.

In most cases, excess algal growth is caused by a problem with nutrient levels. In other words, there is too much fertilizer in your tank! Now is the time to check your water chemistry, looking at the factors that I outline in Chapters 13 and 14. Start with the nitrate, and then check pH, carbonate hardness, and phosphate. Have you conducted routine water changes (see Chapter 16)? Is your circulation and aeration adequate (see Chapter 3)? Check your filtration, as well.

If you find that one or more of these parameters is out of balance, take steps to remedy them. Flip to Chapters 13 and 14 to determine how to solve your water problems.

Get some help

One of the best and most enjoyable ways to control algae is to stock your aquarium with algae-eating critters. In Chapters 10 and 11, I introduced a number of species of fish and invertebrates that eat algae. Blennies, tangs, snails, sea urchins, and hermit crabs are among those species that readily consume algae.

Harvest it!

At some point, removing algae will become a part of your routine maintenance. Even if it's not out of control, algae will cover your glass and obstruct the view of your pets. In Chapter 7, I recommend the purchase of algae scrubbers and tube brushes to remove algae.

If beneficial green algae is excessive, simply remove it from the aquarium fixtures by rinsing them. A vacuum will help remove it from the gravel. If the excessive algae are the blue-green slime algae, make every effort to remove all the algae and the causes of it. Poor water quality must be improved. Test the water, do a partial water change (see Chapter 16), and check the operation of your filters.

Removing algae is a great way to remove excess nutrients from your aquarium, but if the algae are the beneficial variety, don't fall into the sterility syndrome and remove them all!

Identifying Types of Algae

One thing is sure, not all algae are alike. While there are a number of formal classifications for algae, scientists have recognized at least eight major divisions, but not all occur in the typical aquarium. Some kinds are desirable, and others are not. Some are typically referred to as seaweeds, others are planktonic, and some are both.

There is really no point in reviewing all the various kinds of algae, so the following sections concentrate only on those that you're most likely to encounter or purchase for your marine aquarium.

Green algae

This group is called the Chlorophyta, but green algae is a much easier term to remember. With 7,000 species, this is the most diverse group of algae, but only about ten percent of the green algae are marine forms. These are typically the most beneficial of the algae, although some species are less desirable. They are green in color because their chlorophyll pigments are identical to those of higher plants.

Although green algae are thought of as one of the typical seaweed groups, the planktonic spores of some species are not visible to the naked eye but appear as a green cloudiness in the water. These algae sometimes form a green film on the aquarium glass. Larger green algae species may come in desirable plant-like shapes or less desirable hair and mat-like forms. The most desirable species of green algae are cultivated and sold as attractive additions to your aquarium.

The following types of green algae are desirable:

- *Caulerpa* **spp:** This is the most popular and common genus of green algae in the aquarium. Members of this group come in a variety of colors ranging from lime green to bluish brown. They typically have a single stalk with blade-like leaves. These prolific algae are cultivated and offered by many marine aquarium dealers.

- *Halimeda* **spp:** Unlike the *Caulerpa*, members of this genus are calcareous, meaning that they contain calcium. They resemble underwater cacti growing as a series of circular flat plates. These algae are important contributors to the sparkling white sand that you see on Caribbean beaches. In the aquarium, they are indicative of a healthy environment.

- *Valonia* **spp:** These species of algae are called *bubble algae* because they form clusters of spherical bubbles. Although they have an attractive silver appearance, bubble algae can overgrow an aquarium and should be watched closely and regularly cropped.

Hair algae are less desirable. These algae form thick, hair-like mats that can carpet your aquarium. For a fish-only tank, this matting will be simply ugly, but in the reef tank, it can smother and kill live corals. Make efforts to control hair algae.

Red algae

This group of algae, called the Rhodophyta, contains about 6,000 species, and most are marine seaweeds. Although most red algae are multicellular and grow attached to rocks and other algae, there are some single-celled forms.

Red algae are red because of the pigment called *phycoerythin,* which absorbs blue light and reflects red light. Their coloration depends on how much of this pigment they have and may range from reddish yellow to bright red to greenish blue and brown. Because blue light penetrates much deeper than red light, these algae typically live at deeper depths and are well adapted to low lighting conditions.

Most red algae are introduced into the aquarium on live rocks. The most common are called coralline red algae, which secrete a hard calcareous shell the way that corals do. These algae are considered important in the formation of tropical reefs and, in some areas, may contribute more to reef structure than corals do. They are beneficial to an aquarium, encrusting rocks and even spreading to the fixtures and glass.

Brown algae

Belonging to the Phaeophyta group, the brown algae comprise about 3,000 species that are predominantly marine seaweeds. There are no single-celled forms of brown algae (and the simplest is a branched filamentous organism, which is techy information that you don't need to remember).

Their brown coloration results from the dominance of a xanthophyll pigment, which masks other pigments, like chlorophyll. Colors of brown algae range from pale beige to yellow-brown to almost black.

The most common brown algae, called *kelp,* are the largest algae, attaining sizes greater than 200 feet in length. The giant kelp forms expansive seaweed forests off the coast of North America and provides habitat and shelter for many organisms. Tropical waters have fewer species of brown algae.

Some forms of brown algae come attached to live rock when you purchase it. Like the red algae, brown algae are generally beneficial for a saltwater aquarium.

Diatoms

These algae of the group Bacillariophyta are microscopic cells composed of overlapping half shells of silica. These are the diatoms, which are planktonic and benthic algae that spend their lives floating in the ocean or in the sediments. Their silica shells, called *frustules,* are remarkably geometric in shape, but their microscopic size makes them difficult for the average aquarist to see.

In the ocean, diatoms form a major part of the plant-plankton called *phytoplankton,* providing important food for the animal-plankton called *zooplankton.* Chapter 3 discusses how the frustules of diatoms are used in diatom filters as filter media.

These algae proliferate in aquariums with high nitrate levels. They are usually the first algae to establish themselves. Diatoms form a brown slime on the gravel, rocks, decorations, and aquarium glass. Heavy concentrations of diatoms will discolor the water. As the aquarium matures, these algae should disappear. Until they do, you can scrape them away to keep a clear view of your aquarium pets.

Dinoflagellates

Members of the group Dynophyta are single-celled organisms considered by biologists to be either plants or animals depending on whether you're a botanist or a zoologist. Clearly, they have the characteristics of both. Although it sounds like a prehistoric reptile, the name *dinoflagellate* actually refers to their forward swimming motion created by their tails, which are called *flagella.*

Not all species of dinoflagellates are photosynthetic, and some species are planktonic, while others are *benthic;* that is, they live on the bottom. Some species of dinoflagellates are harmful to sea life and those that eat it. Dinoflagellate blooms, called *red-tide,* turn coastal waters reddish-brown, producing serious toxins that can affect human health.

In some instances, excess nutrient levels will cause dinoflagellate blooms in your aquarium. This will result in brown mucous slime covering most of the tank and its contents. If this happens, the algae must be physically removed with a siphon, and you should conduct a 50 percent water change (see Chapter 16).

The dinoflagellates that are of greatest interest to aquarists are those that live in live corals, sponges, clams, and anemones. These are called *zooxanthellae,* and I discuss them in Chapter 11. These algae form a *symbiotic relationship* with their hosts, providing beneficial organic carbon that they produce by photosynthesis.

If you're an invertebrate enthusiast, make sure you have sufficient lighting to keep zooxanthellae dinoflagellates alive. If they die, in all likelihood, their host will die.

Blue-green algae

The blue-green algae are not algae at all: They are bacteria. For years, they were considered algae because they are aquatic and make their own food. This group of bacteria is called the Cyanobacteria, and it has the distinction of being the oldest known group of fossils at more than 3.5 billion years old. Because they are bacteria, blue-green algae are small and single-celled, but they grow in large enough colonies that you can see them. Although called blue-green algae, they can have colors ranging from black to red to purple.

They may be earth's bacterial heroes, but when these algae are in your aquarium they can be both good and bad. Like a lot of bacteria, blue-green algae in your substrate are beneficial to the health of your aquarium, feasting on *detritus* (organic wastes). However, in cases of poor water quality, high nutrients, and poor circulation, they form a dark brownish-red gelatinous mat, called *red slime,* on rocks, gravel, and plants in your tank. They are also capable of producing toxins that will poison aquarium fish. If allowed to proliferate, they will smother the tank. Unfortunately, few critters feed on blue-green algae, so they must be physically removed with a siphon during a partial water change.

Water that's not well maintained and that lacks frequent changes will promote the growth of blue-green algae.

Chapter 16

Keeping Your Aquarium Clean

A fish living in the open ocean isn't generally too concerned about water quality. Waste products and detritus are, after all, diluted by massive amounts of water. In the closed aquarium system, however, this is not the case. You must keep the aquarium clean.

Preventative maintenance, my friend — that's what keep an aquarium is all about. You know that your house, your car, and even your body benefit from routine care and maintenance. Everything lasts a lot longer with fewer problems. Your marine aquarium is no exception.

Ben Franklin said, "An ounce of prevention is worth a pound of cure." Aquariums are a great example of how true Franklin's quote is. This chapter tells you how a little work every day will keep your aquarium healthy in the long run.

Performing the Basics

Cleaning an aquarium involves a conscientious effort on your part. In fact, maintaining a fish tank is not for the lazy at heart. Don't set up a saltwater aquarium if you don't intend to follow through and keep it clean and healthy. All too often, an aquarist's interest wanes after the first couple of months of ownership, and the aquarium occupants ultimately suffer the consequences.

Realize that going into this hobby requires a real commitment on your part. Concern must be shown at every step and on every level. Your fishes' lives depend on your attention to detail!

If you're a parent and your child has an aquarium, it's your responsibility to help him or her to maintain the aquarium. Make a game out of it and try to keep it fun. As soon as it starts to feel like work, you're on your own.

There are basic tasks that you should tend to on a regular basis. They are listed as follows and I cover them in detail in the following sections.

- Vacuum the gravel
- Clean and maintain the filters
- Test your water quality
- Conduct partial water changes

In the "Developing Your Maintenance Schedule" section later in the chapter, I give you a schedule for some of these tasks, but this is not set in stone, and you should customize the schedule as you see fit. The frequency with which you clean your aquarium depends on how dirty it gets, and that depends on the number of occupants, the quality of your filtration, and the amount of food that is left to foul your tank.

Sucking it up

Vacuuming is one of the most important parts of maintaining your tank. You must reduce the accumulation of detritus in the gravel so that your biological filters are not overwhelmed.

Detritus is the combination of fish wastes and uneaten food that sinks to and decays on the bottom of the aquarium. If not removed, this organic waste breaks down into ammonia and overwhelms the nitrogen cycle. This result will, in turn, disturb your water chemistry, snowballing into a series of problems that will ultimately harm your fish and invertebrates.

If detritus is allowed to accumulate to excessive levels, your filter will be clogged and water quality will go downhill fast. Too much detritus will clog the undergravel filter, preventing water flow through the gravel and reducing the filter's ability to do its job.

Aquarium vacuums, sometimes called *substrate cleaners,* are commercially available at your aquarium dealer. Chapter 7 addresses the kinds of gravel vacuums available to the aquarist.

While an aquarium vacuum is a nice piece of equipment, the old-fashioned garden hose works to siphon wastes, as well.

The most efficient way to vacuum your aquarium is while conducting a water change because water is removed in the process anyway. This accomplishes two goals at once: vacuuming detritus and removing water from the tank for replacement. Follow the steps in the "Changing the water" section later in this chapter to vacuum your aquarium while changing your water.

When you vacuum, make sure you gently rake the gravel. Don't mix it up too aggressively, though, or you may disrupt the filter bed.

Cleaning your filters

As I discuss in Chapter 3, many filters have their own maintenance schedule. The level to which you "clean" your filter depends on the kind of filtration that it provides. A filter that's strictly mechanical can be cleaned thoroughly to remove debris, while a biological filter should not be touched except to remove large detritus. Somewhere in the middle is the chemical filter, which should be recharged every month.

Don't forget what I tell you in Chapter 3 about the function of a filter. Filters remove wastes from the aquarium and either retain them (mechanical and chemical filtration) or convert them to less harmful compounds (biological filtration). Regardless of the type, wastes remain in the filters until you remove them through a thorough cleaning.

In the following sections, I touch briefly on each filter that I describe in Chapter 3, giving you a maintenance routine.

Inside box filter

Although you may not be using inside box filters except in a quarantine tank (see Chapter 12), they are easily maintained. Simply replace the activated carbon and the filter floss every month, retaining about half of the latter for the bacteria that they harbor.

Sponge filter

Because the sponge in this type of filter provides the filter medium for mechanical and biological filtration, there is no need to change additional media. Sponge filters are easy to maintain by rinsing them in water every two weeks to a month, but be careful not to wash them out too thoroughly (keep those bacteria!).

Undergravel filter

After a healthy undergravel filtration system is established, this filter can be used indefinitely without being disassembled and cleaned. There is no filter floss or carbon to change, and the only medium is the gravel itself.

Nonetheless, debris does accumulate in the gravel, so the gravel needs to be vacuumed to keep the filter from clogging. This vacuuming is done with routine partial water changes every two weeks (more on this in the "Changing the water" section, later in this chapter).

Every month, make sure that you check the airstones that power your undergravel filter and replace them if they're clogged or crumbling. If you have powerheads, make sure the intakes are clear and the impeller inside is clean. I like to take them apart every month and clean the moving non-electrical parts under running tap water.

Power filters

Power filters are easy to maintain. Most have cartridges that can be replaced every two weeks to a month, depending on bioload (see Chapter 13) and waste accumulation. However, make every effort to retain 50 percent of the used filter media or use a sponge type medium so helpful bacteria are not lost. If your filter has two cartridges, alternate their replacement so bacteria are always present. Activated carbon should be replaced every month, as well.

If your filter is equipped with a biowheel, you can retain bacteria even though you have to replace the internal filter media. Biowheels don't need to be cleaned.

Filter impellers should be cleaned every month under running tap water so that they continue to run efficiently.

Canister filters

The canister filter contains compartments with various kinds of filter media, like activated carbon, filter sponges, filter floss, and ceramic bodies. The use of multiple filter media allows valuable bacteria to be retained when the filter is cleaned every two weeks to a month, depending on waste accumulation and bioload.

When the canister filter is cleaned, the activated carbon is replaced, the ceramic bodies and filter sponges are rinsed and retained, and 50 percent of the filter floss is replaced.

The number of filter components depends on the brand of canister filter that you have — many are available. Read the manufacturer's instructions and follow its recommended maintenance schedule.

Don't forget to check those impellers and clean them, as well.

Trickle filters

Trickle filters offer great advantages over other filter systems relative to filtration efficiency and effectiveness. In addition, they require little maintenance. Like the canister filters, you can find many brands, and the level to which you clean them depends on their components. Every month, replace the carbon and rinse the sponges and filter pads. Bioballs and ceramic bodies can be rinsed every six months to a year.

Protein skimmers

Daily checks are required for the protein skimmer to make sure that it's working properly and to empty the collection cup if needed. Airflow components, like airstones, air ports, and tubing, should be checked regularly, and then cleaned and replaced, as needed. Every month, clean powerhead or water pump impellers, as well.

Follow the maintenance schedule of your manufacturer so that your protein skimmer is kept running efficiently.

Testing, testing, testing (your water)

If you read Chapters 13, 14, or 15, you're probably getting sick of my writing about testing your water. But I can't impress upon you enough the need to keep an eye on your aquarium's health and conduct water chemistry tests.

When you first set up your aquarium, testing the water every day is critical to monitoring the water-maturation process. As you begin to add fish, water chemistry will change radically, and water-quality monitoring is critical to the survival of your fish. After this sensitive period, which can last several weeks, it is still important to test your water. I recommend that you do so at least once every week. This will give you a good understanding of the mechanics of the nitrogen cycle and will tell you when the nitrates, carbonate hardness, pH, and other parameters are to the point at which a water change is needed.

Look out for sudden behavioral changes in your fish, fish disease, fish mortality, excessive algal growth, smelly water, and cloudy water. All of these warrant an immediate water quality test and possible water change.

As I discuss in Chapter 13, the results of your water testing should be written down and compared to previous test results. If there has been a dramatic change since the last test in any water parameter, action may be required as follows.

✔ If the pH is too low, conduct a water change, and see Chapter 14 for more information.

✔ If the ammonia, nitrite, or nitrate is too high, conduct a water change and see Chapter 13 for more information.

✔ If carbonate hardness is too low, conduct a water change and see Chapter 14 for more information.

✔ If your salinity or specific gravity is too high or too low, see Chapter 14 for information on how to adjust it.

Changing the water

Water changes are one of the most important aspects of cleaning and maintaining your aquarium. Waste products build slowly in your aquarium and the resilience of your water is slowly depleted (see Chapters 13 and 14). The only way to solve both of these problems is to physically change your water, removing the wastes and replenishing valuable trace elements.

Deciding how much and how often

The typical preventative water change usually involves 10 to 20 percent of the tank's volume being replaced with properly balanced premixed seawater. The added water, which should be the proper specific gravity, will replace exhausted trace elements and nutrients, as well. The amount you change varies with the quality of your water, the aquarium's bioload (number of critters), and the frequency of water changes.

Some experts feel that a ten percent water change is sufficient every two weeks, while others feel that this volume should be 20 percent. If your aquarium is crowded, your son Paul has a tendency to overfeed the fishes, or you're unable to change your water frequently, a 20 percent change is in order. However, if your aquarium isn't heavily stocked, you're careful when you feed, and you're religious about water changes, ten percent should be sufficient.

I recommend that you start with a water change of 20 percent every two weeks and modify it either up or down depending on water quality.

Siphoning water

The best way to conduct a water change is to use an aquarium vacuum and a large plastic bucket. The vacuum has a large diameter tube attached to a siphon. The siphon is used to draw water from the aquarium, while the vacuum is thrust into the substrate, stirring the gravel and allowing detritus to flow out with the water into the bucket.

The surface gravel should be stirred during every partial water change for two reasons.

✔ It breaks up impacted areas in the filter bed where water flow has become restricted.

✔ It puts detritus into suspension where it can be siphoned out with the old water.

When you change the water, make every effort to efficiently cover as much of the substrate as possible, but don't rush over spots. If you can't cover it all, make a mental note where you left off and start at that spot with the next water change.

These steps explain how to siphon:

1. **Fill the tube completely with water, making sure no air is trapped in the tube.**

   Make sure the siphon and your hands are clean. You can fill the hose by submerging it in the aquarium, but do this only if your aquarium is large enough to accommodate the hose without spooking the fish. Otherwise, place one end of the tube in the tank and apply suction to the other to start the flow.

2. **Make sure the bucket end is lower than the aquarium, or siphoning will not work.**

   If you filled your siphon in the aquarium, plug one end of the hose tightly with your thumb, lift it from the aquarium, and bring it lower than the tank to the bucket.

3. **Release your thumb, and the water will begin to flow rapidly from the aquarium into the bucket.**

   You control the water flow by pinching the hose.

4. **Discard the water in the bucket.**

Figure 16-1 illustrates both siphoning water to and from the tank.

Adding water

When you need to add water, make sure you use premixed and conditioned saltwater that you store in a cool dark place. Aerate the water for about 15 minutes before conducting the water change (see Chapter 3).

To add water, pour the premixed and conditioned water slowly into your tank, making sure not to disrupt the aquarium or its inhabitants. I like to place a plate or bowl on the bottom of the tank to absorb the force of the water entering the aquarium.

Make sure the water you add is the same temperature and specific gravity as that of your aquarium.

Water out of your tap may be loaded with chlorine, chloramine, heavy metals, phosphates, and other ions. Many of these compounds are harmful to fish, so they need to be removed. This process is called *water conditioning*. It doesn't hurt to read the water-mixing sections in Chapter 7 to review how to premix and condition salt water.

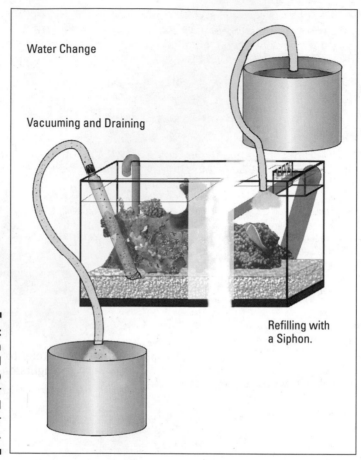

Water Change

Vacuuming and Draining

Refilling with
a Siphon.

Figure 16-1:
Use a
siphon and
vacuum to
clean your
gravel and
change your
water.

Your local water company routinely checks the water supply for these compounds. Check with them to find out what's in your tap water.

Topping off

Don't confuse water changes with adding water that has evaporated from the aquarium. Depending on the amount of aeration and circulation that you have (see Chapter 3), you may have more or less water evaporation. When water evaporates, dissolved salts are left behind, and the specific gravity of the water increases.

Pay attention to this process, because changes in specific gravity cause severe problems for your tank's inhabitants.

Water evaporation is readily solved by adding fresh water, not premixed conditioned saltwater, to your aquarium. The water you add should be conditioned tap water. If you don't have a lot of evaporation, the use of store-bought distilled water relieves you of the need to condition the water.

Distilled water is pure water, that is, pure H_2O without the additives and toxic compounds.

Developing Your Maintenance Schedule

The list in this section gives you a rough guideline for keeping up with preventative maintenance. Use this as a starting point and fine-tune it to fit your needs and those of your new pets. Most of these steps are self-explanatory, requiring just a few minutes of your time.

Every day

Every day, do the following:

- ✔ Turn the aquarium lights on and off. Most aquarists prefer to use an automatic timer. If you choose not to, try to turn the lights on and off in a consistent pattern.

- ✔ Check the fish and invertebrates for signs of stress, disease, or death. Be prepared to remove or treat fish that aren't well.

- ✔ Feed the fishes and invertebrates twice a day, removing any uneaten food.

- ✔ Conduct water tests until the water matures and the nitrogen cycle is established. Routine tests include ammonia, nitrite, nitrate, and pH. Record the test results.

- ✔ Check the water temperature and specific gravity or salinity. Adjust the heater, as needed.

- ✔ Empty the protein skimmer collection cup, as needed.

- ✔ Check the water level and top off, as needed.

- ✔ Check all aquarium systems: heater, filters, aerators, protein skimmer. Make sure they're running properly and smoothly and pay special attention to intakes and siphon tubes. Make sure that nothing is leaking.

Every week

Once a week, complete the following tasks:

- ✔ Remove excess algae, keeping beneficial algae at acceptable levels and getting rid of nuisance algae (see Chapter 15).
- ✔ Clean the glass, both inside and out, but don't use glass cleaner. Remove salt-creep deposits.
- ✔ Conduct water tests weekly after the water matures and the nitrogen cycle is established. Record all test results and add trace elements and buffers, as needed.

Every two weeks

Every two weeks, do the following:

- ✔ Clean filters, as needed. Partially change or rinse the filter media on some filters if the bioload is high, the media is dirty, or the flow is restricted.
- ✔ Change 20 percent of the tank water while vacuuming the gravel.

Monthly

Every month, be sure you complete these tasks:

- ✔ Conduct thorough filter checks. Replace the filter carbon and rinse the filter media and components, as needed and depending on bioload.
- ✔ Clean the protein skimmer.
- ✔ Replace airstones, as needed.
- ✔ Clean the outside of aquarium, removing salt and calcium deposits, dust, and dirt.
- ✔ Rinse any tank decorations that suffer from excess algae.

Quarterly (every three months)

Every three months, conduct a thorough examination of all aquarium systems, including lighting, heating, filtration, aeration pumps, and tubing. Replace or clean parts, as needed.

In the long run

If you maintain a freshwater aquarium, you're encouraged to break down your aquarium completely every year, essentially starting from scratch. This is not the case in the marine aquarium. The effectiveness of a well-established biological filter will last for years.

However, the undergravel filter may become heavily clogged over a long period. In addition, the substrate itself may begin to break down in about two years. However, you can slowly replace the gravel over several months by removing a thin strip of gravel and replacing it with new gravel. The following week, repeat the procedure and continue to do so until the entire substrate has been replaced without disrupting the aquarium. Under no circumstances should you break down a healthy aquarium and replace the gravel in one step.

Dealing with Emergencies

This section makes me cringe as I write it. Nobody likes to think of extreme situations when something goes terribly wrong with an aquarium or the systems that keep it going. But, like all preventative maintenance, contingency plans must be in place, and you need to know how to keep your pets alive.

What do I mean by emergencies? The most common are power failure, water leaks, overheating, and pollution, and each is discussed in the following sections.

By definition, you never really know when an emergency is going to strike. If you did, it wouldn't be an emergency. One thing I've done is establish an arrangement with my dealer, Condo. He temporarily houses my fish and invertebrates during extreme emergencies.

Pay particular attention to your fish and invertebrates after any kind of emergency. These kinds of events cause extreme stress, which can, in turn, lead to disease that will become apparent over the following two weeks.

What, no power?

Power failure is a pretty common emergency, but you can't do a lot to prevent it. Because most power outages are temporary and last less than 24 hours, your fish and invertebrates will be fine if you aerate the water while the power is down. For these situations, it's a good idea to own a battery powered air pump, which helps you maintain dissolved oxygen levels. To keep heat in the tank, wrap a thick blanket or sleeping bag around the tank, as well. Don't feed your fish while the power is down, because your filters aren't working!

Unfortunately, you may live in an area that's prone to frequent power failures, lengthy power failures, or hurricanes, which can knock out power for some time. If this is the case, make the investment and buy a portable generator for your aquarium. This can be an expensive option, but I look at it this way: You've already invested hundreds of dollars in your aquarium and its inhabitants. Why take the chance of losing everything in one power failure? In the long run, you'll save both time and money with a generator.

Oh no! A leak!

Another major emergency occurs is when your aquarium springs a leak. While I know that the likelihood of your tank leaking is pretty low, the chance of little Bernie hurling a baseball through it is not beyond the realm of reality.

If this happens, collect as much of the water as possible into buckets and place your aquarium inhabitants into them. Make sure you aerate the water, and then rush out and replace the tank as soon as possible. Transfer your filtration and all other equipment, including your gravel, to the new tank. Then add your water and fish.

If you try to repair the tank, the process may take too long. And your fish shouldn't live in buckets for more than 24 hours.

Too hot to handle

A malfunction of your heater can lead to aquarium overheating. Most tropical fish and invertebrates can handle water temperatures as high as 86°, but they don't necessarily like it. If the heat keeps cranking, you're going to literally boil them alive!

The best way to deal with overheating is to avoid it. One way to do this is to use two smaller, less powerful heaters instead of one large one. That way, if the heater malfunctions, you can detect it during a daily check and before the water temperature is driven to lethal levels.

If you do walk down your stairs one morning and find your aquarium overheated, immediately remove 20 percent to 50 percent of the water and place floating ice bags in the aquarium. Save the water that you removed in buckets and let it cool. Monitor the water temperature closely and return the water when temperatures in the aquarium and in the buckets are similar.

The solution to pollution

If your aquarium is well balanced and your filtration is working properly, it's unlikely that you will sustain a major pollution event. However, suppose right after you walk out the door one morning, one of your fish dies. Suppose that fish sits in your aquarium for a day or two because you're traveling. See where I am going? Ammonia will skyrocket, pH will drop, and dissolved oxygen will plummet. Pollution city!

When you walk through that door and discover a pollution event because the water is cloudy and not smelling very good, you need to mobilize emergency procedures immediately. I recommend a 50 percent water change. Change the carbon in your filters and conduct water tests. Conduct another 20 percent water change if conditions don't improve. Don't feed your fish until conditions have stabilized and returned to normal. After aquarium conditions return to normal, change or rinse the filter media and replace the filter carbon.

Part IV
Caring for Your Pets

The 5th Wave
By Rich Tennant

"Naturally we need to adjust the chemicals, but it seems to be the only thing that relaxes him after work."

In this part . . .

I show you how to keep your fish and invertebrates healthy. The first step is to feed them correctly; then you have to be able to diagnose and treat ailments. Healthy, happy fish equal a healthy, happy aquarist.

Chapter 17

Feeding Your Fish

In This Chapter

▶ Understanding that nutrition is the key to healthy pets

▶ Discovering the kinds of foods available

▶ Knowing how to feed your fish and invertebrates

*F*ish and invertebrates are alive, just as people are alive. And people need fuel for energy and growth, and that comes in the form of food. In their natural environment, fish and invertebrates have to find their own food. They hunt, they scavenge, and the graze. In your aquarium, your pets are spoiled. They don't have to work too hard to feed. However, this puts the responsibility on you to provide them with a well-balanced diet that keeps them alive and healthy.

One of the most enjoyable parts of owning an aquarium is feeding its occupants. The tank seems to come alive at feeding time, and your children and friends will get a big kick out of it. This chapter helps you provide your fish and invertebrates with the right food. When considering nutrition, living marine animals are no different from your other pets: They need a well-balanced diet.

Giving Them Their Meat and Veggies

The raw materials needed for life and growth are called *nutrients*. Fish, like all other animals, need these nutrients for sustenance, growth, and reproduction. They can get these nutrients only from organic matter that has, at one time or another, been alive.

Keep several considerations in mind when providing food for your fish. In their natural habitat, fish have evolved various feeding strategies to optimize their ability to get nutrients. With all the different kinds of fish and habitats, you can imagine the many kinds of feeding strategies that exist.

In general, fish can be divided three general groups based on the type of feeding strategy that they have evolved: carnivores, herbivores, and omnivores.

Eat or be eaten (carnivores)

Fishes and invertebrates that are predators are referred to as *carnivores*. In their natural habitat, they feed on fishes or invertebrates that they bite, engulf, or crush. These are flesh-eaters. If these creatures were human, they would prefer steak, chicken, or fish. Carnivores eat a variety of animals, ranging from tiny plankton to large species of fish. Invertebrates, like corals, that filter-feed small plankton from the water are actually carnivorous!

In the aquarium, many tropical marine fishes and invertebrates have been successfully fed dead food, commercially prepared pellets and flakes, or live critters.

Pieces of fish, shrimp, and other meats will be taken by most carnivores, but some species will simply not accept anything but live food. Guppies, goldfish, and brine shrimp are commonly offered to these predators.

Just a salad, please (herbivores)

Critters that prefer to eat vegetative matter, which is mainly algae, are called *herbivores*. If these animals were people, they would be the salad-eaters. Some tropical marine species of fish, like tangs, are exclusively herbivorous, deriving all their nutrients from plants and algae. However, from a practical standpoint, there are few strictly herbivorous fishes in captivity, and most can be conditioned to eat other foods.

Studies have shown that all marine aquarium fishes known to feed exclusively on plants in the wild will accept animal tissue in captivity. Regardless, it is important to have a lush growth of algae in your aquarium if you intend to house fish or invertebrates that are herbivorous by nature. You can also augment their diet with household vegetables, like blanched lettuce and spinach.

A little of this and a little of that (omnivores)

If a species of fish is not selective relative to whether it eats meat or vegetables, it is referred to as *omnivorous*. These fish and invertebrates feed on a variety of foods and have no specific dietary preferences. (Most humans are omnivorous by nature, mixing meats, fruits, and vegetables in their diet.)

Many of the recommended species outlined in Chapter 10 are considered omnivorous. As a new hobbyist, don't worry about special feeding strategies when setting up an aquarium for the first time. These fish accept commercially prepared flake and pellet foods, but providing a good variety of foods is necessary to meet all their dietary requirements. Many invertebrate species are omnivorous, as well, scavenging organic matter and algae from the substrate.

Before you buy a fish or invertebrate, make a point to find out the feeding preferences of the species that you're buying.

Recognizing the Building Blocks

Like all living animals, fish have dietary requirements for protein, fat, carbohydrate, vitamins, and minerals. In their natural environment, fish meet their own needs by foraging and hunting. In the aquarium, fish rely entirely on you to meet their dietary needs.

Unfortunately, the nutritional needs of tropical marine organisms are poorly understood. These requirements can differ by species, age, water temperature, and many other factors. The best that any aquarist, including the professionals, can do is to feed the fish a variety of foods that approximate their requirements.

By consuming different types of food, the fish is more likely to obtain all of its nutritional requirements.

- **Proteins:** Proteins are major constituents of all animal tissue, and they are essential in the diet to maintain normal growth. Younger fish, in particular, require more protein in their diets than larger, older fish.

- **Lipids (fats):** Lipids, or commonly called fats, are critical components of cell membranes. They also provide an immediate supply of chemical energy and stored energy. We all probably have a little too much stored energy, if you know what I mean.

- **Carbohydrates:** Carbohydrates are broken down into units of glucose, which is a major source of energy. They can also be converted to lipids for energy storage.

- **Vitamins and minerals:** These important compounds play the same important roles in fish as they do in mammals. They provide the necessary ingredients for proper metabolism and skeletal stability.

Identifying the Types of Food

You can find many different types of food for your tropical marine fish. Carnivores eat flake food, brine shrimp, and almost any kind of seafood — crab, lobster, oysters, and clams. Herbivores adapt to an omnivorous diet, taking flake and frozen foods and vegetables, while grazing on aquarium algae. The omnivore eats all these foods.

Aquarium foods can be grouped into a variety of categories, and experts do it differently. I prefer to classify aquarium foods into three general categories: natural foods, prepared foods, and live foods.

Natural foods

This group of foods includes items that are obtained fresh, frozen, or freeze-dried. They are not heavily processed. They can be fed to the fish fresh, cooked, or dried. Foods under this category are leafy-green vegetables, fish and invertebrate flesh, and frozen or freeze-dried invertebrates.

Leafy greens

It is essential to provide vegetative matter in the diet, because some of the marine species are naturally herbivorous. While the algae in your aquarium may be enough for some grazing fishes and invertebrates, you should also feed vegetables that are fresh, blanched, or thawed after freezing. Common vegetables include lettuce, spinach, cabbage, parsley, kale, and watercress, to name a few.

Some aquarists prefer that you *blanch* the vegetables to aid in their digestion. This means that they are boiled for just a few minutes to soften them up and break down cell membranes.

In general, vegetables are composed mostly of water and are low in energy, protein, and lipid but contain high concentrations of carbohydrate, fiber, and certain vitamins. You don't want to feed only vegetables to your fish, but be prepared to provide them to your herbivorous fish.

Meaty foods of the sea

If you live in the sea, it only makes sense that you eat seafood, which includes a variety of foods comprised of fish and invertebrate meats. They are fed fresh, thawed, or cooked. Cooking these foods doesn't lower their nutritional value. Cooking is also a good idea, because raw seafood can carry infectious diseases that can be transmitted to the aquarium fish. Cooking can involve boiling, steaming, or using foods that are canned in water, which are already boiled.

Feed your marine animals only flesh from other sea animals, because you want to serve them foods that have a similar composition to themselves. In other words, don't scrape your Thanksgiving turkey leftovers into the aquarium.

The variety of meats available is vast. This category includes fishes like herring, anchovy, smelt, mackerel, and tuna, as well as shellfish like clams, shrimp, mussels, scallops, oysters, crabs, and squid. In general, meaty foods contain less water and carbohydrate and substantially more protein and lipid than vegetative matter.

You must include this type of food for carnivorous fishes.

Frozen and dried

These foods often provide the greatest portion of your fish's diet, because many are specifically produced for aquarium use and are widely available. The dietary value of this food is similar to that of meaty foods. Some of the most common commercially available frozen foods in this category include brine shrimp, plankton, krill, and other shrimps. Also, many of the seafoods, like fish, squid, scallops, shrimp, and clams are offered frozen.

Frozen foods are generally packaged in such a way that you can break off a chunk and put it in the aquarium. I prefer to thaw the food first in a small cup of water from your tank, and then pour the mixture into your aquarium.

Most commercial processors treat frozen foods with gamma rays to ensure that they are free of disease.

Freeze-drying has made it possible to preserve a variety of natural foods for aquarium fish. For the marine aquarium, the process has most often been applied to brine shrimp and other small invertebrates, like krill, tubifex worms, and bloodworms. These critters are not processed, and what you see is what you get, the whole animal without water.

These foods help increase the variety of the foods that you're feeding your fish, but shouldn't be the only food offered to them. While it has been shown that freeze-dried brine shrimp have the same lipid concentrations as freshly killed brine shrimp, it has not been proven that they are a complete dietary substitute for live brine shrimp.

Prepared foods

This category of food contains the flake and dry foods that are commercially processed for aquarium fish, but may also include frozen processed foods that contain a number of healthy ingredients. Prepared foods try to approximate the basic requirements of proteins, fats, and carbohydrates. They are also supplemented with vitamins and minerals.

These foods come in many varieties, depending on the type of fish (carni-vore, herbivore, or omnivore), and new formulations are being added every year to better estimate the dietary needs of your pets. Marine algae that are dried in sheets are becoming a popular dried food for marine fishes.

Don't feed foods that are processed for freshwater fish to saltwater fish.

Prepared foods came in many forms, depending on the size and the feeding behavior of the fish. Flakes, tablets, pellets, and crumb forms are available. For example, larger predatory fishes should be fed pellets as opposed to flakes, because they prefer to consume a large quantity. In addition, fish that feed on the bottom may not venture to the surface for flakes, so they must be fed pellets or tablets that sink to the bottom. You can also stick pellets to the aquarium glass for the grazing species in your tank.

Many of the fish reviewed in this book can be fed prepared foods. However, if you want active, colorful, and healthy fish, you must vary their diets. Flake is good as a staple food, but you need to make every effort to substitute other foods (every day) that enrich your fish.

Live foods

Live food is an excellent source of nutrition for the tropical marine aquarium. Fishes and invertebrates that are fed live foods ordinarily grow fast, have vibrant colors, and maintain high survival rates. This is because live foods retain active enzymes that make digestion more efficient. Also, because few fish species refuse live foods, using live foods is the best way to get the picky eaters to eat.

Live foods are an essential requirement of captive fishes, and they must be included as a dietary supplement. The type of live food you give your pets depends on the size of the fish or invertebrate you're feeding.

The most common live foods that may be available at your dealer are as follows:

- **Feeder fish:** Small freshwater fishes, including guppies and goldfish, are popular food items for larger predatory fish, like lionfish. While guppies can tolerate saltwater, goldfish can't, so make sure that they are either eaten or removed before they die.

- **Earthworms:** These backyard dirt dwellers offer an economical food source for many aquarium fishes. They can be served whole or in pieces, depending on the size of your fish, but be sure to rinse them.

- **Blackworms and tubifex worms:** Many dealers carry these freshwater worms that are readily consumed by aquarium fishes. Although they are only worms, be aware that they will not live long in salt water, so feed them sparingly.

- **Rotifers:** These tiny planktonic animals are ideal for filter-feeding invertebrates, but they may be difficult to obtain.

- **Glass shrimp:** Although these little decapods aren't easy to find, they make excellent live food for both fish and invertebrates in your aquarium. Their name comes from the fact that you can see right though them.

Brine shrimp

The most popular live food for the tropical marine fish is brine shrimp (*Artemia* species), a primitive crustacean-inhabiting shallow salt ponds that exist in over 160 locations around the world. Those in your local pet store probably originated in San Francisco Bay or Great Salt Bay in Utah. They are one of the best sources of nutrition available for marine aquarium organisms of any type. Tiny hatchlings, called *nauplii,* are ideal for filter feeding organisms, as well.

Brine shrimp are an excellent source of lipids and protein. Of all the live food available, they are the safest because they don't carry disease. An added advantage to brine shrimp is that you can raise them yourself, because many dealers sell brine shrimp eggs.

To raise brine shrimp, follow the instructions accompanying the eggs. However, I have found that the following simple steps work well.

1. **In a plastic or glass container, make a solution of seawater with a standard specific gravity of 1.021-1.024.**

2. **Bring the water temperature of the hatch solution up to about 75 to 80°.**

   Use an immersion heater, if you must.

3. **Place an aerator in the solution and adjust the air to produce a slow stream of bubbles.**

   Too much air causes the eggs to collect along the edges of the container.

4. **Add the brine shrimp eggs, called *cysts*, at a concentration of about one teaspoon of eggs per gallon of hatch solution.**

   Handle them with care, because they are small and delicate.

5. **After ten minutes, illuminate the container with a 40-watt light about eight inches from the container for about ten minutes. This will initiate hatching.**

6. **After 24 hours, shut off the aerator and allow the empty shells and unhatched eggs to separate from the nauplii (hatchlings).**

7. **After 15 minutes, attract the nauplii to a corner of the container using a small flashlight. The young brine shrimp are attracted to light. This will take about 15 minutes, depending on how far they have to swim.**

8. **When they are concentrated, drain or siphon them into a fine mesh net and rinse them well with artificial seawater.**

You can find containers at your dealer that fit in your aquarium for hatching brine shrimp eggs, as well.

Brine shrimp can be fed to your fish or placed in a container of seawater for growing to larger sizes. If you choose to keep the young shrimp, bring the water temperature to about 86° and provide low aeration. The nauplii can be fed brewer's yeast or powdered rice bran dissolved in water for several days. Aquarists who want to raise the brine shrimp for longer periods should try to obtain one of the encapsulated feeds devised for crustacean larvae that are available commercially.

Putting Food in Their Mouths

The biggest questions when it comes to feeding your critters are how much and how often to feed them. Some fish are gluttons, while others stop when they're full. We all know people from both ends of the spectrum!

It is important that the same person or people feed the aquarium. This ensures that the feeding is done consistently and with an eye for the right quantities. Letting Uncle Bill feed the fish when he visits may result in a lot of waste and water pollution. Also, keep a tight lid on the tank during a party. Inevitably, everybody wants to feed the fish!

It is definitely better to feed them too little than too much. Use the following guidelines (and see Figure 17-1) when feeding and you will develop a working sense of how much and how often to feed them.

✔ **Offer as much food as your fish will eat in five minutes.** Flakes should sink no deeper than one-third the height of the tank. Provide tablets, pellets, or sinking food for bottom fish and invertebrates.

✔ **Feed your fish in very small portions over the five-minute period.** If any food is left over after this time, you're an over-feeder. Bear in mind, however, that some foods, like lettuce or spinach, are nibbled over time, so the five minute rule does not apply.

✔ **If you're home during the day, feed your fish and invertebrates very small portions over the course of the day.** If you're not home, feed them twice a day at the same times every day: once in the morning, once at evening. Keep in mind that some critters are nocturnal, so you may have to feed them after the lights are out.

✔ **Always feed your fish at the same spot in the tank.** This lets you sneak food down to bottom dwellers while the surface fish are distracted.

✔ **Don't overfeed the fish, no matter how much you think they need more food.** Overeating stresses your fish and causes detritus to accumulate in the tank, degrading water quality.

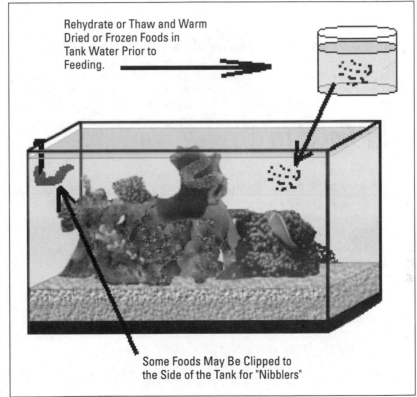

Rehydrate or Thaw and Warm Dried or Frozen Foods in Tank Water Prior to Feeding.

Some Foods May Be Clipped to the Side of the Tank for "Nibblers"

Figure 17-1: Feeding your fish is one of the most enjoyable aspects of owning an aquarium.

Dealing with the oddballs

Although these steps get you going, you'll find a lot of exceptions. For example, some invertebrates, like sea anemones and corals, house photosynthetic bacteria that provide them with nutrients, so you don't need to feed them every day. Their diet, however, should be augmented once or twice a week with fresh, frozen, or live foods.

Also, large carnivorous fish typically consume one large meal at a time, so you don't need to feed them more than once every day or two.

It is better to underfeed than to overfeed your fishes and invertebrates.

Keeping a watchful eye

Watch all your fishes during feeding. This is a good time to assess your fishes' health and take a head count, as well. Try to make sure that each gets its share of food, but this will not always be possible. In the ocean world, it's eat or go hungry, so don't expect a lot of good will.

Remember that fish have different mouth shapes, which allow them to feed at different levels in the tank. Some species will not go to the surface to eat and will wait for food to disperse throughout the tank. Don't rely on surface feedings and the leftovers of others to feed bottom fish. Pellets or other foods that sink to the bottom should be provided to these fish. You may have to offer food through a turkey baster or distribute food via a feeding stick.

Refusal to eat is one of the first signs of illness, so keep an eye out for fish that seem to have no interest in food.

Always remove food from the tank that hasn't been consumed.

Offering a variety

Freshwater fish and saltwater fish aren't the same — you know that. If you've ever had a freshwater aquarium, dry flake food was all you sprinkled in every day. You need to break that habit. Although you may offer a daily staple, marine organisms must be fed a variety of foods.

You can try flake food and frozen brine shrimp as your staples, but mix in different foods as your fish acclimate to your aquarium. Try not to feed your fish right after turning on the light, because they will not be fully alert until about 30 minutes later. In addition, make sure you match the size of the food with the size of the fishes' mouths. You may need to crush or mulch the food for fish with small mouths. Be sure not to grind the food too small. This adds to the water fine particles that are not ingested and that degrade water quality.

Going away?

If you're going to be away from your aquarium for one or two days, the fish will be fine without food. When you return, don't feel that you have to feed your fish twice as much because they missed a meal. If you do, much will go uneaten.

If you plan to travel for longer periods, you have a couple of options. You can arrange for someone to feed your fish. Prepare portions ahead of time and give detailed instructions on how to properly feed your animals. Don't let them do so at their own discretion unless they are experienced aquarists.

The other option is the purchase of an automatic feeder. This specialized piece of equipment dispenses dry food for you while you're away. You wouldn't want to load it with fresh seafood, but many processed foods work well.

Feeding Your Invertebrates

While discussing feeding in this chapter, I've made every effort to reference invertebrates, as well as fishes. Nonetheless, I think it's important to make a few extra points about feeding invertebrates because they are such a diverse group.

The key to invertebrate feeding is to do so sparingly. They don't need as much food as their fishy counterparts.

In general, invertebrates can be divided into three kinds of feeders: carnivorous predators and scavengers, herbivorous grazers, and filter feeders.

Hunting and gathering (carnivorous)

Invertebrates, like lobsters, squids, conchs, and large crabs, are normally predators or scavengers of meat. If you choose to keep any of these critters, you can provide them with many meaty live foods, like goldfish and guppies, as well as seafoods, including clams, mussels, and shrimps. Feed these invertebrates once a day — quantities depend on the size of the animal. Be sure to remove uneaten food after about an hour, because these invertebrates tend to eat slowly.

Scraping (herbivorous)

Herbivorous invertebrates, like small snails and crabs, prefer to graze algae from the walls, gravel, and decorations in the aquarium. They can typically subsist on this while scavenging minute organic matter, as well.

Sifting (filter feeders)

Strict filter feeders, like featherduster worms and soft corals, are generally not recommended for the aquarium of a beginner. However, if you simply can't resist the beauty of these critters in your reef tank, you have to feed them liquidized seafoods, newly hatched brine shrimp nauplii, live rotifers, or commercial liquid feeds. Feed filter feeders once per day: The general quantity is about one drop of liquid food per animal. Note, though, that the food requirements of suspension feeding creatures are quite specific, so make sure you're providing the right food for the species you're keeping.

Several species of filter feeders, like anemones and hard corals, contain photosynthetic algae that provide them with a lot of their nutritional needs. However, don't assume that all their nutritional requirements are met by these algae. In nature, these animals still filter feed, so they must be fed in captivity, as well. Any of the filter feeder foods listed in this section will work. Anemones can be fed small bits of seafood, as well, but this should be done sparingly, only once every week or two.

Chapter 18

Preventing Stress

*I*f you intend to be a tropical fish hobbyist for a long time, inevitably, one of your fish will become infected with some kind of disease. Marine tropical fishes are subject to all kind of maladies. Pathogenic organisms that cause disease include parasites, bacteria, viruses, and fungi. They are present in the ocean and in the aquarium, and it is difficult to eliminate them. Many are introduced with new fish, and many are highly contagious.

However, whether or not diseases actually break out depends on the resistance of your fish. A healthy fish has a strong resistance and an immune system that keeps pathogens in check. A fish or invertebrate with stress is a fish that's vulnerable to disease. In this chapter and Chapter 19, I discuss stress and disease in your aquarium, what causes an animal to become vulnerable, and how to prevent it.

I'm Stressin'

Everyone knows what stress is, but I'm sure that everybody's definition is not the same. What one person considers stressful may be a routine day at the office for another. When I use the term *stress,* I'm referring to the biological interpretation. That is, stress is any condition where the normal biological functioning of an animal is disrupted.

In biological terms, the normal biological function of an animal is referred to as its *homeostasis.* Anything that causes a disruption of the animal's homeostasis is a *stressor,* and the animal is said to *be stressed.*

Stressors can be physical, biological, or psychological. You may be familiar with psychological stress, but you may not think about physical stress. For example, suppose you're working outdoors on a brutally hot day. If you don't drink plenty of fluids and rest in the shade, your body temperature will rise and your homeostasis will be disrupted. Your body will respond by sweating, and if steps aren't taken, heat exhaustion or stroke will result. You're under stress.

This kind of stress can happen to any animal, including your aquarium pets. When an animal's homeostasis is disrupted, its immune system is often compromised, which means that its resistance to harmful pathogens is reduced. If the conditions that produced the stress persist, the situation is called *chronic stress,* and the animal may succumb to disease.

Poor living conditions weaken your fish, cause chronic stress, and ultimately lower the fish's resistance. That's when your fish is most vulnerable to disease, and those pathogens living in your aquarium move right in.

The best way to deal with stress is to avoid it!

Stressful Conditions

In the closed system of an aquarium, fish and invertebrates are exposed to stressors that their wild counterparts may be able to avoid. Your pets are dependent on you to make sure stressful conditions are avoided.

I've summarized stressful conditions in Table 18-1. In this table, you also find the corresponding chapter numbers in this book that you can go to for solutions to these problems. After the table, each stressor is discussed individually.

Table 18-1	Causes of Stress and Problem-Solving Chapters
Stressful Condition	*Chapter(s)*
Poor water quality	3, 13, 14, 16
Handling	12
Injury	18
Lack of nutrition	17
Overcrowding	10
Aggressive behavior	9, 10
Temperature changes	4
Salinity changes	7, 14
Disturbances	1, 5

Poor water quality

First and foremost on the list of stressors is water quality. The water in your aquarium is the medium that your pets depend on to live. Fish and invertebrates can live for days without food, but without clean water, they die immediately. Not only is water to them what air is to us, but they also literally need water like we need water, and they drink it, as well.

Fish also excrete wastes into the very water that they use to stay alive. In the open ocean, this is not a problem, but in the closed system of an aquarium, it can be dangerous. That is why I place a huge amount of emphasis on filtration in Chapter 3 and maintenance in Chapter 16. Clean water means healthy water, which means healthy fish and invertebrates.

When the water is polluted with wastes, pH drops, ammonia and other nitrogenous compounds increase, the buffering capacity diminishes rapidly, carbon dioxide builds, and dissolved oxygen plummets. When these conditions develop, the water then acts as a stressor, and your marine animals become stressed.

Under the stressful conditions associated with poor water quality, fish and invertebrates have to work harder to breathe, their heart rates increase, internal ion balance is disrupted, and internal pH drops. In addition, their bodies react by producing a number of hormones that compromise the immune system. If the level of pollution is extreme, the inability of the fish to offload carbon dioxide in exchange for oxygen will kill it immediately. The animal will literally drown, which is something we generally don't think of when it comes to organisms that live in the ocean!

However, if water quality degrades slowly, the stress becomes chronic and the animal becomes increasingly susceptible to the harmful pathogens that live around and inside its body. This fish will become sick and may die.

 To avoid poor water quality, make sure you have adequate filtration for the size of your aquarium, don't overcrowd your aquarium, and properly maintain your aquarium and its filtration. Use water parameter tests to look for and diagnose signs of water degradation.

Handling

Every time you chase your fish with a net, catch them with a net, spook them, bag them, move them, or remove them from the water, you're stressing your pets — you are the stressor. This kind of stress is typically referred to as *capture stress* or *handling stress*.

While long-term stress is called chronic, this kind of short-term stress is called *acute,* and acute stress can be as lethal as chronic stress.

The physical consequences of acute stress can lead to immediate death from respiratory failure, infections from physical damage, and immune system failure and disease. Fish and many invertebrates have a protective mucous layer that acts as a first line of defense against infection and disease. When this layer is removed or damaged, one of their defenses is compromised, and an avenue for pathogens is opened.

Unfortunately, handling stress can't be avoided. In fact, when you buy your fish, they have already been subjected to a lot of handling stress from capture in the wild, transport to your dealer, capture from his tank, and transport to your home. There is no way around it! The only way to deal with handling stress is to minimize it, keeping the following tips in mind:

✔ **Make sure you buy fish and invertebrates that have had a chance to recover from the handling stress associated with capture and transport to your dealer.** They should have been in your dealer's possession for a least a week. Feeding is a good sign that they have recovered.

✔ **Minimize handling stress by reducing the amount of chase time and net time when you're moving a fish.** I know this is easier said than done, but don't chase a fish around the aquarium in an effort to tire it out. This will exhaust the fish, and the consequences may be lethal. Instead, try to coax the fish with food to an area when it can be snatched with the net or cornered quickly. After the fish is in the net, move it to the container or bag as quickly as possible, keeping it out of the water for only seconds. Have the travel container as close as possible.

✔ **Keep travel time short.** The more time in the container or bag, the more stress. Keep in mind that water quality in the container degrades quickly.

✔ **Use a net that's not only soft on the fish but also large enough to accommodate the whole fish.** This will minimize damage to the protective mucous layer on their skin. If an animal doesn't fit into the net properly, it may flip out during transfer, and physical damage will surely occur.

Injury

Anything that causes injury to your fish and invertebrates applies physical stress that can lead to immediate death or delayed mortality due to infection or disease. An injured fish, like any injured animal, bleeds when its tissues are damaged. Veins and arteries carrying blood throughout the body of the fish can be damaged when the fish is bitten, dropped, or physically abused in some way. The bleeding may be external or internal depending on the nature and the extent of the damage.

If a physical injury doesn't cause immediate death from blood loss, at the very least it will compromise the protective mucous layer of the skin, which can lead to infection. In addition, an injured fish is not a healthy fish. It may stop feeding, and its immune system may become compromised, leading to more serious ailments.

While handling stress can obviously cause physical damage, there are a number of injurious aquarium conditions, as well. Overcrowding, incompatibility, territoriality, and certain social behaviors can also cause injuries to a fish or invertebrate.

Lack of nutrition

If an animal isn't eating right, it won't be healthy and strong. An unhealthy fish will be stressed. It won't be able to power its immune system, and the door to disease will be wide open.

Your fish or invertebrate may not be eating right for a couple of reasons. First, you may not be feeding it the right kinds of food and meeting its nutritional needs. Read Chapter 17. Make every effort to offer the right foods in terms of content, size, and placement.

Another cause of poor nutrition may be associated with the inability of the fish or invertebrate to physically get to the food. Perhaps aggressive tankmates eat everything, or perhaps the fish prefers to feed low in the tank and food is not getting to it. You may have to take extra steps to use personal attention when feeding those fish or invertebrates that are having this problem.

Don't forget that invertebrates with photosynthetic algae, like corals and anemones, need adequate amounts of light to feed. Poor lighting will stress these animals.

Overcrowding

Having too many occupants in your aquarium can have several stressful effects. The immediate physical effect of overcrowding is associated with lack of personal space. Not having enough room leads to territorial disputes, fighting, and injuries. Injuries lead to infection, disease, and death.

Overcrowded conditions inevitably lead to poor water quality. Too many animals means too much waste, which means pollution. Pollution, of course, leads to stress, and so on.

Aggressive behavior

In Chapter 10, I chew up a little space discussing fish compatibility. Some species of animals simply don't get along with each other, let alone with other species. When placed in the same tank, these animals get aggressive.

Aggressive behavior can be exhibited due to territoriality, competition for food, or sexual behavior. It usually results in fighting and injury. Injury, of course, can cause immediate death or lead to secondary infection and disease. Moreover, a fish that's constantly harassed by another fish is prone to jumping from the aquarium, has a general lack of appetite, and lives under chronic stress.

When choosing fish and invertebrates for your aquarium, make sure to choose animals that get along. A single bad seed can cause severe problems for your aquarium and may ultimately live alone.

Temperature changes

If your heater malfunctions, you have a serious problem! If it fails to work, the temperature of the aquarium will plummet, and your fish will be stressed. If it fails to turn off, the temperature will soar, and your fish will be stressed. If temperatures rise or fall to levels outside the thermal tolerance of your pets, the acute stress will kill them immediately. If not, the acute stress may cause secondary physical effects associated with temperature fluctuations that weaken the animal, compromise the immune system, and lead to disease.

However, temperatures don't have to rise or fall to levels that the animals can't tolerate in order for them to be stressful. The rate of temperature change can be just as detrimental. If your aquarium temperature rises or falls rapidly but stays within the tolerance of your pets, the sudden change can kill or cause problems. The same thing happens if you move your animal from a bag of one temperature to your aquarium, which has much cooler or warmer water.

Extreme temperature changes can be avoided if you make frequent heater and temperature checks. Also make sure that water temperatures are the same between two containers when fish and invertebrates are being transferred.

Salinity changes

In Chapters 7 and 14, I discuss the level of salt in your aquarium, which is measured as salinity or specific gravity. While you must maintain salt levels within a specific range, you must also avoid sudden changes within that range. Any changes in salinity stress your aquarium pets.

Stress from changes in salinity is called *osmotic stress* because it disrupts osmotic balance. Osmotic stress disrupts the animal's normal function because it creates an osmotic imbalance that needs to be corrected, and this requires energy. Ultimately, other bodily functions, like the immune system, may fail as energy is redirected to corrective osmoregulation, and disease may result. You can review osmoregulation in Chapter 9.

Sudden dramatic changes in salt levels cause acute osmotic stress that can be lethal if salinity rises or falls outside the osmotic range of the animal. More gradual changes in salinity may not be lethal, but can still cause chronic stress.

Avoid sudden and dramatic changes in salinity by closely monitoring salt levels in your aquarium and conducting regular water level maintenance (top off the tank — see Chapter 16).

Disturbances

Any sudden change in light or sound can stress your fish. This includes that annoying habit some people have of tapping on the glass of your aquarium, thinking that they are going to attract the fish. These disturbances cause acute stress that may not be detrimental if they occur only once in a while, but can be a problem if they're repeated often.

Try to avoid switching the light on while the fish are resting during late-night hours. Avoid sudden changes in noise level and keep people from tapping on the glass.

Recognizing Stress

The first step to dealing with stress and disease in your aquarium is to recognize and identify the problem. You should be able to determine whether an animal isn't healthy by checking its appearance and its behavior. This isn't complicated and doesn't take long. Because you're feeding your aquarium inhabitants every day, feeding times are the best times to give them an examination.

With any kind of stress symptoms, determine whether the problem is affecting only one critter or the whole aquarium. If more than one fish is displaying symptoms of stress, your problem may be systemic. Conduct water tests, check your notes, and run down the list of stressful conditions above to isolate the cause. If only one fish is affected, you probably need to isolate it for treatment to keep any malady from spreading.

So, what exactly are you looking for? Chapter 12 shares telltale signs of unhealthy fish that you want to look for when you purchased them. Those same signs manifest themselves in your aquarium if your fish or invertebrates are stressed or suffering from some ailment.

Acting weird

How an animal acts betrays the way that it feels. Fish and invertebrates simply don't fake their behavior. If they don't feel right, you know it fairly quickly. The following sections discuss a couple of behavioral signs.

Not being hungry

One of the first signs of stress or illness is the loss of appetite. Think about it. How hungry are you when you're sick? The fact that the animal was eating, but suddenly has no interest, tells you that something is wrong. If you suspect that one of your pets isn't interested in food, try offering something that it normally can't refuse, like live food.

Laziness

Another symptom of stress is a general laziness. If any of your pets loses its pep and becomes more sedentary, something is wrong. If it feeds only half-heartedly or avoids other fish, it is clearly fighting some kind of ailment. Other symptoms include hiding and keeping to itself. Lethargic fish typically keep their fins folded close to their body.

Keep in mind that everything is relative when diagnosing your fish. It's the change in behavior that counts. Some species are naturally lethargic or prefer the safety of hiding places. This doesn't mean they are sick.

Gasping

If your fish is spending an inordinate amount of time hyperventilating or gasping at the surface, you have a clear sign of stress. This is not necessarily a sign of disease, but is probably indicative of poor water quality and low dissolved oxygen. In reality, your fish isn't breathing oxygen from the air at the surface but trying to pull oxygen from the richer surface layers.

Rubbing

Any fish that displays rubbing or twitching behavior is stressed by some kind of problem. It's not unusual for an animal that's infested with parasites to rub itself against the gravel and aquarium decorations.

Looking weird

By far, the best way to determine whether your fish and invertebrates aren't well is to check their physical appearance. Anything out of the ordinary should be considered a sign of stress or disease, and you must take appropriate steps. Many of these signs apply to fish and invertebrates alike. Physical characteristics that are indicative of stress or disease include the following:

- ✔ **Discoloration:** Faded colors and discoloration are classic signs of stress. Strange white spots or blotches may be infectious pathogens or parasites. Cuts and scrapes in the skin are signs of injury.

- ✔ **Clouded eyes:** Glazed or cloudy eyes are indicative of stress and disease. The eyes of fish and invertebrates (if they have any) are normally clear and alert.

- ✔ **Frayed fins:** Fins that are shredded or frayed are indicative of fighting or disease. Also, fins that are kept folded or close to the body for extended periods are an indication of a problem.

- ✔ **Abnormal stomach:** When your fish has a *pinched stomach,* it usually means that the fish is not feeding. When the stomach is *distended* (pooched out), the fish is probably feeding too much.

Making a Diagnosis

Suppose one of your fish or invertebrates is showing one of the signs that I outlined in the preceding section. Now what? At this point, you suspect that your pet is suffering from stress and may very well have a disease. You need to conduct more investigative work to determine the cause of the problem.

Find out whether the symptom is being exhibited by just one fish or involves more than one critter. If more than one is showing symptoms, your problem may be systemic — the problem has spread throughout the aquarium. In these situations, consider the list of stressful conditions that pertain to the whole system, like water quality, and evaluate each one.

If, however, only one animal is showing signs of stress, check for the stressful conditions that may be specific to a single animal, like injury or lack of nutrition.

After you isolate a stressful condition, make every effort to stop it. Use Table 18-1 (earlier in this chapter), which gives you the chapter numbers in this book in which you can find solutions to your problem. If poor water quality is a problem, read Part III. If your fish have nutritional problems, read Chapter 17. Whatever is the problem, make sure the stressor doesn't persist.

It is one thing to treat the symptom, it's another to stop the cause. You need to stop the cause. However, in some cases, it is simply not possible to isolate and stop the stressor. Sometimes, everything checks out and you can't find a stressful condition. This may mean that your fish has some kind of ailment and you don't know why. All you can do at this point is treat the ailment (see Chapter 19).

Disease and stress

Some of the symptoms of stress may disappear when you isolate the stressful condition and stop it. For example, a gasping fish may stop gasping when you increase aeration and improve water quality.

In some cases, however, the stressor has taken its toll, the fish's resilience had been diminished, and the fish has contracted a disease. Right from the beginning of your diagnosis, you may know this because many ailments have telltale symptoms. If this is the case, you have to treat the animal and, if the problem is systemic, you have treat the entire aquarium. This is the subject of Chapter 19.

Chapter 19

Diseases and Treatments

*I*n Chapter 18, I tell you that the most effective way to deal with disease is to prevent it by minimizing stress. Unfortunately, even the most effective stress management can't keep disease from striking one or more of your marine pets.

Nasty pathogens that cause disease are in and around your fish in their natural setting and in your aquarium. These pathogens may be bacterial, viral, fungal, or parasitic. Fortunately, many of the diseases caused by these agents manifest themselves with identifiable symptoms. Unfortunately, not many treatments are available for the home aquarist, and you have no guarantees that your pet will be saved.

This chapter helps you recognize and treat those diseases that are most common in the home aquarium.

Reviewing the Treatment Methods

The best remedy for disease in the marine aquarium is prevention. Nonetheless, if disease does strike one of your animals, you have a few methods for treating it. These include direct aquarium treatment with therapeutic agents, the hospital tank, the dip method, and internal medication, all of which are discussed in the following sections.

Always use commercially available treatments instead of homemade remedies. Some experts recommend chemicals, like malachite green or potassium permanganate. These chemicals must be handled in exact dosages, which can be tough for you to do. If a fish is overdosed with one of them, it will kill the fish faster than the disease would have. Discuss all the possible remedies with your local dealer and let that person advise you on the best commercial remedies the store carries. When you apply the remedy, follow the directions exactly.

Don't be afraid to call your veterinarian and ask a few questions. If your veterinarian doesn't handle fish, he or she can usually recommend somebody who does.

Remove activated carbon from your filters when you medicate your aquarium. Carbon will remove many medications.

Direct aquarium treatment

Direct aquarium treatment involves the application of therapeutic agents directly into the aquarium containing the diseased fish. This method is sometimes called the *long bath*. It can be effective against some diseases, but not always. In some cases, medications may be absorbed by the aquarium decorations or filter media, or they may be toxic to filter bacteria. Moreover, fish medications are toxic to invertebrates. You're better off isolating the infected fish in the hospital tank.

The hospital tank

In Chapters 7 and 12, I mention that some aquarists isolate new fish in a quarantine tank. This small aquarium is also called an isolation tank. In this simple set-up, the fish or invertebrate can be evaluated for signs of disease before they're introduced into the main aquarium.

You may choose not to set up a quarantine tank to isolate fish when you first buy them, but I do recommend that you set up a hospital tank to isolate individuals that are suffering from disease. This tank reduces the likelihood of the disease spreading to others in the aquarium. It also provides a refuge to a fish that may ordinarily be harassed by healthier fish. The hospital tank helps you treat the fish without subjecting other fish to the treatment. And it helps you observe and diagnose the ailing fish.

As your expertise in this hobby increases, you may accumulate more expensive fish that you simply don't want to expose to disease. At that point, a hospital tank will be mandatory. It will also act as a quarantine tank, as well, if it has not recently housed a diseased fish.

The hospital tank need not be large: A ten-gallon tank will do. It does need adequate filtration and aeration, but elaborate decorations and gravel should be left out. Try to provide some kind of cover for the fish, in the form of rocks or flowerpots, as a source of security. An external power filter, sponge filter, or internal box filter will be sufficient for the hospital tank.

The dip method

The *dip method* involves removing the infected fish from the aquarium and dipping it into a bath containing a therapeutic agent or fresh water. The dip is brief enough not to injure the fish but long enough to kill the pathogen. Unfortunately, this method doesn't treat the infected agents in the aquarium, just the fish.

The freshwater dip has become as useful to the marine aquarist as the salt-water dip is to the freshwater aquarist. This method involves dipping a fish infested with parasites into a freshwater bath for three to ten minutes. The difference in salt concentration between the aquarium and the treatment bath is enough to rapidly kill the pathogen without harming the fish.

The bath is prepared as follows:

1. **Fill a one- to two-gallon container full of conditioned fresh water, matching the temperature and pH of the main aquarium.**

   The pH can be elevated by adding sodium bicarbonate to the container.

2. **Add a quart of seawater to the bath to reduce the osmotic shock to the fish.**

3. **Net the fish and place it in the container for three to ten minutes.**

   It may show signs of disorientation for a moment, but it should recover.

Internal medication

Some remedies need to be administered internally. This is usually accomplished with injection or by feeding the remedy to the fish. I don't recommend injecting your fish until you're extremely experienced. Feeding the fish food that has been medicated can be difficult, as well. In many cases, the dosage is difficult to estimate, the fish isn't feeding normally anyway, and you can't guarantee that the fish being treated is getting the proper amount of food.

This treatment method is, therefore, only marginally successful. Avoid it if you can.

Getting to Know Common Medications

The treatments available to the home aquarist — copper and antibiotics — is somewhat limited for marine fish diseases. The fact of the matter is that they are successful only some of the time.

Copper

Copper is a pollutant in the marine environment. It is, however, thought by many to produce beneficial effects by killing parasites. Copper can have adverse effects on fishes, it is not very stable in saltwater systems, and its fate in the aquarium is not fully understood. Some experts feel that copper should be eliminated as a treatment of aquarium fish diseases. Nonetheless, it is still widely used in the aquarium trade. I would avoid the use of copper unless you have absolutely no alternatives. If you do use it, isolate the fish in a hospital aquarium (see the preceding section) for treatment.

Copper is toxic to invertebrates, so don't administer copper in an aquarium with any kind of invertebrate.

Antibiotics

Antibiotics are chemotherapeutic agents that seem to be the most effective way of treating some of the common aquarium diseases. When possible, treat fish in a hospital tank to avoid the effects of these compounds on a mature, established aquarium. Don't, however, expect miracle cures from these compounds, because many have not been found to be fully effective against disease.

Recognizing the Bad Guys

Hundreds of possible maladies can afflict fish. Some are specific to certain species, and some can easily be transferred between species. The causes of common aquarium ailments include bacteria, viruses, fungi, or parasites. Not all are common in the average home aquarium.

Bacterial infections

You can find good bacteria and bad bacteria. Regardless, all bacteria are microscopic one-celled organisms capable of rapid reproduction. There are thousands of species of bacteria inhabiting many different habitats. Some are beneficial to the aquarium in the nitrogen cycle, but some can cause infection, as well.

Fin rot

✔ **Causes:** *Aeromonas, Pseudomonas, Vibrio* bacteria

✔ **Symptoms:** This external bacterial infection causes an erosion or rotting of the fins and the fin rays. The base of the fins usually reddens, as well. In advanced stages, the disease spreads to the skin, causing bleeding and ulceration, and to the gills.

✔ **Treatment:** The occurrence of this disease is thought to reflect deteriorating water quality. Immediate steps should be taken to improve water quality. Remove uneaten food, do a partial water change, and change the activated carbon in your filter. The antibiotics furanace, augmentin, and ciprofloxin may be effective.

Fish tuberculosis, wasting disease

✔ **Causes:** *Mycobacterium* bacteria

✔ **Symptoms:** External signs of this disease are often lacking. A fish that seems outwardly healthy may be internally infected. Fish that are infected may live a year or more before succumbing. Skin lesions, emaciation, labored breathing, scale loss, frayed fins, and loss of appetite are all clinical signs of this infection. Unfortunately, by the time these are manifested, it is probably too late to save the fish.

✔ **Treatment:** These bacteria are transmitted orally through raw infected fish flesh, detritus, and feces of infected fish. These bacteria can also infect skin wounds and lesions. The best treatment is prevention by not feeding raw fish and shellfish to your aquarium occupants. Antibiotics, including kanamycin, erythromycin, and streptomycin, have shown some promise against these bacteria if the disease is diagnosed. If the aquarium is heavily infected with this disease, it must be sterilized and the water discarded.

Vibriosis, ulcer disease

✔ **Cause:** *Vibrio* bacteria

✔ **Symptoms:** A variety of symptoms are associated with this disease, but they depend on the species of *Vibrio* and the species of fish. These can include lethargy; darkening of color; anemia; ulcers on the skin and lower jaw; bleeding of the gills, skin, and intestinal tract; clouded eyes; loose scales; pale gills; and sudden death.

✔ **Treatment:** These bacteria commonly inhabit the intestinal tracts of healthy fish. They become dangerous only when stress allows infection. Poor water quality, crowding, excessive handling, and copper treatments are common causes of stress in aquarium fish. Vaccination against infection is possible but not feasible for aquarium fish. Immersion treatments with antibiotic compounds, including furanace, erythromycin, halquinol, and nitrofurazone, have met with some success.

Viral disease

These simple microscopic organisms thrive by invading the cells of their hosts. In most cases, there are no treatments for the few viral diseases of the marine aquarium.

The most common viral disease is called cauliflower disease or lymphocystis:

✔ **Causes:** *Cystivirus* virus

✔ **Symptoms:** Fin and body lesions that are raised, whitish, warty, and have a lumpy texture, like cauliflower. These lesions may take three to four weeks to reach their full size. Diseased fishes typically show few signs of distress and continue to feed and behave normally. The infection is generally not fatal, but it can be transmitted to other fish in the tank.

✔ **Treatment:** There is no effective treatment of this viral infection other than to isolate the fish immediately and let the fish's natural immune system deal with it. This may take as long as several months. Some aquarists scrape the lesions off the animal.

Fungal disease

Fungi are plant-like organisms, some of which are parasitic on fishes. These can potentially cause disease.

Ichthyophonus disease, whirling disease

✔ **Causes:** *Ichthyphonus* fungus

✔ **Symptoms:** This fungus invades the internal organs of the fish, infecting the kidney, heart, spleen, and liver. Clinical signs include emaciation, spinal curvature, darkening or paling of the skin, roughening of the skin, fin erosion, and skin ulcers. Erratic swimming behavior can be a symptom of the disease, as well. Internal examination after death reveals white nodules on the organs.

✔ **Treatment:** This fungus is a parasitic organism with a complex life cycle. The fungal cysts are usually ingested by the fish, where they burst and enter the bloodstream, infecting internal organs. Typically, fish with this disease die up to two months after infestation. Treatment is very difficult due to the internal nature of this disease. The infected fish should be immediately removed from the aquarium to prevent other fishes from becoming infected.

Exophiala disease

✔ **Causes:** *Exophiala* fungus

✔ **Symptoms:** Lethargy, disorientation, and abnormal swimming are signs of this fungal infection.

✔ **Treatment:** This is a poorly known fungus, and no treatment is known. Isolate the fish to prevent other aquarium fishes from contracting the fungus.

Parasitic infestations

Parasites exist in a variety of forms, including tiny one-celled organisms called *protozoa,* as well as larger invertebrates, like crustaceans and worms. A parasite does not usually kill its host, but it can cause lesions that become secondarily infected by bacteria. The location of parasites on their hosts can be internal or external. The latter can be more readily identified in the aquarium, while the former is difficult to detect.

The following provides a general overview of those parasitic diseases you're most likely to encounter in your aquarium.

Marine velvet disease

✔ **Causes:** The dinoflagellate protozoan *Amyloodinium ocellatum*

✔ **Symptoms:** The gills are usually the first site of infection, spreading to the skin, which becomes dull, patchy, and velvetlike; white spots are visible on sections of intact skin. As the disease progresses, the fish's behavior may include fasting, gasping, scratching against objects, and sluggishness. Lesions caused by the dinoflagellate can lead to secondary bacterial infection.

✔ **Treatment:** This organism has three stages to its life cycle with one of them being parasitic. No completely effective treatment is known, although some antibiotics are effective. These include malachite green, nitrofurazone, and acriflavin. A freshwater dip sometimes dislodges these parasites from the host but does not kill them. Treatments are often prolonged, and the entire tank must be treated to fully eradicate the infestation.

Marine white spot, cryptocaryoniasis, marine ich

✔ **Causes:** The ciliate protozoan *Cryptocaryon irritans*

✔ **Symptoms:** Early signs include fasting, cloudy eyes, troubled breathing, excess skin mucus, and pale skin. White spots then appear on the skin, gills, and eyes, and death follows within a few days, most likely due to gill damage.

✔ **Treatment:** The white spot organism can be difficult to control. Like marine velvet, the encysted stage of this parasite is resistant to most treatments and remains in the gravel of the aquarium. The freshwater dip may be effective in killing the parasites on the fish but does little to treat the aquarium. Therefore, you must maintain levels of treatment in the tank. Copper products seem to have limited effectiveness, and the antibiotic chloramin T can be used as well.

Uronema disease

✔ **Causes:** The ciliate protozoan *Uronema marinum*

✔ **Symptoms:** External ulcers, muscle and skin bleeding, lethargic behavior, sloughing of the skin, and internal infection are signs of this disease. Death may be rapid due to impaired circulation in the gills.

✔ **Treatment:** Little is known of this parasite, and there is no known treatment.

Tang turbellarian disease, black spot

✔ **Causes:** *Paravortex* flatworms

✔ **Symptoms:** Although the name implies that only tangs are infected, this is not the case. Many species of fish can be infected by this flatworm. In the parasitic phase, these organisms look like numerous dark spots distributed unevenly over the fins, gills, and body. Other signs include fasting, listlessness, paling or whitish skin, and scratching against objects. Secondary bacterial infections are known to occur, as well. These signs are common to other infestations by flatworms.

✔ **Treatment:** Flatworms are a type of worm in a phylum of their own, called Platyhelminthes. As with most parasitic infestations, crowded facilitates allow the disease to spread to other tankmates. A freshwater dip, trichlorfon immersion, and praziquantel immersion may be effective.

Trematode infestations

✔ **Causes:** Monogenetic trematode worms

✔ **Symptoms:** Many species of these worms are too small to see without a microscope. They normally infect the gills, eyes, skin, mouth, and anal opening. Infected fishes usually rub themselves against objects in the aquarium, trying to dislodge these parasites. This often causes damage that leads to secondary bacterial infections.

✔ **Treatment:** These infestations are difficult to eradicate because the life cycles of these animals are poorly understood. Immersion in fresh water, mebendazole, praziquantel, or trichlorfon have demonstrated effectiveness against trematodes.

Crustacean infestations

✔ **Causes:** Copepod, isopod, and argulid crustaceans

✔ **Symptoms:** Most of these tiny, crab-like organisms are visible to the naked eye. Copepods remain fixed in the same position, while isopods and argulids move over the surface of the fish. These groups feed by piercing the fish, causing tissue damage. Fishes with heavy infestations swim erratically, rub against objects, and jump. Bacteria will infect lesions.

✔ **Treatment:** Remove fish that are infested with these parasites immediately. Also remove aquarium decorations and either dry them to kill egg masses or immerse them in 2 percent bleach solution for two hours. Treat infested fishes by immersing them in fresh water, trichlorfon, or malathion baths.

Other health problems

Head and lateral line erosion

✔ **Causes:** Poor water quality, nutrient deficiency, possibly a parasite

✔ **Symptoms:** Like the freshwater disease called hole-in-the-head, holes develop and enlarge in the sensory pits of the head and down the lateral line on the body. The disease progresses slowly, and the fish does not seem to behave differently. Advanced stages can lead to secondary bacterial infection and death.

✔ **Treatment:** There are no specific treatments for this disease, although some recommend the use of the freshwater antibiotic flagyl. Check your water quality and make necessary adjustments. You should also make sure that you're meeting the nutritional needs of your fishes. Diversify their diet and add vitamin supplements to their food.

Poisoning

✔ **Causes:** Multiple causes, including buildup of nitrogenous compounds (ammonia, nitrite), household chemicals (smoke, cleaners, fumes), and tap water constituents (heavy metals, chloramine)

✔ **Symptoms:** Low levels of toxins in the aquarium stress fish, thereby lowering their resistance to other diseases. Higher levels cause abnormal behavior, including darting movements, jumping, and gasping at the surface.

> ✔ **Treatment:** Make sure that activated carbon is used to remove toxins and conduct a 20 to 40 percent water change. If pollutant levels are high, move the fish to a hospital tank until the main aquarium water problems are corrected.

Why Invertebrates Don't Get Sick

The answer to this conundrum is quite simple: Invertebrates do get sick. But you probably noticed that all of the diseases outlined in the preceding section were associated with fish. The fact of the matter is, invertebrates contract parasitic, fungal, bacterial, and viral diseases, but little is known about how to diagnose and treat them. Although fish and invertebrates share common pathogens, the extent to which the same remedies are effective isn't well known.

Until more research is conducted on invertebrate disease and home treatment, the most effective tool is prevention. High water quality, adequate aeration, optimal lighting, and good nutrition are key to keeping your invertebrates healthy.

A worst-case scenario

In some instances, your fish is so ill that you know it's going to die. At that point, you have a decision to make. You can either put the fish out of its misery and euthanize it or let nature take its course. This can be a difficult decision because many times you have a lot of time and money invested in a fish, and you have probably become somewhat attached to your pet. I always make this decision by deciding what's best for each individual fish.

If you decide to dispatch the animal, the most humane way to do so it to sever its spinal column and kill it immediately. This can be done by either cutting off the fish's head or passing a knife through its back just behind the head.

Don't discard a dead fish or invertebrate by flushing it down the toilet. This may transmit disease pathogens to local fishes. Instead, place the dead animal in the trash or bury it in your backyard.

Chapter 20

Observing Your Fish

· ·

In This Chapter

▶ Watching your fish be fish

▶ Keeping an aquarium log

▶ Taking photos of your aquarium

· ·

After you get your aquarium up and running, it's time to sit back and enjoy your pets. They will interact with each other and they will interact with you. This is truly the most enjoyable part of aquarium keeping.

You control every aspect of your aquarium. The health of your pets is in your hands, and you have to pay attention to them. Doing so requires patience, time, and a little start-up money. But as a result of that investment, maintaining your aquarium will be fun. At times, you may want to throw your hands in the air in disgust, but these times will pass, and you'll likely realize that being an aquarist has rich rewards for you and your family. This chapter gives you some hints on how to get the most out of your new hobby.

Seeing Is Believing: Fish Can Be Fun

In Chapter 1, I share some great reasons to have a saltwater aquarium. In this section, I briefly review those reasons and give you a few ideas about enjoying your fish.

Fish watching

When you watch your aquarium and your pets, they'll be better off. Get to know all the subtleties of your fish and invertebrates and get a feel for their individual personalities. I, for example, like to name them after people that I know. I have a cantankerous hermit crab that I named after my grandfather and a very pretty little damsel named after my niece Anna.

Watch your fishy friends and family members interact and make a game out of it. As you do this, you'll know immediately whether something is wrong because Maggie isn't fighting with Vickie or Anna is hiding all the time. This game may sound goofy, but it's fun to play, especially with your kids.

Each animal in your aquarium is your pet, and, like any pet, watching it daily tells you when it acts normally and when something is wrong. You can diagnose problems as they arise and not after it's too late.

Relaxing

Perhaps you can't help but think that keeping an aquarium will involve a little work. But after you have a good understanding of the basics and if you keep up with the maintenance, you'll be able to relax with your aquarium.

Suppose it's the dead of winter, you're home from work, dinner is finished, and you want to relax. Well, look at your choices. Sit down and watch a bunch of mindless television shows, read a good book, or kick back in front of the aquarium and watch as the drama unfolds. Fish and invertebrates are entertaining creatures, and just sitting and watching them can be relaxing. As far as I'm concerned, relaxation is one of the best reasons to have an aquarium.

Studies show that spending time in front of the aquarium reduces stress.

Having fun with your family

If you have children or nephews and nieces, include them in as many aspects of the aquarium as possible. Not only do they enjoy it, but they learn the responsibility of taking care of pets. You can even teach them how to properly feed the fish.

Daily, weekly, and monthly maintenance duties become easier if they are shared by all. In addition, if everybody has a personal stake in the aquarium, the aquarium will be better off: Family pets often get more attention than those owned by a single person.

Showing off

Don't forget to show your fish and invertebrates off to all your friends. The beauty of a well-maintained aquarium is naturally impressive. Don't be surprised if your friends come over just to see your aquarium, no offense, not you! I guarantee you that anybody who enters the room where you have your tank will be drawn to it immediately.

Remind your friends that they shouldn't tap on the glass or feed the animals.

Experiencing marine biology in your home

I have been studying marine biology for over 20 years, and that doesn't include my amateur years as a young aquarist. Believe me, those early aquarium years with my brother Burt and my friends Dave, Condo, and Carlo were extremely important in helping shape my future. If you, too, are an aspiring marine biologist, there's no better way to get started than to own an aquarium. Because many studies on fish biology have been conducted on fish kept in aquaria (see Chapter 1), an amateur biologist can learn a lot about fish in his or her own home.

Keeping a Log

When I discuss water chemistry in Part III of this book, I stress the need to write down the results of the water-quality tests. This way, you're able to follow the water-maturation process. Keeping a log is important — and not only for water chemistry results.

A well-kept log helps you pinpoint when and how situations progressed in your aquarium. It also provides you with an interesting history of your aquarium that you and your family will probably enjoy reading now and at some point down the road.

An aquarium log need not be complicated. Mine is just a simple notebook. I mark the date on the left side of the page and make all kinds of notes on the right. You can also subdivide your notebook into sections for each general category. For example, the fish section can have an individual page or two for each animal so that the history of that critter is all in one place.

Keep your notebook close to the aquarium and encourage all the fish watchers to make notations. This way, patterns of observations can be established even if you're not there all the time.

The following sections give you some idea for the types of notes to make in your log.

Comings and goings

Write down when you add fish and invertebrates to your aquarium and when you remove them. This allows you to follow the progress of any new additions or the effects of taking a fish or invertebrate away. For example, if you suspect that one particular fish is bullying the others, but you haven't personally seen it, you may need to isolate that fish for a week. You can then follow the progress of your other fish to see whether conditions improve. To do this, you have to make note of when events happen.

Take notes about new arrivals — in particular, how they interact with others or with the aquarium. For example, "Just placed new lionfish in tank, and he immediately consumed the clownfish" or "New damselfish is shy and seems to hide a lot; need to keep an eye on it."

Fish interactions and behavior

Write down your observations on animal behavior and interactions. This does not pertain only to when you add or remove a tank inhabitant: Make notes whenever you see something worth noting!

Suppose you're relaxing and fish watching when suddenly your triggerfish nips your cardinalfish, and the latter quickly swims away and hides. You should write this down for a couple of reasons. First, this agonistic behavior may be an isolated incident or a recurring situation. You won't know unless you make note of it. Second, if your cardinalfish starts to show signs of stress, you'll know why.

Most of the fish and invertebrate interactions you see will probably be associated with aggressive or agonistic behavior (see Chapter 10 for a discussion of agonistic behavior). In many aggressive relationships, a pecking order is established, and the fish sort it out themselves. If not, one of the fish should be removed before the situation gets out of hand. If the aggressor is a general aquarium bully, it must go. However, if the fish being picked on is getting injured, it must be relocated to a more peaceful setting.

Feedings

Question: What is one of the first signs of stress? Answer: loss of appetite. If you notice that a fish or invertebrate isn't eating, write it down. If a fish or invertebrate is eating too much, write it down. If a fish is eating only one kind of food, write it down. If a particular food type is not liked at all, write it down.

Face it, you can't remember everything. Writing down these observations helps determine whether there are any consistent patterns worth following.

Because feeding is such an important aspect of keeping your fish and your aquarium healthy, don't be afraid to keep detailed notes on feeding behavior, food types, feeding times, and food quantities.

New equipment

Any time that you replace or add equipment to your aquarium, note it in your log. This way, if anything changes dramatically after adding that equipment, you'll know why. Suppose, for example, your dealer recommends a different fluorescent light bulb for your aquarium to improve invertebrate health. You buy it, use it for several months, and find that your invertebrates are no better off. By checking your notes, you can pinpoint the amount of time you've been using the bulbs and evaluate their efficacy.

It doesn't take long to write down, "Added new airstones to undergravel filter." Take the few seconds to do it, and you'll have an excellent maintenance record.

Problems

If something goes wrong, make note of it. This way, you can follow patterns, if they develop. Filter failure, heater malfunction, and even air tube clogging are routine incidents that can stress your fish. If you know when they happened, you may be able to find the cause of any future problems.

Here's an example of a hypothetical but possible situation. You come home from a long weekend away and find your butterflyfish hiding in the corner of the tank and not interested in food. You have not been there and don't know whether something went wrong. Fortunately, your good friend Kimberly took care of the fish, fed them, and made sure that aquarium conditions were stable. So, what happened? You pick up your log and noticed that Kimberly found cooler water temperatures on Saturday and she had trouble getting the heater to work. She also observed that the butterflyfish was not interested in food. Bingo, temperature stress and a possible heater problem. See what I mean?

General notes

You don't need to be feeding your fish, adding or removing an animal, having a problem, or adding equipment to make notes in your aquarium log. Any note that helps you or remind you to do something is helpful. For example, my notes from last week say, "Need to stop watching fish and finish that book!"

This general note-taking will come in handy when you decide to write your own book about saltwater aquariums. Just remember me when you become a famous author!

Taking Pictures

"Take da pitch:" That's the way my father says "take the picture!" Don't ask why. The point is there may come a time when you want to photograph your aquarium and its inhabitants. Photography happens to be one of my other favorite hobbies, and I've spent literally thousands of hours and thousands of dollars underwater trying to get photos of fish and invertebrates in their natural environment. It's amazing how much time, effort, and money I could've saved had I just photographed the animals in my aquarium — and I wouldn't have had to get wet!

I can think of a number of great reasons to take photos of your pets: to show off their aquarium inhabitants, to follow the history of a particular animal, to preserve the memory of a critter, or to publish photos. Whatever your reason, I strongly encourage aquarium photography. Like maintaining the aquarium itself, photographing your fish can be frustrating, because your subjects don't always cooperate. But the process is also a lot of fun.

Nowadays, you can find many types of cameras on the market. Over the years, I've come to prefer a 35mm single lens reflex (SLR) camera for all my photography. But the times, they are a changing, and digital cameras seem to be the future of photography. Digital cameras make it easier to edit and to e-mail your photos, as well.

Regardless of the kind of camera you choose, make sure you use a strobe when taking photos of your aquarium. The lights in your aquarium generally don't provide sufficient lighting for photography. In addition, the quality of the lighting usually results in strange colors, like green or orange in your photos. Therefore, you need to add strong lighting from a flash unit or electronic strobe. Keep in mind that the more light that you add, the better the photos.

This is not a book on photography, so I don't cover any photography basics. However, the following are a few pointers to taking good aquarium photos:

✔ Use the slowest film possible to maximize the quality of your photos. Slower film has less grain, and it can be enlarged to greater sizes, but you need more light.

✔ Color positive film, also called slide film, may be less forgiving, but it has the highest color quality and is less expensive than color negative film (print film) to process.

✔ Mount the camera on a tripod or something sturdy so that you avoid camera movement and blurred photos at slower shutter speeds.

✔ Match the camera lens to the size of the subject and composition of the photograph. A 50mm lens is good for larger fish, but a macro lens may be required for smaller subjects. A zoom lens gives you both options and allows you to vary your composition.

✔ Make every effort to direct the flash at a 45-degree angle to the glass of the aquarium. If you don't, your photos will have a bright white spot from the reflection of the flash.

✔ Pay attention to focus and depth of field so that what you see is what you get. The depth of field determines what's in focus and what isn't. For example, you may want the blenny on the coral in focus, but not the decorations behind it. You can manipulate your depth of field with your aperture setting.

✔ Compose your photo so that it has a subject. I have lots and lots of photos of my aquarium that look busy because there is no center of interest. Now if I'm taking panoramic photos, I try to compose it with an element of central interest. In the case of close-ups, I try to fill the frame as much as possible with the subject.

✔ Be creative. You may shoot something that you love, but everybody else looks at it and shrugs. So what? We all swim to a different current or something like that, so go with what pleases you.

Part V
The Part of Tens

The 5th Wave   By Rich Tennant

In this part. . .

Every *For Dummies* book ends with top-ten lists, and I'm not about to break the trend. I've tried to summarize some aquarium basics in these lists so that you don't have to dig around in the book.

Chapter 21

Ten Fish to Avoid

....

In This Chapter

▶ Knowing which fish will only cause you aggravation
▶ Steering clear of the bad apples

....

In Chapter 10, I list a number of individual species that aren't well suited to the beginner's aquarium. In this chapter, I emphasize some families of fish that tend to be a problem in captivity. Of course, each group may contain one or two exceptions.

Sharks

It's a natural desire to have sharks in your aquarium, but you want to avoid them for a number of reasons. Most of the over 350 species of sharks are simply too big for the average aquarist. Did you know that only a handful of shark species have been successfully kept in captivity, and that includes large, public aquaria? Besides, most sharks are predatory carnivores that will eat everything in your aquarium.

Skates and Rays

Skates and rays are flattened relatives of the sharks, and like their cousins, I don't recommend them for the average aquarium. Both groups grow to large sizes and prefer to eat invertebrates, so keep them out of your aquarium.

Stonefish

These fishes possess venom glands near the base of their needle-like dorsal fin spines. The neurotoxin of these fish is the most deadly of the fish venoms and can be fatal to humans. They typically camouflage themselves as rocks, which means that they aren't very attractive, either. Leave stonefish care to the experts.

Moray Eels

Moray eels are cool-looking fish that belong to the family Muraenidae. Morays are generally nocturnal fish that feed on other fish and invertebrates (including yours!) at night, spending most of their daytime hours in holes and crevices, so they're not much fun to observe. Also, in the wild, these fish grow very large and easily attain lengths in excess of five feet.

Lionfishes and Scorpionfishes

These predators hover or lie in wait for their prey, suddenly lunging at and engulfing them. Their camouflaged coloration aids them in doing so. For obvious reasons, these fish must be handled with great care. In captivity, they will readily consume smaller tankmates. The novice is best to avoid them — they don't belong in a reef tank.

Boxfishes and Trunkfishes

These box-shaped fishes of the family Ostraciidae release poisons into the water when threatened and are, therefore, poorly suited for the average aquarium. Some of the boxfishes are also intolerant of their own kind. Who needs this in an aquarium?

Groupers and Sea Basses

The family Serranidae is comprised of fast-growing, large, predatory fishes. Most species require a large aquarium that's populated with other large fish. Otherwise, groupers and sea basses will quickly outgrow your aquarium and will probably eat many of your smaller fishes in the process. Don't let their small size in the pet store surprise you: They grow up and grow up fast! In addition, many of the groupers are nocturnal, spending most of their day hiding or lying on the bottom. That's not fun to watch!

Parrotfishes

These fishes prefer to feed on algae, using their beaks to bite off pieces of dead coral to get at it. For this reason, parrotfishes aren't well suited to the reef aquarium. In general, these fish grow relatively large, which also makes them a poor choice for the average fish-only aquarium.

Snappers

Snappers are another group of fast-growing, highly active fishes that, as adults, aren't suitable for the average marine aquarium. They are predatory by nature, require a lot of space, and will quickly dominate an aquarium.

Seahorses

Seahorses are delicate and exotic fishes that are difficult to feed and require very high water quality, so keeping them alive is challenging for the beginner. Because they don't compete well for food with other species, seahorses live best in a quiet aquarium by themselves.

Chapter 22

Ten Invertebrates to Avoid

In This Chapter

▶ Staying away from trouble-causing invertebrates

▶ Making buying decisions that will save you grief

*W*ith so many kinds of invertebrates, I have a tough time singling out just ten that aren't for the average saltwater aquarium. In fact, there are thousands that aren't suitable, but in this chapter, I list ten that you may encounter at the fish store.

Octopi

Octopi is plural for octopus, which are really cool cephalopods. Every aquarist I know is intrigued by them! Unfortunately, most octopi are large, crafty, and predatory in the tank. They are also quite delicate, rarely living very long in captivity. Why waste the money?

Crown of Thorns Starfish

This species of starfish is not a friendly invertebrate. Instead, it is a predator on the reefs, eating corals left and right. If you plan to have a reef tank, avoid these funky-looking starfish.

Bristleworms

These polychaete worms are rarely purchased, but they usually end up in your aquarium hitchhiking on live rocks. They are named after the bristles that line their sides. These bristles are sharp and can easily irritate you if you handle them. While small bristleworms are relatively harmless, larger ones can damage corals and must be removed.

Mantis Shrimp

Mantis shrimp are nasty ill-tempered crustaceans capable of inflicting a serious injury with their powerful spear-like arms. They are efficient predators of other invertebrates and fishes. This is one shrimp that doesn't act like one.

Jellyfish

Jellyfish aren't the most common aquarium invertebrates for a number of reasons. Although public aquaria do display jellyfish, they go through a lot of work to do so. Jellyfish require far too much work for the average aquarist in terms of water quality, aquarium conditions, and food. If someone offers you jellyfish, just say no!

Queen Conch

The shell of this large gastropod is probably the most popular curio in the tropics. The beauty of this animal and its shell often entices the new aquarists to add a small one to their aquarium. Don't do it! These snails get large. If you want a queen conch, collect just a shell.

Lobsters

If you place a lobster in your aquarium in the evening, by morning you will no longer recognize your aquarium. These feisty decapod crustaceans are disruptive and territorial, not to mention cannibalistic. Do yourself a favor, don't add a lobster to your peaceful community aquarium.

Bivalves

Clams, scallops, mussels, and oysters belong in this group. There are all different kinds of bivalves, and many of them are beautiful additions to the aquarium. They are included here because they are strictly filter feeders and this makes them difficult for a beginner to accommodate. Practice aquarium upkeep before you add these challenging species with special feeding requirements.

Sea Cucumbers

Although a some species of sea cucumbers are okay for the aquarium, as a beginner, avoid these critters. When some sea cucumbers are stressed, they release toxins into the tank, and you don't want that.

Fire Coral

Although these cnidarians are actually not coral, they are named after the feeling you get when you touch them. When these animals sting you, you feel as if you've been burned. For this reason alone, you don't need any species of fire coral in your aquarium.

Chapter 23

Ten Simple Metric Conversions

The units of measurement in this book are given in customary U.S. measures. However, in the rest of the world and in the scientific community, the accepted units of measurement are metric. The simple conversions in this chapter help you translate your American aquarium into one that's recognized worldwide.

Temperature

To convert Fahrenheit to Celsius (which is the temperature scale used in most of the world), use the following formula:

$$^\circ C = (^\circ F - 32) \times 0.5556$$

To convert Celsius to Fahrenheit, use the following formula:

$$^\circ F = (1.8 \times {}^\circ C) + 32$$

Length Conversion

The metric system is based on units of ten, and the basic unit of length is the *meter*. Measurements are made in meters or increments of meters, and so named with different prefixes. The basic prefixes are milli (1/1000), centi (1/100), and kilo (1000) and each represents an increment of ten. Therefore:

1000 millimeters (mm) = 1 meter (m)

100 centimeters (cm) = 1 m

1000 m = 1 kilometer (km)

The U.S. uses inches and feet to measure length, while the metric system uses centimeters and meters.

✔ To convert inches (in) to centimeters (cm), multiply by 2.54.

✔ To convert feet (ft) to meters (m), multiply by 0.3048.

✔ To convert centimeters to inches, multiply by 0.3937.

✔ To convert meters to feet, multiply by 3.28.

Weight Conversion

Just as the meter is the basis for length, the *gram* is the basis for weight. So, the prefixes for length also apply for weight. Therefore,

1000 milligrams (mg) = 1 gram (g)

1000 g = 1 kilogram (kg)

The two standard units of weight are pounds in U.S. measures and kilograms in metric measures.

✔ To convert pounds (lbs) to kilograms (kg), multiply by 0.4536.

✔ To convert kilograms to pounds, multiply by 2.2.

Always take into account the weight of your aquarium when it is full with water.

✔ One gallon of saltwater weighs 8.4 pounds.

✔ One liter of saltwater weighs 1.01 kilograms. See the "Volume Conversions" section for more on liters.

Area Conversion

The surface area of anything is simply the product of the length and the width or

Area = length × width.

Using the U.S. system, area is usually reported as square inches (in^2) or square feet (ft^2) because the unit of measurement is squared (inches × inches = inches squared).

✔ To convert square inches (in^2) to square centimeters (cm^2), multiply by 6.4516.

✔ To convert square centimeters (cm^2) to square inches (in^2), multiply by 0.155.

Volume Conversions

Volume is equal to the product of length, width, and height or

Volume = length × width × height.

In the U.S. we usually report this as cubic inches because multiplying inches times inches times inches results in the inches cubed (in^3). We also report volume in U.S. gallons. The metric system uses cubic centimeters and liters.

- ✔ To convert cubic inches (in^3) to cubic centimeters (cm^3 or cc), multiply by 0.061.

- ✔ To convert cubic centimeters to cubic inches, multiply by 16.39.

- ✔ 1000 cubic centimeters = 1 liter (l) = 1 kilogram (kg).

- ✔ To convert gallons to liters, multiply by 3.78.

- ✔ To convert liters to gallons, multiply by 0.2642.

Part VI
Appendixes

The 5th Wave   By Rich Tennant

"It's that wierd Ahab friend of yours. He probably wants to come in and stare at the Albino tigers again for about 9 hours."

In this part. . .

1 provide you with a list of useful resources for increasing your knowledge as a marine aquarist, and I give you a glossary of aquarium-related terms.

Appendix A

Resources

• •

*H*ome aquarists number in the millions throughout the world. As long as you have an aquarium, you will never be alone in this hobby. As you become more involved in aquarium keeping, you may be surprised at how many people share this avocation. I find myself going to my local pet dealer to see new fish arrivals, talk about aquarium problems, and exchange ideas with fellow aquarists. I've picked up some of the most valuable information on fish keeping from amateurs who enjoy the thrills of this hobby. The resources for the home aquarist are almost limitless, ranging from books to the Internet.

Books

While I'd like to say that the book you're holding in your hand is the only one you're going to need, I can't. This book is really just the beginning and literally thousands of books have been published on aquarium keeping. Some are good, some aren't. I happen to think the one you're reading is very good. Books have been written to address virtually every aspect of the hobby. They cover broad topics, like basic aquarium set-up, and specialized topics, like the proper husbandry of a certain species. If you have any questions about aquarium keeping, it's covered in a book.

The list of books below includes others that I think are helpful, but this is a mere smattering of what's available for the new and experienced aquarist. Each one of the books listed below has its own bibliography, which will help you delve further into the field.

- ✔ Bailey, M. and G. Sandford. *The Ultimate Aquarium.* Smithmark Publishers, New York, NY, 1995.

- ✔ Bower, C.E. *The Basic Marine Aquarium.* Charles C. Thomas Publishing, Springfield, IL, 1983.

- ✔ Burgess, W.E. *A Complete Introduction to Marine Aquariums.* TFH Publications, Neptune City, NJ, 1989.

- ✔ Burgess, W. E., H.R. Axelrod, and R.E. Hunziker III. *Dr. Burgess's Atlas of Marine Aquarium Fishes.* TFH Publications, Neptune City, NJ, 1990.

✔ Dakin, N. *The Book of the Marine Aquarium*. Tetra Press, Blacksburg, VA, 1992.

✔ Delbeek, C. J. and J. Sprung. *The Reef Aquarium: A Comprehensive Guide to the Identification and Care of Tropical Marine Invertebrates, Vol. I.* Ricordea Publishing, Coconut Grove, FL, 1994.

✔ DeVito, C. and G. Skomal. *The Everything Tropical Fish Book*. Adams Media Corp., Avon, MA, 2000.

✔ Eschmeyer, W. M. *Catalogue of the Genera of Recent Fishes*. California Academy of Sciences, San Francisco, CA, 1990.

✔ Fenner, R.M. and C. Turk. *The Conscientious Marine Aquarist: A Commonsense Handbook for Successful Saltwater Hobbyists*. Microcosm Ltd., Shelburne, VT,1998.

✔ Gratzek, J.B. *Aquariology: Fish Diseases and Water Chemistry*. Tetra Press, Blacksburg, VA, 1992.

✔ Hargrove, M. and M. Hargrove. *Aquariums For Dummies*. IDG Books Worldwide, Inc., New York, NY, 1999.

✔ Helfman, G.S., B.B. Collette, and D.E. Facey. *The Diversity of Fishes*. Blackwell Science, Inc., Malden, MA, 1997.

✔ Kay, G and N. Dakin. *The Tropical Marine Fish Survival Manual*. Quarto Inc., London, 1995.

✔ Lundegaard, G. *Keeping Marine Fish: An Aquarium Guide*. Sterling Publishing Co., New York, NY, 1991.

✔ Melzak, M. *The Marine Aquarium Manual*. Arco Publishing Inc., New York, NY, 1984.

✔ Michael, S.W. *Reef Fishes: Volume 1*. Microcosm, Ltd., Shelburne, VT, 1998.

✔ Mills, D. *Aquarium Fish*. Dorling Kindersley Publishing, New York, NY, 1993.

✔ Moyle, P. B. and J. J. Cech, Jr. *Fishes: An Introduction to Ichthyology*. Prentice-Hall Inc., Englewood Cliffs, NJ, 1999.

✔ Sandford, G. *An Illustrated Encyclopedia of Aquarium Fish*. Howell Book House, New York, NY, 1995.

✔ Scott, P. W. *The Complete Aquarium*. Dorling Kindersley Publishing, New York, NY, 1995.

✔ Shimek, R. *The Coral Reef Aquarium, An Owner's Guide to a Happy Healthy Fish*. Howell Book House, New York, NY, 1999.

✔ Skomal, G.B. *Setting Up a Saltwater Aquarium, An Owner's Guide to a Happy Healthy Pet*. Howell Book House, New York, NY, 1997.

✔ Spotte, S. *Captive Seawater Fishes: Science and Technology*. John Wiley & Sons, Inc., New York, NY, 1992.

✔ Spotte, S. *Marine Aquarium Keeping*. John Wiley & Sons, Inc., New York, NY, 1993.

✔ Sprung, J. and C.J. Delbeek. *The Reef Aquarium: A Comprehensive Guide to the Identification and Care of Tropical Marine Invertebrates, Vols. II.* Ricordea Publishing, Coconut Grove, FL, 1997.

✔ Stoskopf, M. K. *Fish Medicine.* W.B. Saunders Co., Philadelphia, PA, 1993.

✔ Stratton, R.F. *Aquarium Filtration.* Yearbooks, Inc., Neptune, NJ, 1998.

✔ Tullock, J.H. *Your First Marine Aquarium.* Barrons Educational Series, Inc., Hauppauge, NY, 1998.

Clubs

In virtually every state, aquarium buffs have formed clubs and associations in which ideas and techniques are endlessly bantered about. The best way to find these organizations is to ask your local pet dealer or jump online and do a search — many clubs have Web pages.

Not only are these kinds of organizations great for gathering information, but they also can help you acquire equipment and healthy home-bred fish.

Magazines

Monthly aquarium magazines provide you with some of the most up-to-date information on keeping an aquarium. Timely articles on breeding, feeding, disease, and species-specific husbandry will both entertain and inform the new aquarist. In addition, product information and classified advertising are excellent features of any aquarium magazine. The photos are pretty cool, as well.

The most popular magazines that have proven to be good conduits of information include

✔ *Aquarium Fish Magazine,* P.O. Box 53351, Boulder, CO 80322, 303-666-8504, www.animalnetwork.com/fish/.

✔ *Freshwater and Marine Aquarium,* P.O. Box 487, Sierra Madre, CA 91024, 800-523-1736, www.mag-web.com/fama/.

✔ *Marine Fish Monthly,* 3243 Highway 61, East Luttrell, TN 37779, 800-937-3963.

✔ *Practical Fishkeeping,* Bretton Court, Bretton, Peterborough, PE3 8DZ, United Kingdom, www.practicalfishkeeping.co.uk/home.asp.

✔ *Tropical Fish Hobbyist,* One TFH Plaza, Neptune City, NJ 07753, 908-988-8400, www.tfh.com.

Internet

The amount of the aquarium information on the Net is unbelievable. It's the place where people gather to exchange information about the hobby. This is by far the fastest way to obtain and exchange information on keeping a salt-water aquarium. If you have access to the Internet, you have unlimited access to a vast amount of information on this hobby. Internet resources include chat groups, equipment, photos, links, husbandry information, classified ads, events, and on and on and on.

Some Internet service providers have even established networks for fish enthusiasts. Membership in a network gives you access to hobbyists, professional aquarists, researchers, breeders, and vendors of aquarium products. You can even get immediate advice from staff about sick fish.

With so much information on the Internet, you may be overwhelmed with all the options. Don't forget that many experts and vendors have home pages, as well. Any good search engine can also help you access these resources, but here are a few that I like:

- **Aqua Link:** www.aqualink.com/
- **Aquaria Central:** www.aquariacentral.com/
- **Aquarium Global Resource:** www.aquariuminstruments.com/global/
- **Aquarium.net:** www.aquarium.net
- **Aquatic Book Shop:** www.seahorses.com/
- **Fish Base:** www.fishbase.org/search.cfm
- **Fish Index:** www.fishindex.com/
- **Fish Info Service:** http://info-s.com/fish.html
- **Fish Information Service (FINS):** www.fishlinkcentral.com/
- **Fish Link Central:** www.fishlinkcentral.com/
- **Reef Aquarium Farming News:** www.garf.org/news.html
- **Sea and Sky:** www.seasky.org/sea.html

Appendix B

Glossary

acidic: Condition of the water in which the measured pH is less than seven. It is generally created by carbon dioxide buildup or decomposing organic matter.

actinic bulbs: Bulbs that produce light at the blue end of the spectrum, near ultraviolet.

activated carbon: Material used to mechanically and chemically filter aquarium water.

adipose fin: Small, fleshy fin between the dorsal and tail fin on some species of fish.

aeration: The introduction of air into the aquarium to create water movement and increase oxygen content.

aerobic bacteria: Bacteria that use oxygen for metabolism.

airstone: An air diffuser that produces tiny bubbles for aeration and water circulation.

algae: Simple, photosynthetic, aquatic organisms that range in size from one-celled microscopic types to large seaweeds.

alkaline: Condition of the water in which measured pH is greater than seven.

alkalinity: Carbonate hardness.

ammonia: The primary nitrogenous waste of fish that is highly toxic at elevated levels.

anaerobic bacteria: Bacteria that don't require bacteria for metabolism.

anal fin: An unpaired fin on the ventral side of the fish located between the anal opening and the tail fin.

aquarist: A person who owns and maintains an aquarium.

aquascape: To set up the inside of the aquarium.

barbel: Whisker-like growths on the mouth of some bottom-feeding fish, used for detecting food.

bioload: The volume of waste-producing animals, in terms of size and number.

biological filtration: The utilization of bacteria to convert toxic nitrogenous wastes to less-toxic compounds, thereby filtering the water.

brackish: Mixture of fresh and saltwater; pertains to fish habitats, like estuaries.

brine shrimp: Tiny saltwater crustaceans of the genus *Artemia,* which are excellent fish food, either live or frozen.

buffering: The ability of a solution to resist changes in pH.

calcareous: Containing calcium carbonate.

calcium carbonate: A crystalline mineral found in high concentrations in invertebrate skeletons and shells.

carbon dioxide: A common waste product of respiration in living things. It is used by plants during photosynthesis.

carnivore: Term describing fish that prefer to eat the flesh of other living creatures; meat-eaters.

caudal fin: The unpaired tail fin.

chloramine: Tap-water additive that kills harmful bacteria but may be toxic to aquarium fish.

community tank: An aquarium containing different species of compatible fish.

diatoms: Microscopic organisms with silica skeletons.

distilled water: Pure water that can be purchased at most pharmacies and food stores.

diurnal: Active during the day.

dorsal: Pertaining to the top of the fish.

dorsal fin: The unpaired fin(s) along the top of the fish.

family: The name for a group of related genera.

filter: A device that removes impurities from the aquarium.

filter feeders: Animals that filter plankton from the water for food.

foam fractionation: The separation of proteins from the water by a foaming action; the method used by a protein skimmer.

genus (genera): The name for a group of closely related species.

gills: The respiratory organs on fish that extract oxygen from the water.

habitat: The physical environment of a particular species.

hardness: The amount of dissolved minerals in water.

herbivore: Term that describes fish that prefer to eat vegetative matter; plant-eaters.

hydrometer: Instrument used to measure specific gravity in the aquarium.

ichthyology: The study of fish.

invertebrate: Animals that lack a spinal column.

kalkwasser: Lime water used to increase the buffering capacity of water.

lateral line: Sensory organ composed of receptors (lying along the surface of the fish's body in low pits or grooves) that detect water displacement and give the fish the sensation of touch.

length: Dimension of fish measured from the tip of the snout to the beginning of the caudal fin; used to calculate tank capacity for fish. Technically referred to as standard length.

live rock: Rock encrusted with live flora and fauna.

live sand: Sand containing live flora and fauna.

marine: Pertaining to the saltwater environment.

mechanical filtration: The physical removal of debris using filter media.

mineral: Naturally occurring inorganic substance in water.

mulm: An accumulation of decayed organic matter and detritus.

nauplii: Newly hatched brine shrimp.

nitrate: The end product of nitrification that is utilized by plants in aquariums; the least harmless of the nitrogenous compounds.

nitrification: Chemical conversion process carried out by bacteria in which toxic ammonia is converted to nitrite and nitrate.

nitrite: The intermediate compound of nitrification resulting from the conversion of ammonia by bacteria; can be toxic to fish in high concentrations.

nitrogen cycle: The conversion of toxic ammonia to nitrite and nitrate by bacteria.

nocturnal: Active during the night.

omnivore: Term that describes fish that have non-selective feeding habits and will eat a variety of foods.

operculum: Bony covering of the gill opening; also called *gill cover*.

osmoregulation: The biological control of salt balance in an organism.

osmosis: The movement of water through membranes.

ozone: Unstable molecule composed of three atoms of oxygen; sometimes used to disinfect aquariums.

parasite: A living creature that thrives on or in another living creature.

pectoral fins: Paired fins on each side of the body behind the gill opening.

pelagic: Term used to describe animals that live in the open ocean.

pelvic fins: Paired fins forward of the anal fin near the anal opening.

pH: A logarithmic scale used to describe the amount of hydrogen atoms in a solution.

photosynthesis: The process by which plants produce compounds for energy-utilizing carbon dioxide and energy from the sun to produce oxygen.

plankton: Microscopic organisms living in the water column.

power filter: A filter driven by a motor.

powerhead: A water pump.

rays: The main supporting structures of fins.

salinity: Measurement that refers to the amount of dissolved salts in water.

salt: A term commonly used to refer to sodium chloride, but also refers to various mineral compounds.

salt creep: The accumulation of salt deposits on the outside of the aquarium.

scales: Hard, bony structures that cover the skin and serve to protect the fish, reducing the chance of injuries and infection.

school: An organized group of fish swimming together in synchrony.

shoal: An unorganized group of fish.

spawning: The act of breeding.

specialty tank: An aquarium set-up that recreates a specific habitat with all its natural occupants of plants and fish.

species: The name applied to highly related living organisms capable of inter-breeding; a subdivision of genus.

species tank: A tank containing only a single species of fish.

specific gravity: Ratio of density of seawater to that of pure water; used as an indicator of salinity.

substrate: Bottom material, such as gravel or sand.

swim bladder: Internal organ that regulates buoyancy in fish.

symbiosis: A mutually beneficial relationship between organisms.

taxonomy: The scientific classification of life.

temperate: Geographic areas that are seasonal.

thermometer: A device that measures temperature.

thermostat: A device within the aquarium heater that regulates the output of the unit.

tropical: Geographic areas that are warm throughout the year.

ultraviolet (UV): Short wavelength light used to disinfect seawater.

ventral: Pertaining to the underside of the fish.

Index

Notes

Notes